RISING FROM THE RUINS

JOAKIM ANDERSEN

RISING
FROM THE
RUINS

THE RIGHT OF THE 21ST CENTURY

ARKTOS
LONDON 2018

Published in 2018 by Arktos Media Ltd.

www.arktos.com

Printed in the United Kingdom.

Originally published as *Ur ruinerna: 2000-talets höger växer fram*. London, 2017.

TRANSLATION	Gustav Hörngren
EDITOR	John Bruce Leonard
LAYOUT	Daniel Friberg
ISBN	978-1-912079-45-2 (Softcover)
	978-1-912079-44-5 (Hardback)
	978-1-912079-43-8 (E-Book)

Contents

A Note from the Translator

This book collects a broad range of perspectives from the rich heritage of modern political thought and action relevant for a 21st century Right. By necessity it is terse. Nonetheless, owing to its peculiar arrangement, it is vivid. As a backdrop, Andersen sets forth a perspective of society and civilization as a high culture or living organism or entity. There have been several civilizations before ours, and there are common traits shared by their life-processes. Ours is no special snowflake; it too takes part in the structure of various phases and sub-phases of rise and decline. This is what's called the *civilizational perspective* assumed by the author, and in relation to which he selects and arranges strains of thought (to establish a diagnosis) and methods of activism (to treat the rot) to form a tool box for today's fighter of the Right.

Aiding me in the work of translating this book, and to whom I owe a debt of gratitude, is first and foremost Jacob Bohlin, but also Lina Everby, Josef Lagerskog, Simon Gustafsson, Matti Ravander, Nicholas Miles, and Erik Westman. Besides being true friends they have done a considerable part of the gross translation, thus contributing to getting this important work out to an English-speaking audience.

Gustav Hörngren
Örebro, Sweden, January 2018

Entering the New Paradigm

We've recently experienced a couple of eventful years, marked by populist victories and globalist defeats, ranging from the Trump presidency to referendums on EU membership in Great Britain, immigration in Hungary and the constitution in Italy. This trend is bound to continue in the years to come. The populist and nationalist Right, or what we refer to as the true Right, will continue scoring political victories and the liberal globalists will suffer further defeats in the years ahead. It is clear that we have entered a new paradigm.

Many of you might ask how we can best make use of this momentum. What should we do next? I have some points of advice:

1. **Keep doing what we've already been doing.** In terms of metapolitics, crush the final remnants of political correctness and keep building our own platforms for news, debate, politics and socializing. Since our current strategy is obviously working, let's do more of the same, but let's intensify our efforts and get even more professional.

2. **Maintain a positive attitude.** Even if our streets might be burning from "cultural enrichment," remember that our liberal-leftist opponents have already lost. They have just not stopped breathing yet. Keep this in mind, and spread positive, encouraging messages to raise morale in our ranks and potential recruits. People want to join the winning side. Show them that we *are* winning and that we're never going to tire of it.

3. Have large families. Feminism and the degeneracy of potential partners are not valid excuses. We are currently fighting a demographic war, a war which we have been losing. Let's turn that around and make sure that nationalist and traditionalist Europeans are the ones who pass their heritage on in the largest numbers. Get married as early as possible, and have four children or more, thus ensuring that future Europeans are *our* descendants, rather than those of colonizing minorities or deranged political opponents.

4. Emerge from the shadows. Many of us have suffered under the soft totalitarianism of the PC establishment for several decades. Not so much anymore. It is understandable that some of you cannot openly take a stand for our ideas due to extremely sensitive career choices. If that is the case, consider changing your career in order to become more independent and less vulnerable to attacks from our opponents. There are of course cases of individuals who can do more good by keeping below the radar and working covertly from within the system. But more often than not this is just a lame excuse to make people feel better about themselves, and the real reason is often pure cowardice.

The time of cowardice has come to an end; the time to make a stand and to challenge our enemies openly has arrived. Embrace this necessity, and stand with us. Those who know the gravity of the situation but choose to stay passive and hidden are little better than the very people working against us. Ask yourself: is it really a worthy goal to spend the rest of your life accumulating wealth working for a bank or multinational company while our civilization goes up in flames? Choose your path wisely.

Those who read this are likely not cowards or passive bystanders, and by reading this book you will get a unique overview of the most interesting currents of anti-globalist resistance rising up from the ruins to save our European civilization in the eleventh hour. The author, Joakim Andersen, is not only a long-time friend and associate of mine, he is also perhaps the foremost intellectual of our movement in Scandinavia, as well as one of the more significant ideological influences, not only for me, but for numerous others as well. I was therefore greatly honored when he asked that I write this foreword to his very first book.

As mentioned before, we are living in the eleventh hour, and it is imperative that you do as much as possible to contribute to our forthcoming, inevitable victory. Disregard all the defeatist claims that "it's already too late." It is never too late. Our current demographic situation is certainly less than ideal, to put it mildly, and it is most likely unavoidable that through low birthrates and violent ethnic conflicts, we will see our European populations severely decimated during the coming decades. But that is certainly no reason to give up. During some of its highest peaks, our European civilization consisted of ten percent of today's population or even less; as long as there are still Europeans breathing, it is always possible to rebuild. And so we will. There are simply no other options.

With this book, and the other titles recommended in the reading list at the end, you will get the proper ideological and strategic foundation to become a more productive member of the alternative, true Right and our fierce resistance to the globalists' destructive and failing agenda. Make use of this knowledge, and put it into action.

Heroic deeds await you.

Daniel Friberg
Budapest, January 3rd, 2017

Preface

Greetings, dear reader. This book was originally intended as an introduction to the growing resistance against the liberal order (broadly speaking the true Right). It was written in Swedish and intended for Swedish readers, and many of the examples in the book are taken from Sweden. For some readers this might provide an insight into Swedish history; the Young Right and the Gothicists especially should be every bit as inspiring, as the current establishment in my country is bad. Readers less interested in Sweden can skip those parts without missing anything essential to the book. The book can be read in two ways. It can be read from beginning to end; it is then a dramatic story about a failing liberal order and its challengers. But you can also jump between chapters, choosing the parts that seem useful in your circumstances. The book is intended as something of a toolbox or armory, describing several different milieus and groups. I do not agree fully with any of the groups described, and probably neither do you, but all of them have developed useful perspectives and methods.

The book was written during the end of 2016 and the beginning of 2017, and as usual Minerva's owl flies at dusk. I make several attempts at predicting the future in the book—a future that we are living now. It is therefore interesting to re-visit the analyses made in the book. My hopes regarding the Alt-Right seem to have been realized; the Alt-Right has become ever more consolidated in "the real world" with initiatives such as Charlottesville and its vital Scandinavian "chapter." My fears about the effects of the split with the Alt-Lite on the other hand seem to have been exaggerated; as the debate between Richard Spencer and Alt-Liter Sargon of Akkad demonstrated, the Alt-Lite is not able to ignore the Alt-Right. When it comes to Donald Trump, it is still difficult to know his historical role, in order to make a proper analysis of "Trump vs Trump." Parting with Bannon was not a promising move, and the Wall has not been built yet. On the other hand, he seems to be gradually removing the threat from the Deep state, he refused to demonize the entire Alt-Right after Charlottesville, and he hasn't bombed Russia yet. These are interesting times, and hopefully the perspectives and methods presented in this book might help you in understanding and influencing them.

Chapter 1

Ragnarök

Garm grisly howls
in front of Gnipahellir;
will shackles burst asunder
and the wolf free, unleashed

— *Völuspá*, The Prophecy of the Seeress

We live in exciting times. The question is always, of course, *how* exciting? Is this the breakdown that will lead to a total collapse, or is it a temporary dip, soon to be followed by a new period of growth and security? Is there something looming in between these two alternatives—not a complete collapse, with hordes of mutants battling each other on the highways, but also not "more of the same"? What *paradigm*, model of thinking, describes our times the best? Is it the irrepressible belief in progress of a Condorcet, the man of the enlightenment—or is the answer to be found with our ancestors? The latter named the apocalypse *Ragnarök*. This time would be preceded by a period of moral and natural catastrophes, during which "brethren shall fight" and "sisters' children their kinship spoil"; "harsh is the world, whoredom plenty." Then the wolves would break their fetters, and from the kingdoms of the giants and the dead the gods' sworn enemies would march to the final battle which has been building up for such a long time. An old order succumbs in blood and fire, and a new one ensues.

As with all myths, our ancestors' *Ragnarök* can be interpreted in different ways. One possible interpretation is based on the notion that the gods had built a world order that carried within itself the seeds of its own destruction. Not least of all with respect to the

3

gods' asymmetric relationship to the giants (the *jötnar*), in which the gods among other things kill giants and steal their women, but never the other way around. This is an asymmetric relationship that, on the one hand, in each individual case seems logical and necessary, but yet, on the other hand, makes for bad blood and increasingly bad feelings. Many elements in the myth bring to mind our own times. "Whoredom plenty" and "sisters' children their kinship spoil" speak for themselves: both virtue and kinship have lost much of their meaning, and have been replaced by hedonism and cosmopolitan vanity. In the myth there are also the cohorts of Hel, comparable to the cohorts of the living dead—people bereft of memory and with empty chests, "individuals" oscillating between "labor" and "entertainment." We also recognize in our times the dragon-like Nidhogg that gnaws away at the roots of the World Tree; regardless of whether this indicates environmental destruction or global finance capital, or if it is rather the ecological or the humanitarian foundations of our civilization that are being gnawed away. The World Serpent (*Jörmundgandr*) can bring to mind those dark undercurrents in the collective psyche that thrive beneath the rational and civilized surface—undercurrents such as material greed, narcissism, and collective death-drive. Against these stands Thor—the friend of the honorable middle layers. Then there is Fenrir, a multifaceted *gestalt*, who among other things represents the demonic masculine, but who also reminds us how the polarization, in its final stages of disorder, runs the risk of erupting in open violence. At that point the antagonisms can no longer be resolved through compromises; often those involved won't even be interested in making such an attempt. The witch Gullveig can remind us of the sway that money holds and the consequences thereof, as well as how difficult it is to fight money-power and materialism. The giantess Angrboda is instead reminiscent of the demonic feminine advancing its positions in society and the collective unconscious. Psychologically interesting here is the connection between Angrboda and the wolves and ogres bred forth in the Iron Forest—for the sake of tearing the world order of the gods to pieces. In our times there is a similar alliance between cat ladies and other—albeit less supernatural—threats against the order. The fire-giant Surtr with his fiery sword that incinerates the world is an uncanny reminder of nuclear war. Against all these stand the gods—various aspects of the order. There is the powerful but simple Thor, as well as Odin, in whom several aspects are united; he has prepared his people for many generations for what looms ahead. There are also many significant goddesses like Freyja, Idunn, and Frigg, who remind us of how highly our ancestors regarded their women. In short, there is an impressive lineup, even on the side of the gods. But by the final battle they lack the swords of Baldur and Freyr—a problem that has dire consequences.

This, it seems, is *one* possible interpretation among many (even though, as we will find, it is an unexpectedly useful one for understanding our times). Loki's children, not least, are indispensable elements of every order, as necessary as the gods themselves, and possibly once gods in their own right (Fenrir as Time/devourer, The World Serpent as the upholder of the world, and Hel who guards the passage between the living and the dead). Even Odin has strong connections to the giants and their primordial wisdom. Asatru is not dualistic in the same way as Christianity. Still, the myth reminds us of the fact that every order has a beginning and an end, and as such makes for a wholesome counterweight to the ahistorical optimism of our times. Within every order grows conflicts and processes that one day will lead to its perdition. Angrboda breeds forth her ogres, Freyr loses his sword, relations between gods and giants become continually worse. The Marxist thesis, that the undertakers of capitalism emerge from the very bosom of capitalist society, is but one example of this pattern among many; the conviction that something better will follow, however, is an expression of Marxism's modern deterministic and optimistic character. *Ragnarök*, as well as related myths, reminds us that an accident rarely arrives alone. In Indian analogues both social, moral, and natural catastrophes are central; in the final stages the rulers become directly harmful to their subjects, raising taxes without reservation; people move *en masse* across the earth; violence spreads; money and sex become central, while truthfulness, honor, solidarity, and a sense of duty are confined to the background; starvation and disease will haunt mankind, as permanent winter and other natural disasters afflict the earth.

But the myth can also serve as a wholesome counterweight to an exaggerated pessimism and determinism. The gods—however you choose to see them—intervene when disorder gets too far out of hand. In many Indo-European myths the gods' avatars—in the shape of Kalki or Saoshyant—step in to punish the godless just when everything looks pitch-black. A new order and a new Golden Age follow, and the process goes full circle and starts to repeat itself again. The possibility for regeneration does exist and it is up to us to identify the possible sources for such a possibility. This is to a large extent what this book sets out to do. We will acquaint ourselves with numerous more or less promising challengers of the status quo. We will also attempt to discern the various factors of success and the stumbling blocks connected to their strategies. But first we shall get to know the ruins and the demons that roam about them.

Among the Ruins

> It is not just that human trash accumulates in cities—it is that cities turn what accumulates in them into trash.
>
> — DON COLACHO

A useful simile for our time is the ruin-landscape. In his time Julius Evola directed his message to "the men among the ruins"; the East German national anthem also alluded to the ruins from which the state had arisen. For the time being, this is not so much about physical ruins, although exceptions do exist, like Detroit, the bomb-tattered Donbass, Aleppo, and an increasing number of deserted, actual ruin-landscapes. But if we leave the strictly material viewpoint aside and speak instead of the immaterial foundations of our civilization the view is different; then we truly are living in a landscape of ruins. Classical culture and humanist ideals; the faculty to experience beauty; the bonds between man and society, nature, or the Sacred; the faculty to experience romance; fantasy; the art of conversation; and much more besides lies in shambles. Traditions, knowledge of history and human-ist, anciently rooted ideals are today left in ruins by the pressure of numerous attackers equally fatal as Nidhogg. This also suggests why it is that movies and television series about the Zombie Apocalypse have gained such popularity, because anyone void of memory, mannerisms, and human ideals is in many ways a living dead, whose only motiva-tion in life consists in a short-sighted hunger for what other people can offer (brains or what have you). During dark and gloomy days the modern world can truly appear like a city of ruins inhabited by living dead. However, to embrace any outlook darkened to this extent might also be an indication that we ourselves are seized by the rot.

The ruins, the *desert* of Nietzsche and Baudrillard, gradually in-creases its span, both in the material and the immaterial realms. In spite of all talk about growth and tolerance, in spite of the hypnotizing exuberance of things and all of consumerist society's impressions, many sense the emptiness beneath the glossy surface. Numerous examples of the unfolding ruin-landscape can be given. In the human sphere we could mention the fact that two out of three Americans are obese or that the testosterone levels among American men has dropped by 17% between 1987 and 2004. The culture too is in a shambles, as we realize as soon as we put on the radio, only to have our ears struck by moaning "gentlemen" and passive-aggressive female singers. Both the economi-cal and the political systems have mutated beyond all recognition; in spite of economic growth, the salaries of the American middle class have been stagnating for decades. Reactions against this are, as a rule, branded as "populism" or worse; and by contrast, those responsible for the 2008 crash have not been incarcerated, but retain their power and fiscal means. The boundaries between Goldman Sachs and the White House appear—to put it mildly—rather fluid, not only under the Bush's and Obama's administrations, but also under the Trump administration. Wikileaks' often staggering disclosures are actively silenced by the established media or branded as "fake news." Countries such as Iraq, Libya, and Syria are destroyed by American politics, and others might follow. In the European heartland regions emerge that are no longer European; in London, Malmo, and Amsterdam, the native stock is today a minority; suburban areas that most Swedes shun increase in numbers and become even less inviting each year. Nevertheless, the accusations of "Nazism" continue to shower on anyone that dares to speak of these phenomena. Our relation to nature is severely damaged. Hundreds of species or so go permanently extinct pretty much daily, while toxins and chemicals continue to harm people. Many never leave the big cities, and have the majority of their experiences fed to them through digital monitors.

Many push this away whenever they are reminded of it, and return as soon as they can to television pop music contests or to some glass-of-wine-after-work-posting or the like on Instagram. It is, however, becoming increasingly difficult to keep the growling wolf at bay; the hum of the television in the background is, time and again, drowned by the unpleasant developments of larger society. The bourgeoisie that felt at home during the last half of the 1900s now finds itself increasingly disoriented, and desperately seeks authorities who can promise that everything will become ordinary again and that the growing number of critics and Cassandras are really just bad people—even when the authorities in question are warmongers or corrupt, or just proposing blatant half-measures. Anyone frustrated by the disinclination of his contemporaries to see reality *as it is* can perhaps find consolation in the fact that, not to long ago, the same frustration afflicted Freudian-Marxists like Herbert Marcuse:

> The blissful consciousness—the belief that the present state of affairs is rational and that the system provides us with the good things in life—reflects the new conformism which is an offshoot of technological rationality translated to social behavior.

Nevertheless, there are other paradigms, other lenses if you will, other than the "blissful consciousness" of the liberal or the bourgeois, through which that-which-goes-on can be viewed. We are now living through the last days of an era. In many ways we find ourselves in an *interregnum*—the period between two stable orders. The old and accustomed no longer works, the engine is about to cut out. The 20th century won't come back: *"Toto, I've got a feeling we're not in Kansas anymore."* Liberals and mainstream conservatives view this as something negative and frightening; they drug themselves with consumption and conceited poses to avoid doing any real thinking about the future for themselves and their children (if they even bother to have any). But we can also view that-which-goes-on as something positive, as in the proverbial "exciting times." What we do today can have a much greater effect on the future than whatever we might have done forty or fifty years ago. We are able to shape the coming era, the era that will follow the present interregnum. There is also the possibility that we will fail to do so due to insufficient will or insufficient understanding. In that case other powers will shape the future order (or disorder) for us—or even worse, our efforts might avail the creation of a monster. To shape history, one must first grasp history, and our task is, in this sense, every bit as complicated as Odin's. Like the Allfather we must fight the enemies of the order, but we cannot do so blindly.

The Civilizational Perspective

> ...everything that takes place around us has occurred time and again in
> the past.
>
> — JOHN GLUBB

We can view that-which-goes-on from a shorter- or a longer-term
perspective; focus on the surface or deep down. We can turn our focus
to day-to-day and party politics; this can certainly be interesting, but
we will easily overlook more long-term trends. Universal infantiliza-
tion, for example, and other things that aren't brought up in media
or the political debate. We can also take on a (very) long-term perspective. Through it we can discern how man tamed his environment
and at the same time ended up like a tamed animal himself; this is
the perspective of the primitivists and the barbarians, perpetuated by
Robert E. Howard and Jacques Camatte. Or we can discern the gradual
deterioration of society, man, and spirituality; this is the traditionalist
perspective, expressed by Julius Evola and René Guénon. We can also
discern how *Seele* has become suppressed by *Geist*, how life and soul
have been replaced by dead things; this is Ludwig Klages' perspective.
(We will return to him later on.) Or we can discern how dead labor
seized control of the living, while they lost the control of their own
lives; this is the perspective of Marxism, even if it, in many ways, is
only a limited aspect of Klages' more comprehensive understanding of
history. Capitalism is but one aspect of *Geist*; the same holds true for
the dictatorship of the proletariat.

A truly large-scale perspective gives us a valuable distance to the
present, and is certainly good to become familiar with, but it can also
become too daunting and too discouraging: how can we reverse trends
that have been going on and gaining momentum for millennia? To
resolve the dilemma of a perspective adequate to the task at hand we
will take on a *civilizational* perspective. We then view our civilization,
or more aptly the Faustian high culture (*Hochkultur*) that Oswald

Spengler described, as a unified whole, even as a living organism or entity. The main value in this is the realization that our civilization is not something we can take for granted, and that a whole lot of what we appreciate in life is dependent on our Faustian high culture. Every living organism can suffer injury, illness, or die a premature death; it can even be affected by identity crises and depressions. Politics ought to take this into consideration, rather than contributing to an early downfall of our Faustian high culture. Conservatism, as Heinrich Leo and Klages saw it, carries within itself a protection of the living, including not only plants, animals, and human beings, but immaterial entities as well, such as local communities, tribes, and cultures. Through Spengler, Gobineau, Toynbee, or Günther a feeling of care and veneration towards our culture, its achievements, and the tribes that created it can be kindled. The civilizational perspective helps us understand why, for instance, the gradual abolition of the family or the Church can be harmful. Even if a liberal just views this as the consequences of the "freedom of choice" of "individuals," there *can* be negative consequences for our high culture as a whole if the functions of the family are taken over by the state, or if the faith of our fathers is abandoned. A civilization is a complex, organic whole comparable to an ecosystem in which all things from religion and patriarchy to social codes and dress codes have a greater importance than we might think. Everything is interconnected; if we remove or change some ingredient it can have an effect on the whole. This perspective also helps us to understand why a vital high culture needs its collective memory and its borders against the outside world. Our view is summarized by the French thinker Eric Zemmour:

> I believe that history has laws, that they are relentless, murderous, and that we've defied them with a guilty *naïveté*.

But the civilizational perspective also helps us identify in which life-phase our high culture is now. Much has been written of the phenomenon of "rise and decline." In *The Decline of the West* Oswald Spengler laid out a wider perspective and described the thousand-year life-processes of high cultures. These high cultures have been relatively few; Spengler mentions the Babylonian, the Egyptian, the Chinese, the Indian, the Mesoamerican, the Classical, the Arabian/Magian, and our own European or Faustian. The high cultures are strikingly reminiscent of living entities; they have their own unique personalities and ways of viewing the world; they have evolved within the different tribes which have shaped them. Just like living entities they undergo a natural development, which Spengler compares to the shifting seasons. The young high culture experiences spring and summer, and is, in this stage, still creative and vital. The aging high culture enters the phase of civilization; at this stage creativity is replaced by rigidifying forms and "world-cities," something Sorokin terms *colossialism*. It is easy to prefer the culture and values of the spring, but Spengler described this development as logical and unavoidable. If one is born during the winter, one must learn how to deal with the conditions of winter, and take the good with the bad, so to speak. Our civilization, for instance, would have had outstanding conditions to explore the solar system if its development had not gone astray on misguided paths. The difficulty of the individual's making a difference in a high culture is summarized by Asimov in his *Foundation Trilogy*:

> Gentlemen, the decline of the empire is a massive phenomenon and not easy to combat. It is dictated by an expanding bureaucracy, lost initiative, solidification of castes, loss of curiosity and hundreds of added factors. It's been going on for decades...

The British officer and historian John Glubb, nicknamed "Glubb Pascha" after his career in the Middle East, chose instead to describe the rise and fall of empires—*The Fate of Empires* being one work among others. It is a cycle whose length spans about 250 years. Hence, Glubb's cycle for the empire's life is just an aspect of that which Spengler described in his work. In fact, every high culture witnesses the rise and fall of several empires (Glubb's work is also, unsurprisingly, significantly shorter than Spengler's). Glubb divides the life of the empires into *eras*—different periods or stages, of which there are six. To wit: first there is the era of the pioneers, then follows an era of expansion and conquer, then an era of commerce, then an era of affluence, then an era of intellect, and finally an era of decadence. During different eras different values dominate, and different role models or paragons appear. To expect warrior values in the era of decadence is to set oneself up for disappointment. That 1968 occurred during the era of the intellectuals is hardly a surprise; the same holds for the growth of the welfare state during the later eras of the empire. This has been the case for all empires, from the Arab Dominion to the British Empire. We can blame the symptoms, but ultimately they are only symptoms.

Julius Evola, for his part, sketched the traditional theory of the regression of the castes. From his point of view there has been a steady trend of ever lower quality types of personalities usurping positions of power; from priests and warriors to merchants and servants or masses. Something rather similar occurs during Glubb's empire-eras, which in themselves are shorter elements in Evola's significantly wider time-range. An interesting detail is that the signs of caste regression that Evola sees include architecture, in which the temple (priests) has been followed by the castle/fortress (warriors), then the city-state (merchants), and now the rational and soulless buildings that serve as homes for the masses. Similarly, the regression of the castes affects ethics, family, religion, and work. Evola's traditional perspective can thus serve as a starting point for a fruitful critique of culture: "a Marcuse of our own, only better," as Almirante put it in summarizing Evola's importance.

In many ways these models resemble each other; each brings up questions of the power and dominance of *money* as a central problem that enters the scene at a certain point in time. Evola spoke of merchants, Spengler of the dominance of money, and Glubb of the era of commerce. Still, all of them were aware that money-power will eventually usurp political power and that greed, materialism, and individualism will spread as a consequence. Relatively speaking, Glubb put more focus on the era of the intellectuals, but Spengler and Evola brought them up as well. It is worth mentioning that all three of them, in different ways, spoke about the possibility of renaissance and regeneration. Spengler talked about Caesarism: that era in which money-power had dissolved traditions to such a large extent that *politics* could re-enter the scene, and with it the tradition and kinship as fundamental principles. Glubb mentioned how Rome had a second Great Power period: after the republican period the imperial period ensued (and later still the Byzantine, we should add). Evola brought up the era of heroes, that for a limited time could stunt the decline and give us role models like Heracles and Perseus. History is not wholly deterministic; insight, action, and will can break even far gone processes of decline. *Ragnarök* as a paradigm thus has its limitations if interpreted too literally. The dividing line between wishful thinking and analysis can, in many cases, be rather fluid as we prophesize total and imminent perdition. The destruction of an order does not necessarily have to be physical in nature, just as the ruins do not have to be material. Hence, the process might be difficult to discern for many who dwell in the midst of it.

Chapter 2

The Late 20th Century as Historical Formation

Historical capitalism is a materialistic civilization.

— IMMANUEL WALLERSTEIN

Let us look at the 20th century. It might be practical to study the current era and the order which, objectively speaking, is running towards its own demise. We could call it a *historical formation*, drawing inspiration from Carl Schmitt or Karl Marx; we could also talk about it as a *nomos* or a *mode of production* (*Produktionsweise*). Such a formation is a complex whole; although it is relatively stable, it carries within itself the seeds of its own destruction. The historical formation in question, the late 1900s, were intentionally constructed by the victors of the Second World War in order to prevent many of the elements of worry and uncertainty built into the previous formation from erupting in new catastrophes. The construction comprised a number of spheres, from the social to the geopolitical. Welfare-statism, liberalism, party-based parliamentarism, the bourgeois public sphere, Atlanticism, and market economy were but some of the constitutive elements. We can call it the *liberal order*. While its construction was completed after the war, its foundations really began to tremble around 1970. Today it is stuck in a state of multiple, unavoidable, and insoluble crises.

Nevertheless, nothing lasts forever; every historical formation carries within itself a set of antagonisms that will eventually erupt in strife and crises. That the liberal order has succeeded in providing any real solutions whatsoever to earlier problems is doubtful, to say the least; the worrying elements still loom beneath the surface, unresolved, biding their time. Indeed, there is much that indicates we are now living through the last death throes of a historical formation. How we relate to this last statement plays a cardinal role in how we think politically. The definition of a liberal today is normally someone who is still loyal toward the historical formation of the late 1900s and views its crises as manageable, or who alternatively denies them all together; the rest of us, who, like Tomasi di Lampedusa, realize that *"If we want things to stay as they are, things will have to change,"* are instead ready to forsake what was in order to build something new. This lends us a decisive advantage and a psychological head-start. It can be tough and wearisome to have to deal with historical uncertainty, not least because the time-delay between action and result is often significantly longer than in everyday life. If we fail to realize this we will suffer political burnout, something that each and every one of us will have to find ways of dealing with. But at least we understand more of that-which-goes-on around us and are able to *act*, and not just *react*. Many of our contemporaries have a similar relationship to society that the members of a Melanesian *cargo cult* have to American abundance and technology: they don't understand how it works, but nonetheless take it for granted. Such is not our relationship to our society and our civilization; we view them as complex, unified wholes, not as givens.

The historical construction that comprised the latter half of the 1900s—the liberal order—consisted of several parts that today are afflicted by problems whose solutions cannot be found within the circumscribed feasibility that the current system provides. Some of these problems are classical examples of alienation, in which something that man created turns against him (the welfare state, the global economy, the industrialized culture, et cetera). Comparisons with *Frankenstein's Monster* or *The Sorcerer's Apprentice* come to mind. Other examples that illuminate the system's built-in antagonisms, which today have grown unmanageable, include the ambiguities between free speech and ethnic peace, between democracy and liberalism, and between the people and the establishment. The whole thing is reminiscent of the conflict between gods and giants in our own mythology; step by step it is intensified, even if neither party really wants it to be. Other problems still provide examples of how the resources that founded the liberal order in the first place have been exploited without being renewed; this includes not only social and moral capital, but genetic capital as well. The goose that laid the golden eggs has been killed. Liberalism and money-power has, like Nidhogg, gnawed away for decades at the roots of the present order, to a point that things now have become untenable. Reforms can no longer untie the Gordian knot, and this will, soon enough, be true regardless of what area we look upon. It is precisely into these various areas of the liberal order that we will now steer our inquiries; not only are all of them in a state of crisis, but they are amplifying each other's crises.

The Spiritual Emptiness

> Turning and turning in the widening gyre
> The falcon cannot hear the falconer
> Things fall apart; the centre cannot hold
> Mere anarchy is loosed upon the world.
>
> — W. B. YEATS

The most basic thing in every society is a sense of meaning, and more often than not this has been handed down to us by religion. This notwithstanding, the sense of meaning can be contested as well as undermined. The period of the early 1900s was marked by an increasing spiritual and existential emptiness. Conrad wrote *Heart of Darkness*; T. S. Eliot spoke of "hollow men," describing the nihilism that loomed at every turn, threatening to rear its head; Nietzsche had already proclaimed that God was dead; Carl Jung spent a whole lifetime trying to cure the spiritual crisis of Western man. Without Christianity the

Western World has been likened to an empty shell, and to a corpse. Jung saw that an imitation of alien traditions was not a solution, and he expressly warned about the fascination of the primitive, which all too easily can seize the soul of civilized man. There are no shortcuts available; a solution *for us* must be based in our own history rather than in imitation or regression.

The old faith was not replaced by something new, despite attempts to do so from all around; everything from state and economy to race and class was deified. A sufficient amount of residues from Christianity and its values did, however, remain during the early 1900s to render the situation manageable, and following the war a period of economic growth and consumer-based economy took hold and seemed to imbue life with new meaning. Nonetheless, dissatisfaction with this stinted solution was gradually seeping in—a fact which adds to the explanation of the many elements involved during 1968. It also explains why the bourgeoisie had so little to put up against the young rebels. The system was—to borrow an expression from John Zerzan—*"running on emptiness"*; emptiness was its fuel. 1968 was a natural consequence of this deficit of existential capital, but it did not provide any solutions. At best, the result was a bunch of *ersatz*-religions (substitute religions), such as political correctness, radical feminism, and ethnomasochism. These didn't succeed in rendering life any more meaningful than materialism and consumerism could. Many of the positive, constructive elements found in the youth-revolt quickly disappeared into oblivion, while many of the negative prevailed. What, for instance, began as *nature boys* and a willingness to live authentically and responsibly, ended with politically correct opinion-dictators with house mortgages. The *ersatz*-religions, together with the vested interests of money-power, later brought about an untenable situation, while the spiritual emptiness rendered sound reactions conspicuous in their absence. This is perhaps most transparent in the area of immigration, in which the commandments of ethnomasochism align with the interests of money-power. Moreover, the *ersatz*-religions are also intentionally blocking a renaissance of older cultural and religious forms, since the "faithful" associate this with "Fascism."

The bottom line is that the liberal order, in which we live now, is meaningless; it is horizontal but lacks a vertical dimension. It offers everything from "work" and televised pop music contests to Swedish crime-fiction and African dance, but no deeper meaning. This has been expounded, more or less succinctly, by many thinkers and writers through the years. Baudelaire turned against *"that which we call professions"* and stated that the three venerable creatures were *"the priest, the warrior and the poet"*; Marcuse, instead, talked about *"the one dimensional man"*; Palahniuk's *Fight Club* is also a stinging indictment of modern meaninglessness. Pseudo-solutions tolerated during the 1900s have only exacerbated the situation, with mass migration, neomoralism, and suppression of public opinion as a result. Rather than being renewed, the existential capital that was in place before the liberal order took off came to be chipped away bit by bit, and not seldom made into a target for blatant assaults. The bonds with our ancestors, with our myths, and with religion were actively undermined, while those items of historical knowledge that might have rendered continuity were likewise actively abolished. Their roles in society were usurped by existentially empty consumerism and various harmful ideological complexes.

Culture and Anthropology

As we grow older and think back to those who've been involved in our lives, their egotism seems indisputable. We see it all as it really was; that is, harder than both steel and platinum, and more durable than time itself.

— CÉLINE

A resource of critical importance for every civilization and society are its members. Are they men who live to *"ride, shoot straight, and speak the truth"* or are they timid couch potatoes who shun all mental and physical effort like the plague? Are they able to face up to reality or do they chose to drug themselves with consumption, distractions, and agreeable lies? A traditional starting point is that the human stock is constantly deteriorating. Yamamoto Tsunetomo wrote in *Hagakure* that the ancestors were both morally and physically superior to their descendants. But the fact that things were better in the past was perhaps not only because we ourselves were younger and more spirited. In fact, the anthropological crisis can be discerned even by those without a strong reactionary bent; if we regard things like self-esteem, greatness, knowledge, and truthfulness as more important than material wealth, conformity, or safety and similar values, it is dubious, to say the least, that we live in an era of "progress." Quite the contrary; it seems that growth of material wealth is inextricably linked to a recession of immaterial wealth, as people become feebler and timider, more helpless and incompetent with the passing of each year. We can, like Jean Thiriart and Erich Fromm, question whether the goal is to *be* or to *have* (or indeed, even to *appear as*). The anthropological crisis—which taking inspiration from Renaud Camus, we could call *the Great Worsening* or, following Max Nordau, describe as *the Degeneration*—is inextricably linked to several of the other crises underway. It is partly caused by the proletarianization and urbanization described by Marx and Hans Günther, as men free in their own hearth are reduced to merely employed or welfare-subsidized citizens; it is linked to the decadence which John Glubb related to the period of material exuberance, and it is to a large degree interlinked with the spiritual emptiness and the decline of culture in general.

Cultural decline has occurred gradually and is interlinked with the invasion of money-power in the cultural and the artistic spheres, which in turn have lost their connection to the Sacred. Theodor Adorno of the Frankfurt School described the emergence of the *culture-industry* as reducing culture to consumer goods and people to consumers. From a slightly different perspective the two situationists Debord and Vaneigem described how the sheer quantity of consumer goods, advertisements, and such things had created a *Society of the Spectacle*. The Marxist and filmmaker Pasolini called consumerism a *new Fascism*, by which, it seems, he alluded to its homogenizing and coercive character. He wrote:

> ... moreover, this Power has created a cultural homologization in Italy: we are talking here about a repressive homologization, induced by the vulgar pleasure-doctrine and "le joie de vivre"... Television's ideological bombardment is never explicit: it resides in things, it is always implicit. But never before has a "model of life" benefited from so effective a form of propaganda as being broadcast through television. The type of man or woman that is important, that you should mimic or emulate, is neither described nor extolled: it is represented! The language of television is by nature the language of physical mimicry—the language of behavior. And this is subsequently mimicked to the fullest extent in reality's own language of physical mimicry, in the language of behavior. The heroes from TV-propaganda—adolescents on motorcycles, the girls on the refrigerators—stake out and map out the boundaries for reality's heroes; they become the same.

Later a similar brand of thought concerned with "the vulgar pleasure-doctrine" would receive the name *libéralisme libertaire*, to which we will return later.

Christopher Lasch, the Marxist-turned-populist, described how narcissism was spreading through culture and society, how we got a *Culture of Narcissism*. We can compare this to Glubb's observation that during the decadent phase the celebrity is elevated to a role model, instead of, for instance, the warrior or the intellectual. Presumably most of us readily recognize the narcissist personality type in everything from advertisements to Facebook updates among our acquaintances, as well as in the authorities; perhaps even in ourselves. Lasch and Glubb indeed go together. But we can extend this even further. Philosopher

Bernard Stiegler has described how the narcissistic personality type is followed by the *dispersed* man, deprived of the faculty of *deep attention* (*"unable to read my books!"* as an appalled Stiegler realized). This personality type is deeply connected to the current form of political correctness, and the lack of historical knowledge. It is the dispersed and narcissistic personality type who becomes politically correct. Evola too wrote about this personality type:

> The throne where the "inner sovereign" ought to sit … that place is empty. One lives day by day, in a silly way. Hence, during the brief moments of clarity: aversion and loathing.

The personality type that Lasch, Evola, and Stiegler describe lacks an inner core—it is "transient," as Evola put it. At the same time culture is invaded by what Jung and the historian Lothrop Stoddard calls the *primitive*, which has a dangerous ability to lure civilized man. This is once again passed down by the culture-industry, which is in turn powered by the *ersatz*-religions. Primitive and vulgar pop culture and ethnomasochism spur each other on, while political correctness shields the process from critique, owing to the fact that much of popular culture has its roots in the ethnic, in the lower classes, which are exempted from incrimination. Meanwhile, pop culture and its "life models" actuate the process of ethnomasochism and the presumption that certain groups are more "authentic" than one's own. The sum of these processes has culminated in what Nietzsche called *der Letzte Mensch*, a personality type who regards strength and consequentiality as Fascism and is deprived not only of a will-to-power but also of a life filled with true meaning.

The result is a society and culture of the masses. At the same time we are moving from a more text-based society to a visual, image-based society. As a consequence, difficulties in differentiating between surface and depth, even difficulties in discerning the dimension of depth at all, pervade. During the 1800s world-conceptions influenced by occult materialism, concerned with inquires of what *really* went on beneath the surface of various occurrences, flourished. Marx claimed that the central issue was the struggle between the classes; Gobineau alluded to the dilution of the blood; Freud would later study the unconscious, and some years earlier Adam Smith had studied the market as an invisible hand. Their projects were not without shortcomings, but the value lies in their approach. Similar projects seem difficult to complete in our times; contemporary man can *associate* and *react* but not perceive the dimension of depth. Carl Hamilton wrote in *Det infantila samhället* (The Infantile Society[1]):

> The culture of voice and visuals is intuitive, not intellectual; it is cmotional, not rational; concrete, not abstract. It struggles in conveying ideas (complex, abstract, one-dimensional) but excels in conveying persons and events (concrete, vivid, three-dimensional).

Culture and human stock are closely interrelated; when culture deteriorates humans in general are affected, and like ripples on water, this will give speed to, and render decay possible in, other areas as well, like politics.

Family and Gender Roles

> The revolutionary of our times ... fights against the father and the father's right.
>
> —OTTO GROSS

Linked to the cultural crisis and the Great Worsening, is the crisis of the family and the *androgynization*—the abolition of gender roles. In his time, the Christian culture critic Ivan Illich showed that in traditional societies there are always "men" and "women," with their

---

1   No English translation exists. — Tr.

distinct social spheres or domains. In modern society only "human beings" exist, individuals equipped with one or the other of two types of reproductive organs, but otherwise essentially "unisex." In traditional—Illich called them *genderified*—societies men and women have distinct domains; these may in some respects vary from one society to another, but the separating boundary is always there. The boundary is crossed only under exceptional circumstances (such as natural disasters or carnivals). Furthermore, these exceptions tend to confirm the general rule. Nowadays, we often regard the relationship between these two domains through lenses that Illich called "sexist," which means that we view women as oppressed and discriminated against for having their own domain. This, noted Illich, is to a large extent a modern myth—his point being that women had an autonomy within their domain, in the same way as men had autonomy within theirs. This modern myth serves the purpose of portraying modern society as superior to every other alternative. Illich also linked the abolition of separate gender domains to capitalism. As long as the male and the female are essentially different, the capitalistic logic that can be described as *exchange* or *transaction* will not work. Illich, taking on the role of a civilization critic, linked the genderified society to a state of autarky, and the sexist/capitalist to a state of scarcity. The psychological difference between these two states is cardinal. A traditional family of peasants in, say Mexico—Illich spent a lot time there—doesn't necessarily view itself as "poor," in contrast to the world-conception predominant in modern society by which the conviction of poverty and scarce resources is rife. Illich saw the latter as something historical and fabricated, something that deprives peoples and their societies of their autonomy.

Why this tendency, described by Illich, favors the interests of money-power ought to be clear; women too are proletarianized through it, and families now need a double income. At the same time there is a political aspect to this situation: historically, groups of men have been latent sources of resistance and insurgency. These alliances of men (in German *Männerbund*) in the church, administration, and military were the cohesive force of old Europe. Their logic does not quite fit with the logic of money-power and liberalism. For this reason, the process of demasculinization has run parallel with the dissolution of these kinds of male fellowships. To quote Hans Blüher:

> A state finds itself in the deepest corruption when the power slips through the *Männerbund's* fingers, and it ends up with coalitions whose purpose is strictly managerial.

The *Männerbund* always possesses a revolutionary potential; regardless of whether we speak of the abolition of debt bondage, the freeing of slaves, punishment of crooks, or the dethroning of unrightful rulers. This, among other reasons, is why it is regarded as an adversary by money-power and liberalism, why it is actively counteracted by them in an attempt to dismantle and domesticate it. White, European men are chiefly targeted by such efforts; they've been actively demasculinized to a degree that any masculinity in a man of European descent stirs up associations with Fascism among the politically correct crowd. At the same time European men are accused of lacking depth and authenticity. This means that their *thumos* is actively combated as well—but more about that later.

For reasons economical as well as political an active war has been waged against family, against the *Männerbunds*, against masculinity, and against femininity in Europe and the United States. The result is a ruin-landscape, in which strife between the genders and the generations has been incited. Divorces and broken families have grown in numbers, childbirth decreased. Studies show that after decades of feminist politics women are less happy than ever before. Levels of male testosterone have decreased, and culture as well as politics are described as being informed chiefly by female attitudes. In his time

Julius Evola talked about an emerging *gynocracy*—a rule of females and female attitudes. This, however, is not the whole truth; instead we can claim, taking our starting point in Klages and Illich, that male domains and male logic now imbue the female domain as well. What we see is that the lowest forms of both masculinity and femininity have come to dominate society, rather than any of one particular gender. Together with Klages we might just as well view that-which-goes-on as a devaluation of the feminine; our reaction then should not be to abet the devaluation any further, nor adopt lower forms of masculinity. We must recover and embolden others to recover the higher forms of masculinity and femininity offered in the myths and the history of our ancestors.

If a civilization is to survive, not only men and women, but children too are needed. The policies pursued in Europe and the United States renders this impossible; hence the choice between perdition or a different set of policies. Childbirth is decreasing, which David "Spengler" Goldman links to the spiritual emptiness. He writes:

> We live in a world in which most of the industrial nations find themselves in a demographic death-spiral, a Great Extinction of the Nations unlike anything we've seen since the 7th century. Most of the nations of the world would rather die out than adapt to modernity.

During the early 1900s radicals such as Otto Gross turned against what they called "the fathers" and their order. Freud described the circle around Gross as an "infection"; back then they were a vanishingly small minority of bohemians and rebels. A century later their conception-of-the-world has come to dominate large parts of society; a rainbow coalition of feminists, queer theoreticians, anti-racists, and other such groups are organizing themselves around the struggle against "the order of the fathers." This, combined with the logic of money-power and of the state, has lead to intergenerational conflicts and broken continuity. In earlier times parents could transfer important experiences to their children; upbringing contained rites of passage—like confirmation and conscription—that gave meaning and continuity. Things are different today, when instead Angrboda breeds her wolves and ogres.

The Free Citizen

> In the end a bureaucracy always costs the people more than an upper class.
>
> — DON COLACHO

Principal to any understanding of a historical order is the understanding of its people. Certainly, this entails understanding their values; but it also includes a sociopolitical side: what rights they have, whether they have ownership of their farmlands, and so on.

To a large extent history can be understood as the story of groups constituted by free, independent, and armed men who found or conquer kingdoms and then disappear or are reduced to clients, debt slaves, or subjects. This is a central theme in the civilizational critique of Robert E. Howard, in which the barbarian is someone who views civilization from the outside, and is not yet subjected to state or capital powers. The historian Brooks Adams instead described how the foundation of Rome was the free peasant. It was from the peasants that her hard-to-beat legions could be recruited. But political and economical processes availed in the out-competing by slave plantations of the free Roman, who often would succumb to debt slavery. Without him the empire became dependent on mercenaries and would later succumb itself. Similar processes recur throughout history, among elsewhere with the English *yeomen*. Adams describes a process that goes from *decentralization* to an increasing *centralization* of both economical and political power (Marx's *means of production*, Bakunin's *state*, Charles Tilly's *"capital and coercion"*). But centralization will then tip over into

disintegration: the family breaks apart, architecture, art, and culture
degenerate. The social organism is hollowed out, which entails that it
can no longer produce soldiers. Money-power and oligarchs that can't
be kept in check hollow out the foundations.

Hans Günther was one of the leading thinkers in that environment which was described by the term *völkisch*. Today interest in that
environment has returned among parts of the Alternative Right, but
the degree of ardency with which Günther is read there is uncertain.
This notwithstanding, *völkisch* originally meant focus on the people
rather than the state. It also meant interest in the people's traditions,
ancestry, and history; through these the personality of the people was
expressed. The *völkisch* movement strove towards a return to nature
and an organic German culture. Often there were connections to
nationalism and antisemitism, but there were also currents inspired
by a freer and more organic medieval Germany. From this environment came the German-Jewish "*völkisch* anarchist" Gustav Landauer.
Through his synthesis of freedom and organic community, of love
to the home-region and a willingness to replace the state with other
forms of cooperation, he became a particularly interesting writer for
both anarchists and nationalists. The *völkisch* environment had many
faces, and its adherents were in many ways the identitarians of their
time. Günther, nonetheless, wrote worthwhile passages about about
everything from Nordic heroism, Europe's racial history, and the
significance of language-politics, to the significance of an aristocratic caste, Nordic religiosity, and the problem of urbanization. His
Nordicism would today be of great value, as he, in many of his writings, has described Nordic exceptionality and peculiarity as something
positive—in stark contrast to our times, in which it is described by the
various things it *lacks* ("*the rhythm in the blood*," for instance, as well
as immigrant celebrities' wonderfully exotic perkiness). He also care-
fully described a positive alternative to political correctness, taking his
starting point as Indo-European human ideals like *humanitas* and the

stormenska. According to Günther, ideals like these could not come to fruition through either liberalism or Hitlerism (which he experienced first hand). The latter, he believed, lacked knowledge of human nature as well as compassion; it was only nominally *völkisch*, and this only for a brief period of time. Günther also raised the question of destiny for the free citizen in the modern world. He described how a *people* of free men have transformed into a *mass* inhabiting the big cities. For its part, Marxism describes how the petty bourgeoisie succumbs and becomes part of the proletariat; *proletarianization* entails that fewer work for themselves. The process is the same, but viewed from different angles. Günther, among other things, was not as optimistic as Marx. From his genetical viewpoint it is more difficult to recreate what has been lost than it is from Marx's strictly sociological perspective. Günther also held that with the emergence of big cities the mass began to dominate culture and politics, and thus to impede the return to a democratic republic of freedom and property-based families. He even described National Socialism as split between the city's and the countryside's representatives, between mass and people.

The question is raised in our times—more often than it used to be—of the *crisis of the middle class.* The middle class and its values are the basis of economy and society, yet all of this is under assault by a growing *Lumpenproletariat* as well as by oligarchs and elites. Especially in the United States, the state of the middle class is critical. We can view it as a resource which is difficult to renew, yet which is critical if the system is to work. At the same time, it is a resource that is all too readily exploited, among other things through taxes and economic policies that favor the very rich as well as their poor support troops. It might take a while, but eventually large blocs of the middle class will discern this and turn against the system. This, among other things, is what lies behind the Trump phenomenon and much of so-called populism in general. Be that as it may, seen from a historical perspective, it is an already substantially weakened middle class that is now reacting. Compared to Adams' or Günther's study-objects, most European middle-class men, for instance, have long since been unarmed, nor are they the owners of their homes, and they are employed by some large bureaucratic organization. Nevertheless, their reaction might come to change all this and hopefully to have a ripple effect.

The status of the middle class is one of the system's most explosive inner tensions; on the one hand it is central to a working economy, and on the other hand it is politically marginalized to such a degree that an alliance of various special interests are exploiting it. All through the 1900s these special interests have grown in both appetite and power, and we have reached a boiling point. Not least of all as they are replacing the populations of Europe and the United States.

Ethnic Replacement and Group Solidarity

> ...during the last 30 years the so-called migrant has, through a unique pathological inversion of the values in the public discourse, become the subject of a kind of deification ... His value supersedes that of the native.
>
> — AKIF PIRINÇCI

The foundation of the 1900s' economic prosperity was the middle class (including the working class) or the people. In most cases this group was overwhelmingly ethnically homogeneous, of European stock, and molded by values which were the fruits of a long intra-European history and which were furthering of stability and growth. This resource was taken for granted. In addition, the de-Nazification that ensued after 1945 and which the liberal order was built on, made it much more difficult to point this out. Hitler was the demon that in many ways was the liberal order's foundation: anything resembling him was avoided. Hence, Europe was in part ruled by Hitler despite his defeat, but in accordance with the logic of the inverted image—Hitler's pet issues were also the anti-fascists' pet issues. This demonology reached its dire consequences as money-power and the *ersatz*-religions, in unison, albeit for somewhat different reasons, invited the hordes of the Third World into Europe. Furthermore, this occurred in a historical phase when the natural solidarity of the European peoples was already undermined by urbanization, atomization, and the culture-industry.

Both Glubb and Spengler described how ingroup solidarity—the feeling of unity—loses ground during the phase of decline. Even the North African philosopher of social matters, Ibn Khaldun, described this using the term *asabiyya*. History is a cycle in which tribes with strong group solidarity conquer larger empires, and thereafter, as a result of prosperity and affluence, lose their social cohesion and their warrior values, with the result that they, in turn, get conquered by a new group, and the cycle reiterates. Historically, the case has more often than not been that smaller groups conquer a larger empire, and then get absorbed by it. The mass migration happening today, however, seldom involves "smaller groups," and is thus qualitatively different from the earlier cycles. In the Swedish political debate it is considered obvious that the new arrivals will merge into the Swedish *ethnos*; we lack a conceptual structure with which to pose the question of what will happen if, instead, they have a stronger *asabiyya* than the Swedes. Often this is what is being alluded to when people speak of Islamization. In today's debate we lack the concepts with which to grasp ethnic relations and ethnic rivalry, and are referred instead to the unwieldy concept of "racism."

The Spenglerian F. P. Yockey described how a high culture can assimilate people from completely different regions. This is the case especially if the high culture's ideals appear attractive; the new members will then often defend it with even more conviction than those born and raised in it. They can then be assets who view the high culture with somewhat new eyes; possibly, the new arrivals will be more resistant towards the degenerative processes. But when larger groups are considered, and in particular when we are dealing with a high culture in crisis, the situation is different. In this case an apter description would be *colonization* rather than assimilation; quantitative change will switch over into qualitative change. The result will be ethnic conflicts and the emergence of ethnic lower classes that brutalize the same native middle class that feeds and houses them. Ethnic lower classes, to make matters worse, that rapidly grow in size. This too is a built-in antagonism, one of the utmost explosive potential. The European peoples have never before been pushed back this hard; in the United States, for instance, they are approaching minority status while, at the same time, being blamed for racism. Out of Sweden's ten million inhabitants approximately seven million are ethnic Swedes; many of these significantly older than the new arrivals.

In *World on Fire* Amy Chua describes how market capitalism together with democracy and multi-ethnic societies makes for an extremely risky combination. Different groups will, for the most part, be unequally economically successful, be this due to different genetic or to different cultural conditions. Among the less successful groups, this will kindle an ethnic *ressentiment* towards the richer groups. The latter also tend to lose out in numerical strength, like the Chinese in the Philippines or the Lebanese in West Africa. The same *ressentiment* can be identified in Europe today; many countries have been delineated with the built-in possibility of ethnic conflict. At the same time this population replacement is instigating a process of *white flight*—the indigenous population withdrawing from greater and greater areas of their homelands. The ensuing development of these areas suggests, much more often than not, that not only is the indigenous population the real foundation of stability and prosperity, and a resource which today is treated with anything but responsibility, but also that its renewal is very slow at best.

Moreover, the multi-ethnic society also furthers the process of diminishing *asabiyyah* and social capital. Professor Putnam has written that *"trust between races is relatively high in the homogenous South Dakota and relatively low in the heterogenous San Francisco and Los*

Angeles … In societies marked by diversity people have less trust in their neighbours." But trust within one's own group also decreases in diverse societies; the loss of social capital affects the whole society. Putnam has also noted that the studies that have been made suggest that when the social capital is large, children will grow up to be healthier, safer, and better educated; and people in general will live longer and happier lives. In addition, both democracy and the economy will work better. Similarly to the crisis of the middle class, this is one of the utmost explosive antagonisms built into the system, and one that is nearly impossible to resolve or even to discuss in an adult manner for that matter.

The Welfare State Becomes Amorphous and Therapeutic

> … the most dangerous lie of our century: the red bureaucracy.
> — BAKUNIN

A common misconception is that the welfare state is socialistic. In the form of *Folkhemmet*[2] it was often a more or less conservative project, while the goal of original socialism was rather for the proletariat and the people, in unison, to seize control of their destiny (including the economy). Along with many socialist thinkers, the classical liberal de Jouvenel has identified the difference between the welfare state's redistribution policy and a genuine socialism. The welfare state is a compromise between labor and capital adopted for its presumed effectiveness. The alternative was social vexation strong enough to cause the whole system to collapse. However, when we view the welfare state strictly as a compromise between capital and labor, we tend to overlook the prevalence of certain actors, among whom are those people who work within it, and those who work for the state as such.

---

2   Swedish; literally translated as "a home for the people." — Tr.

The tax-proportion of the economy has increased during the 1900s, as have the activities of the state. From its original preoccupations of war and court, the state has today become a welfare state. Further yet, it has now developed into a *therapeutic* state. The therapeutic state even attempts to shape its citizens' conception-of-the-world, as well as their opinions, to alter their ethnic stock, et cetera.

Paul Gottfried, the godfather of American paleoconservatism, has described this process as ultimately being a conflict between economic and political liberalism. The liberalism of the 1800s was first and foremost an economic liberalism, supplemented by bourgeois mores, over which self-discipline, Christendom, and some paleolithic aristocratic values still reigned. But there was also a political liberalism, whose demands included that of democracy. Some liberals thought that universal suffrage would come to work as a weapon against the old upper classes and the free market. They were wrong, and the classical liberals who have been warning about how universal suffrage would lead to socialism were somewhat more accurate in their predictions. What emerged was a kind of state hitherto unthought of, completely different from the nightwatchman state, and considerably different from the kind of socialism fought for by the socialists. Gottfried calls it a *managerial state*, a term which bears connotations of technocracy. It is a state with a much wider area of responsibility, and one which intervenes in the economy to plan and redistribute wealth. This state would come to employ a whole class of bureaucrats and administrators; together with their kin in big corporations and mass organizations, they are sometimes called *the New Class*. Like all classes it had its own vested interests and developed its own conception-of-the-world. Gottfried describes its situation as ambivalent:

> It possesses considerable material power but does not own the productive forces. Although the influence of the class is massive and demonstrative, this is not the case for the individual members.

The next step was the *therapeutic* state. Now it wasn't enough—especially not considering the recent horrifying experience of the Second Word War, the Third Reich, et cetera—to merely administer society and its citizens; people had to be *educated* into becoming democratic and tolerant citizens. With Adorno's most biased and dubious study, *The Authoritarian Personality*, an important step was taken toward the therapeutic state, in which certain ideological stances were seen as the result of mental illness. The prior tendency of an expanding state, which de Jouvenel named the *Minotaur*, now received further legitimacy and even more projects to delve into.

But a state of this magnitude contributes to the Great Worsening through an active combat against older norms, and through mitigating the consequences, not only of bad luck and business cycles, but also of poor life choices in general. The New Class has a hedonistic and cosmopolitan conception-of-the-world, which permeates the therapeutic state. There have been discussions among eugenicists in history as to whether capitalism is really dysgenic, that is, favoring the wrong dispositions. Socialistic eugenicists such as Ludwig Woltmann deemed this to be the case; in a capitalistic order the rural population succumbs, and inequality cements over time. Even the more reactionary Ludwig Klages entertained similar thoughts, namely, that the survival and thriving of people with more *Geist* and less *Seele* have been favored by the history of the last few centuries. The Danish researcher, Helmuth Nyborg, has shown how falling IQ-scores are linked to the expansion of the welfare state, which at a certain point becomes dysgenic—culturally as well as genetically. A point is reached in the end at which a complex society no longer can be sustained by its inhabitants; a process that according to Nyborg is reinforced by immigration. The German geneticist Volkmar Weiss has, with his theory of population cycles, shown how this can issue in population collapse and a "great chaos."

Academy and Ideology

> A people striving for self-rule must arm itself with the power of
> knowledge.
>
> — James Madison

The Great Worsening also takes expression in the academy, while
simultaneously being informed by whatever changes take place there.
That which we call *PC*, political correctness, is to a large degree a child
born of the academic world, in which everything from queer feminism
to "Critical Whiteness Studies" have originated. At the same time we
shouldn't underestimate the significance of activist groups in the real
world; ethnomasochism hardly would have emerged if it weren't for
the influence that the civil rights movement in the United States and
the anti-colonial struggle of the Third World had on the 68-rebels who
were both impressed by and sympathetic towards these groups.

Reactionaries like Carvalho and Evola had, for a long time, been
skeptical towards intellectuals as a group, but it was only later, and in
combination with political correctness, that these intellectuals became
a factor of unquestionable harm. The more subversive intellectuals
conquered the academical world, and using it as a base they began to
mass produce ever new generations of politically correct civil servants,
journalists, librarians, children's show hosts, et cetera. The situation
has been described by Carvalho:

> The bureaucracy with which the kshatriya state controls society be-
> comes a time bomb. On the one hand, it is clear that the bureaucratic
> intelligentsia soon will seize control over the state, while at the same
> time it will dream of unburdening itself of an increasingly idle and
> costly aristocratic caste. On the other hand, there will be the cohorts
> of those that have been rejected. Their ambitions were built up by their
> education, but frustrated by the job supply.

The therapeutic state is thus entwined within a bureaucratic caste and the academic world that produces it. A shared set of experiences and a uniform conception-of-the-world separates them from the old aristocracy and the rest of the crowd. But this is not enough; not everyone who received a higher education will be able to find employment within the state; some will be left out in the cold. Carvalho called them the *potential bureaucracy*, and described them as a subversive, frustrated, and vain group. Modern history confirms his analysis of the role played by the unemployed intellectuals. "Workers movements" and its associated "revolutions," for example, have not seldom been led by people who are not workers themselves. Academy has a Janus face: on the one hand, it transfers from one generation to the next a tradition of learning, *humanitas*, and critical thinking; on the other hand, it is entwined with a specific caste with its specific interests, and is used by it as a tool. How the academy's goals have transmuted from truth and education to a certain form of "justice," has been outlined by, among others, the social psychologist Jonathan Haidt. At any rate, ideological diversity has become a distant memory in many academic environments.

It is in this environment that things like political correctness and *ersatz*-religions originate. When the new generation of students lacked interest in education and scholarly achievement and were interested instead in power and politics, as was to a large degree the case during 1968, this entailed consequences for the academical world itself; it led to a dumbing down of academy and society. From then onward, the constantly renewed cohorts of the politically correct could infiltrate and take over new parts of society, from Amnesty International to Greenpeace. An inflation in the sphere of formal education began—something that could be compared to a bubble. But when the bubble bursts the subversive tendencies of the potential bureaucracy will be strongly felt.

The Iron Law of the Oligarchy

...the whole world, in its protest against False Governments, hasn't succeeded in finding any other solution than to throw itself into No Government or anarchy (kinglessness), which is how I view this universal suffragism...

— THOMAS CARLYLE

The political order too is reminiscent of a car about to break down, making it's way forward, ever more sputtering and uncertain. The order was built on party-based parliamentarism, at first in combination with genuine statesmen like de Gaulle. Nonetheless, as Robert Michels and Simone Weil, among others, have shown, the party-based order is unstable; it is prone to skew recruitment and to produce the emergence of an establishment with interests different from those of the electorate. According to the ponerologists, a skewed recruitment has indeed shaped our political order, which has become a *pathocracy* dominated by psychopaths. Both Spengler and von Treitschke observed that the normal route to money-power-rule is through democracy—a rather unsurprising claim for those who've been following the American presidential election and the related big-money donors. Without money it is hard to win any elections today. We should be aware of the connection between these three processes: the modern party system that favors, among other things, psychopaths, who in their turn are easily bought by oligarchs and foreign interests, is giving rise to an exceedingly unpleasant establishment. To quote de Jouvenel:

A society of sheep will in due time breed a government of wolves.

In his time, the political scientist Vilfredo Pareto spoke about the interchanging back-and-forth of elites of lions and foxes. Our times, it seems, are shaped by shortsighted manipulative foxes who, in addition, have monopolized parliament and parties to such a degree that we cannot talk about rule by the people anymore, other than in a strictly nominal sense. The established power blocs cement and grow closer to each other until the conflict stands, not between different parties, but between the establishment and the people. At the same time it will overstep the bounds of party-politics and threaten to blow up the party-based political order.

This, however, is not the only antagonism built into the political order. In his time, the jurist and political theorist Carl Schmitt noted that each political order is ultimately built upon a single central concept. Monarchy, for instance, is built upon *honor*. When honor loses its high standing the monarchy becomes an empty shell, and it is only a matter of time before it is replaced by something more fashionable. The parliamentarism in the Weimar Republic, however, was built on two concepts, whose coexistence is problematical. On the one hand, it was based on the liberal view of the value of discussion, and on the other hand on the democratic view of the identity between ruler and ruled. The situation today is similar, except now there are *three* concepts: democracy, discussion, and the commandments of political correctness. The conflict among these entails, among other things, that the historical bourgeois separation of private and public sphere dissolve, and that liberal freedoms, such as the freedom of speech, be practically abandoned. The latter in particular is a consequence of the multi-ethnic society, in which social peace is predicated upon the inability of certain groups to criticize others groups.

The Economical

> Today we are free, but a day will come when our republic becomes an impossibility. It will be impossible because the riches will be gathered in the hands of the few.
>
> — JAMES MADISON

The order of the late 1900s was a mixed economy, but with a capitalistic base. Built into capitalism there are tendencies of increasing inequality,

which will, if not counteracted, erode the free middle classes. Brooks
Adams spoke about centralization to describe this process, and Peter
Turchin of the Principle of Matthew (*"for he that has will have more
given to him"*[3]). Indian-influenced economist Ravi Batra has shown
that large disparities lead to lending crises, during which the rich lend
money to the very poor, in spite of the latter being unable to properly
pay back.

This tendency was kept in check during the conflict with the
Eastern bloc, in part to show the superiority of the Western model
as it was pitted against the Eastern. Around the 70s, however, that
model had reached the end of the road, and was gradually dismantled.
Privatizations and deregulations were implemented in an attempt to
make the system work better, but their real effect was to cause power
to shift from the political to the economical sphere. Deregulations
between individual state economies on behalf of the financial sector
were particularly upsetting; jobs were exported to the Third World, the
First World was de-industrialized, and global financial capital came
to dominate the real economy. The result has been the prevalence of
recurring crises and the cornering of the middle class. In this connection, Alain de Benoist has said that the middle class is the enemy of the
financial capital; there are vast amounts of people all over the world
who can do their work significantly cheaper. He talks about *deterritorialized* capitalism—that is, a capitalism that no longer accepts state
borders. Legalization of the mobility of financial capital, increasing
free trade, and migrant flows have brought about a situation in which
the Swedish worker is more or less directly competing against workers
from developing countries. To understand this process, the myopic
view of liberalism is insufficient; we would do much better to turn to a
historian of economics like Fernand Braudel. Braudel spoke about the
contra-market, that level of things on which *"the great predators roam*

---

3   Matthew 13:12. — Tr.

about and the law of the jungle reigns." He also described this level as
the anti-market. When Goldman Sachs receives massive bailouts from
the American government while the same individuals hold top positions on both sides, this is an example of what Braudel had in mind.
Manuel DeLanda notes, with regard to Braudel, that *"capitalism and
the market have always been different things."* Many classical liberals
and anarchists were well aware of the intimate cooperation between
state and large-scale capital interests (Noam Chomsky's "socialism for
the rich"). The many connections between "the great predators" and
the politicians today act as fuel for crises and bubbles. Matt Taibbi has
described how this took place both before and after the 2008 financial
crisis, and how Obamacare really was designed to benefit "Big Pharma"
and "Big Insurance." The effects are crises and deeper disparities.

Many assessors, in particular from Marxist environments, deem
that capitalism as a historical phenomenon is currently being thrown
into a crisis that it won't escape alive. Immanuel Wallerstein, a valuable thinker in this context, has foreseen the death of capitalism and
liberalism before 2050, partly as a result of a decreasing supply of
cheap labor in the form of semi-proletarians—workers with small
farms. He has also looked into the cornered situation of the middle
classes; historically, they have had a stabilizing function with respect
to politics, which today is being decimated in favor of the global capital. Wolfgang Streeck notes instead how capitalism in the industrial
countries is dragged down by slow growth, increasing indebtedness,
and larger disparities and inequalities. These three processes are
codependent, by which he means that too great disparities will make
fewer consumers of significant purchasing power, hence less need
for innovations. Streeck also identifies how the economy has become
disconnected from politics, and how an uninhibited greed now has
become widespread. As a throwback to Marx, he notes how the new
financial capital has managed to short-circuit the classical formula
"M-C-M"—money that is turned into a commodity, that is turned

into more money—to just "M-M". But when money itself creates new money, thereby side-stepping the physical economy, this brings dire consequences for the rest of society.

Occupied Europe

> All real nobility, all culture resides in being. The one who chases money is bound to lose out in terms of being. A Samurai owned nothing, save his sword and his cultivation. He lived his life in line with Bushido, the way of the warrior. Among ourselves, in a not all too different manner, it used to be stated: "He who swears by Prussia's banner, owns nothing except that which is his own." Look at the United States, and you will find the country of uninhibited material greed.
>
> — Von Lohausen

After 1945 Europe became occupied by two non-European powers, the Soviet and the United States. The older Eurocentric order had succumbed from a lack of solidarity, and from what Oswald Mosley called "petty nationalism." In the competition among European states, non-European powers were invited to participate, which for some countries had certain short-term benefits, but which proved catastrophic in the longer term. Europe had lost her independence and her colonies, Western Europe became Americanized and Eastern Europe was forcibly transformed into a number of people's republics. Aggravated by Americanization, the negative processes within culture and politics were strengthened. Among the contributing factors were Hollywood and various academic ideologies like queer theory or "anti-racism." In the long run, this resulted in Europe becoming more like the United States, and, among other things, importing its racial conflicts. The link between geopolitics and culture is evident.

The order that was instituted after the second World War was bipolar, with two superpowers, each with its respective sphere of interests. Western Europe was dominated by what has been called *parti américan*—leaders with their loyalty towards the United States.

The United States was the *hegemon* of the capitalist world economy, its police and guarantor. This notwithstanding, the statement that all success carries within it the seeds of its own decline is true also for hegemons. The leading power tends, among other things, to invest large sums of money in the military; meanwhile newer powers can grow considerably under its protection. The aging hegemon also lends large sums of money to the newer powers during this phase. This is the situation that the United States is in today. But a hegemon in decline can be an imminent danger to its surroundings. It may be giant with clay feet, but it is still a giant.

A Europe dominated by *parti américan* combined with a United States in decline means problems. American foreign policy never had European interests in mind to begin with, a truth which is more apparent today than ever. Two American goals are to render an independent Europe impossible on the one hand, as well as alliances between Europe and Russia on the other. Several quite recent American initiatives have affected Europe negatively, like the wars in Northern Africa and the Middle East, which have led to massive migrations and the emergence of Jihadist bases at the very threshold of Europe. The activities in Ukraine haven't benefited Europe either. But the many politicians who are loyal to the United States have been a driving force in the European involvement in these anti-European projects, notwithstanding the open geopolitical wounds across the European lands which they have left in their tracks.

The politics pursued by America in many regions aggravates that process which goes by the name 4GW—fourth generation warfare. The term was coined by, among others, the paleoconservative William S. Lind, and refers to a reality in which the state's monopoly on force has been undermined, often by non-governmental operators that challenge state power as war rules and boundaries between civilians and military blur. Moreover, it is also difficult to defeat a 4GW-operator; the Jihadists on European soil, for instance, don't have a capital city to capture. Accordingly, Lind has deemed 4GW a threat to every state, and issued a warning to every state against the use of non-governmental operators as a weapon against other states, lest chaos spread everywhere. Nonetheless, this kind of tactical use of chaos plays a central role in American geopolitics.

In brief: the present world order was dubious to begin with; today it is even less functional than before, and threatens to fall apart.

Ecology

> The wild boar, the alpine ibex, the fox, the weasel, the duck, and the otter—all those animals with which legends, so dear to our hearts, are intimately connected—are decreasing in numbers, where they haven't already gone extinct.
>
> — LUDWIG KLAGES

The foundations of any human order reside in nature. Erosion, toxic waste, peak oil, et cetera, threaten human society. Jared Diamond's thesis in *Collapse* is that many historical societies declined as a result of environmental factors, often in combination with an increase in population. This leads to strife and unrest. In our times, the richer countries can export the ecological effects of their exuberant and unsustainable lifestyle, but these will often, in various ways, find their way back around. The growth and consumption society is unsustainable; we keep wiping out animal and plant species, while simultaneously doing damage to our genetic make-up with everything from toxins to plastics.

An aspect which is equally central to the modern world is man's loss of touch with nature and with the living, which has been replaced with an artificial environment where everyone is always surrounded by other people. This hyper-socializing can be linked to political correctness; strict codes of conduct appear necessary in a world populated by alien masses. Both Günther and Don Colacho turned against urbanization and its effects. The latter noted coldly how anyone who has witnessed a landscape both before and after the leap of "progress" would understand how hideous this progress really is. It is about alienation in a very fundamental sense, an alienation which also makes possible the adoption of ideologies that are estranged from reality. In his cultural critique Günther brings to mind the young Marx and his thoughts on alienation and essential being (*Gattungswesen*). Günther too based his reasoning on the notion of man's essential being, and how life in the cities turns him away from that being and makes him estranged or alien to it. In the city, we live in an artificial environment and turn ourselves into domesticated animals. Günther meant that the instances of technological progress in our times were often just "apparent progress," coincidental with anthropological and genetic regress. Moreover, there are areas in which "progress" is impossible; Günther brought up humanness and *humanitas*; today a horse is more authentic in its horseness than modern man in his humanness. Differing from Marx, Günther held that different groups of people also differed in their essential being; what is natural for one group could very well be strange (in German *artfremd*) for another. Specifically, he held that the Nordic man is particularly vulnerable to urbanization.

Here we also find a critique of modern technology, based on its effects on man. Edward Abbey even turned against the use of a flashlight when experiencing nature, claiming that such a device would isolate us from nature. Evola stated that technology becomes a surrogate for knowledge and power and thus replaces authentic knowledge and power. The more powerful his tools, the weaker man becomes; the inner sovereign gets replaced by a cell phone, a television set, or some other screen.

Many exponents of the ecological perspective have been "reactionaries"; this has been the case for the immigration-adverse anarchist Edward Abbey, the Nordicist Madison Grant, and Ludwig Klages. Klages in particular is worth a deeper look, as he outlined an in-depth critique of the modern world. He was a philosopher, a psychologist, and a prominent graphologist. Together with Alfred Schuler and Karl Wolfskehl, he formed for some time the "Cosmic Circle" in Munich, partly associated with Stefan George, but at the same time in opposition to the overly patriarchal focus of George's following. Klages was a proliferate and original thinker; among other things, he used the term "id" before Freud, and also coined the term logocentrism—nowadays perhaps most ardently used in certain strains of feminist theory. To his school of psychological thought he gave the name *characterology*. He also received a great deal of notoriety for his works in graphology.

One of the great takeaways from Klages' thought is what he called the biocentric conception-of-the-world. For him the distinction between "idealism" and "realism" appeared rather irrelevant; instead, a considerably deeper, and much less known, historical conflict is brought to the center. Klages put *life* at the center, but identified at the same time a life-adverse power that has come to gradually infiltrate the world, to finally conquer it. He used the German terms *Seele* and *Geist*, roughly translated as Soul and Spirit. Life and Soul are connected, but the nature of *Geist* is abstractions, ideologies, thoughts about "sin," "will to power," and the like. The description of how *Geist* like a vampire becomes ever more pervasive has a lot in common with Nietzsche's description of how *ressentiment* and slave-morality spread, but to Klages even Nietzsche appeared dangerously similar to the vampire. There is a kind of kinship between the more Gothic Marx and Klages; the former readily compared capital to a vampire, while the latter likened *Geist* to an otherworldly vampire.

Klages described the modern world as degenerated, but he did so in terms that might surprise some. The will to power is an expression of *Geist*; the same holds for the insatiable capitalism that turns lives into things, and for the modern science that reduces them to facts. Klages was no friend of Christianity either. Instead he considered life and the faculty to experience it central. To the Soul he imputed the love of nature, the home, the fatherland, the animals and the plants, memories, ancestors, and the cosmos. Much of what liberals hold dear—everything from the "enlightenment" and 1789 to "growth" and "equality"—was, on the contrary, met with suspicion by Klages. His concerns were rather such things as the empathic quality, the faculty to experience animated reality as something other than lifeless things. This faculty has a lethal effect on the modern world. Briefly put: Klages must be seen as a representative for the Deep Right.

Chapter 3

The Toothless "Right"

When the ideas of 1968 hit Sweden, the so-called Swedish bourgeoisie stood intellectually and culturally almost without a defense … Whether the bourgeoisie thought of themselves as liberal, conservative, or culturally conservative it stood without an erudite and living holistic understanding on the basis of which it could have thoroughly countered the Left. The defenders of the bourgeoisie, to a large extent, lacked an intellectual and cultural self-awareness—they had to ponder and back-track before they really knew what it was they represented.

— Claes G. Ryn

When during the ongoing mass migration Fredrik Reinfeldt urged the Swedes to open their hearts (in reality their wallets), there were many who struggled to recognize the old right-wing party. The same occurred when leading Republicans actively worked against their own candidate in favor of Hillary Clinton. There are also many who, in hindsight, have reacted to the ease with which the student rebels during 1968 could sweep major parts of the existing order off their feet. The resistance of today appears confused and impotent, and the resistance of yesterday often was so. Many times it didn't even have a serious intention. What actually happened to the "Right" anyway?

But to begin with: what is the Right? It is not without certain consideration that this book was given the subtitle *The Right of the 21st Century.* The terms Right and Left are defined differently de-pending on whom you ask. Several of the groups that we will study more closely in the subsequent chapters do not describe themselves as Right, and even question the usefulness of the terms themselves. Notwithstanding this, there is a historical tradition of ideas, or a sensibility perhaps, that could be called the authentic Right, and to which the groups that we will look into are more or less closely related. This tradition of the authentic Right has little to nothing in common with what today is called the Right. Most elements of today's "Right" were originally viewed as Leftist, including everything from the fondness for the free market to inwardly homogeneous and externally hostile nation-states.

The traditionalist Julius Evola defined the basic attitude of the authentic Right as *"defending the values of the Tradition—spiritual, aristocratic, and warrior values."* It is about a striving towards the higher—transcendence of the mundane towards the supernatural—in different spheres. The man of the Right isn't necessarily conservative; it all depends on whether there is something of value to conserve. Evola contrasts the attitude of the Right with things such as the modern-world-phenomena of materialism, economism, feminism, democracy, and belief in progress. The political ideal, for Evola, is rather a monarchy in an organic society. Economically, Evola viewed capitalism as legitimate, *"as long as it doesn't abuse its power."* Based on Evola's definition it is clear that most political parties and movements of today belong to the Left. Our society is quite bereft of "spiritual, aristocratic, and warrior values," and it is not very organic either. Instead it is made up of a mass of atomized individuals who, at regular intervals, participate in political elections, and in the meantime oscillate between producing and consuming. A principle value of Evola's definition is that a particular conception-of-man is implicit to it, a particular anthropology. A man of the Right strives to live in line with spiritual, aristocratic, and warrior values, such as honor, grandness, and courage.

What Evola often forgot to emphasize was the element of solidarity, cooperation, reciprocity, and autonomy in an organic society. Ownership, for instance, was not capitalistic in nature; there were different forms of public property, as well as safety nets in the clan, the guild, or the village. Significant parts of life weren't *economical*

the way they are today. Similarly, relations were feudal rather than
liberal, also those between superiors and subordinates. The superiors
had a responsibility toward the lower ranks. But to get a complete
view of the authentic Right's conception-of-the-world we are well
advised, once again, to turn to Hans Günther—perhaps the most
fruitful thinker within the *völkisch* and Nordicist sphere. The term
völkisch is linked to a defense of the people (the *Volk*) and its traditions, but originally there was also an aspect of anti-capitalism
involved. Günther considered the ideas of the 1800s, *"Darwinism
and liberalism,"* to be anti-heroic, a betrayal of the little man. While
the Middle Ages were built on fidelity and mutual responsibility, the
French Revolution meant that *"the penny-clutching bourgeoisie was
let loose,"* and that *"human rights replaced human duties."* The fury
that pours out in Günther's description of this process even tops that
of Marx. He describes how the Earl, when at war, used to ride in
the front line; how the artisans in each city came together in guilds
and lodges to negotiate prices and salaries; how the poor were taken
care of. All of this was torn into pieces by the ideas of the 1800s.
With Günther's thinking in mind, the reason becomes clearer why
so many social reforms, like the safety-net that Bismarck created, or
the factory laws Marx was interested in, were pushed through by the
aristocratic or the Christian Right. It also reminds us of how many
peasant-revolts occurred in the name of "the old law"— a *völkisch*
traditionalism directed against the advancements of money and
centralized state-power.

The authentic Right turned against the reduction of society and
culture to economy and market. In England there was for a long time
a Tory-tradition that was skeptical of capitalism; latter-day representatives include the Canadian George Grant and the British Phillip Blond.
In the Swedish speaking parts of Finland an aristocratic tradition still
exists, represented by names like Örnulf Tigerstedt. Marx described
this Right in derisive terms like "feudal socialism," even though their

conception-of-the-world was as multifaceted, if not more multifaceted, than his. Many members of the Labour Party, in its early days, cited John Ruskin as their foremost source of inspiration—more, in fact, than those who cited *Das Kapital* or the Bible. Alain Soral has defined the Right with a starting point based on the fundamental values *"honor, virtue, respect for elders, and hierarchy."* Alain de Benoist has described the historical Right as *"at the same time popular and aristocratic,"* *"anti-individualistic as well as anti-utilitarian ... with an honor-based ethics."* For this Right, "utility," economical or not, individual or collective, was subordinated to things like honor.

A central theme in the tradition of the Right is the insight of inequality: people are not equal. This has been described as anti-egalitarianism and anti-universalism, and will necessarily lead to a hierarchical view of society. In his time, the reactionary de Maistre had a concise way of putting it: *"I have seen Frenchmen, Italians, Russians, et cetera,"* he said, *"but as for a Man, I declare that I have never met him in my life."* In de Maistre's time large-scale immigration to Europe was unheard of, but given his perspective he would have regarded such a phenomenon with skepticism. Today this question is urgent in a very different way than was the case during the early 1800s, as the European peoples are now exposed to processes that in a very short time, relative to history, will wipe them out if nothing changes. Another marked difference between our times and de Maistre's is the incessant pushing of a uniform economical and political model for all countries; this also never became an urgent question for de Maistre. The tradition of the authentic Right has always upheld an organic society, with both unity and autonomy, as the ideal. The totalitarian state appear strange to the authentic Right, as does a society reduced to market mechanisms.

The Right and the Alternative Modernity

An unhinged freedom is nothing but slavery, for without boundaries the
weak will succumb to the strong.

— VON TREITSCHKE

A century ago, the European Right was standing, in a way, both weak
and strong at the same time. It had imbued and developed new ideas
and perspectives, to a large degree under the influence of Nietzsche.
The Right at the turn of the last century was in many ways reminiscent of that Internet sphere that today goes by the name "the Dark
Enlightenment." Researchers and philosophers took no conventional
truth as a given, but were constantly engaged in debunking several
convenient illusions of the time. Freud disclosed the belief in the
rational individual as a myth, and was interpreted by, among others,
Ludovici and Blüher; Gustave Le Bon explored the psychology of the
masses; Oswald Spengler concerned himself with the rise and decline
of cultures, including our own; Sorel wrote about the nature of violence
and the significance of myth; Vilfredo Pareto studied the rise and decline of the elites; Lombroso laid the foundations for a criminological
anthropology that included a significant interest in the role of physiognomy; Günther and L. F. Clauss described the Nordic peculiarity and
discovered paths in physical anthropology; geopolitical thinkers like
Ratzel and Kjellén disclosed the actual ways in which history works,
and how states conduct themselves in their relations with one another;
et cetera. All of this taken as a whole could be described as an alternative modernity, especially in combination with trends in the world of
fine arts, like the works of Pound, Marinetti, and Wyndham Lewis. It
was certainly difficult to accommodate this alternative way of relating
to the world with liberalism's conception-of-the-world; religion too
was not always accepting towards it. Its conclusions were nonetheless
interesting and it contained a significant potential. In its best moments
it was a genuine conservative revolution, in which timeless values

found expressions in new shapes and forms. In its worst moments it was realism combined with chauvinism.

The Swedish Young Right (*Unghögern*) was a good example of this kind of revolutionary conservative Right, represented by, among others, Rudolf Kjellén. He coined terms like *Folkhem* [loosely translated as "the people's home," but with connotations more along the line of a "desirable home"—Tr.] and geopolitics, and he joined his conservatism with necessary social reforms. Kjellén studied both geopolitics (the state as a *Reich*) and ethnopolitics (the state as a people). He took great interest in those processes by which new peoples are born and older peoples die out. In viewing the state as a household he endorsed autarky as a principle:

> A *Reich*, just like a person, ought for the sake of its economical independence, as a prerequisite of political self-determination, to a certain degree "rely upon itself."

Embedded in his geopolitical thinking there are some interesting similarities with modern ideas of a united Europe, not least as history tends to make ever increasing spatial demands as it progresses. This is illustrated by the continual expansion in size of the leading trading powers, from Venice, the small city, to the small delta of the Netherlands, over to the insular kingdom of England and further yet to the North American continent. Also in line with this is the development from Prussia to larger Germany, which could very well in the next large step forward become Europe. Eurasia and Eurosiberia are both logical extensions of Kjellén's perspective.

Classical liberalism's view of the state as a nightwatchman was also rejected by Kjellén. He took the exploitation of Norrland[4] during the early 1900s as an example, when financially strong interests mis-

---

4   The northern part of Sweden, comprising 60% of the country's total land area. — Tr.

treated natural resources and tricked the local population. If we regard the state as simply a nightwatchman, these kinds of things become unproblematic, but if we regard the state as household and as people the situation is different. This meant that Kjellén and the conservative nationalism that he was associated with welcomed, if necessary, state interventions in market economy, state-driven education and culture politics, as well as welfare politics. Kjellén was also critical of the democracy of his time: a democracy based on individualism becomes *"disintegrating, destructive, and leveling. It will gravel the ground were the old class society stood, but it won't build anything new and positive."* Besides Kjellén, the Swedish Young Right had representatives including Adrian Molin and Vitalis Nordström.

Nevertheless, the Swedish Young Right lacked many aspects found in the Deep Right. There was seldom any talk of any deeper spirituality; effective organization and a stronger state were rather the main focus of attention. Something similar could be said of the British Nietzschean thinker Anthony Ludovici. He claimed that the modern man, as a result of far-gone dysgenic trends, has been given a "chaotic constitution," biologically inferior to the complete and seamless individual of older times. Where the "conservative" of our times strives for a society ruled by the market, Ludovici instead asserted the duty of every elite to protect those that are poor; where the "conservative" of our times demand mass-immigration, Ludovici instead asserted that no one can call himself a proper conservative if he isn't even concerned about preserving his nation's identity in the form of blood and ancestral lineage. He also adopted a negative stance toward the mass use of automobiles, as well as Christianity and any ideological justification of equality, democracy, or women's suffrage. Among his role models we find not only Nietzsche and King Karl I, but also many Freudian psychoanalysts, as well as sociologists like Veblen, and the aristocratic Tories. Meanwhile Ludovici had already, to a large extent, stepped away from classical conservatism, as his interest in the spiritual aspect was rather small; his interests, influenced by Nietzsche, were mainly the historical and biological prerequisites for creating an aristocracy.

Thinkers like Kjellén and Ludovici certainly produced much of value, but during their time the Right was afflicted by vested interests and class interests; even men of the Right were tempted to put the interests of their own *part* before the interests of the *whole*. This can be seen clearly in the bourgeois parties that have gradually shifted to promoting the interests of money-power rather than immaterial values. Here we also find the explanation for the breach in the Swedish Right during the early 1900s, into what would become The Swedish Conservatives (Moderaterna) on the one hand and the nationalist movement on the other. Similar processes can be identified in Oswald Mosley's relation to the British Right. Both the Swedish Young Right and Oswald Mosley have, *post facto*, been blamed for racism and antisemitism, which served the purpose of making the breach appear more natural and legitimate. The real breach of interests, however, was economical—the Swedish Young Right, Mosley, and others were prepared to put restrictions on money-power in order to create a true *Folkhem* and real solidarity, while the more established part of the contemporary Right was not; hence the breach. The Young Right had a populist vein which the established powers saw as a threat.

This breach had dire historical consequences. On the side of the Swedish Young Right, Mosley, and others, a great number of clear-minded and creative rightist thinkers and activists gathered. After the Second World War they could be associated with the losing side and thus marginalized. But the established Right out of which they were thrown had at the same time discarded some of its most valuable members and perspectives. This didn't show all that much during the 1940s, but would become gradually more apparent over time. The establishment, at the time, depicted the Right as a group of dull old men without vision; in short, obsolete. During the 1960s, the New Left was quite correct in accusing the Right for its intimate connections with money-power—a major adversary of life and soul. And one of the few who actually did have a vision including everything from geopolitics to politics—de Gaulle—was instead faced with a color-revolution. Nonetheless, many solid men of the Right still prevailed in the aftermath of the War; men like de Gaulle, flanked by both Simone Weil and Maritain, men who had a vision that went beyond liberalism. These were men that had often had to live through war. But they would come gradually to disappear. The human capital that they constituted was never renewed. Emerging instead was an economical, moralistic, and, taken as a whole, boring "Right" that, over time, became the cuckservatives and the neoconservatives of our times, characterized by their loyalty to money-power, and their inability to discern what a true Right really is.

Jonathan Bowden pointed out that what really was needed by the Right to counter the radical Left were *"Far Right ideas"*—concepts and ideas from the hard, authentic Right. Concepts like "mass society," *Männerbund*, civilization, *Volksgemeinschaft*, and degeneration were needed. Instead it limited itself to liberalism or "liberal conservatism," leaning heavily towards a strictly economical perspective. Consequently, the assailants could gradually advance their positions, seize control of language and discourse, and define what is moral and not moral. Indeed, it was many times the radical Left that borrowed *"Far Right ideas,"* which lent them an air of excitement and an appearance of being relevant critics of civilization.

The Right and the World War

It is said that wars are caused by "nationalism," that is the love to a nation. This is an illusion. Almost every modern war has been caused by economical factors and the exploitation of national sentiments to further individual goals. The causes of war are to be found in conflicts of interest and envy among powerful financial institutions. The financiers secure power in their countries by appointing "statesmen" in the governments,

"statesmen" who are already doing their biddings. When struggle ensue
they incite every base instinct of hate and murder in the people.

— OSWALD MOSLEY

The Second World War was an outright catastrophe for the more
authentic Right. They were, not seldom, put through the same "de-
Nazification" by the victors of the war as if they had been actual Nazis,
despite the fact that many men of the Right had played an important
role in the resistance—hidden Jews, and what not. The society at large
underwent what Schrenk-Notzing has called a "character cleansing,"
where everything that could be even remotely associated to Nazism
was effectively marginalized. In many countries this was related to
the occupation by either the United States or the Soviet Union, and a
cultural, ideological, and political Americanization or "Sovietization."
This process was also applied to the neutral Sweden.

At the same time we should keep in mind that the challenges
posed by the early 1900s had been poorly handled by large parts of
the Right. Peter Viereck proclaimed that the original sin of the Right
was its adaption to the "hysterical Right." Today this includes the
accommodation of blustering fundamentalists and chauvinists; during the previous century it included not only the accommodation of
people with other fixed ideas, but also a tendency towards nihilism
concerning methods in relation to utopian goals, similar to parts of the
Left. It is easy to condemn this in hindsight, but the choice often stood
between compromising with the mass and its representatives on the
one hand, or irrelevance on the other. A general lack of higher values
didn't make things easier either.

The conclusions that we can draw from this are that the authentic
Right should neither let their conception of-the-world be reduced to
economism and moralism, nor should it let itself become the mer-
cenary of money-power. In addition, it will also be necessary, in the
words of Jonathan Bowden, to use *"Hard-Right ideas."* The Right must,
whenever needed, have the courage to think outside the liberal order,

view liberalism as a historical product and a limited part of society as a whole—a limited part that sometimes must be subordinated to the interests of the whole, partly for its own sake. Nevertheless, the Right must not in an opportunistic manner adapt to hystericals or reduce itself to pure *realpolitik*. An element of the Deep Right must be included, whether we may speak of Evola's Traditionalism or Klages' *Seele*. An element of the Deep Right and an element of populism.

Chapter 4

The New Left —
A Failed Attempt

We have turned ourselves into Americans. It is thus natural that we find all of America's miserable problems over here; from the drugs to the mafia, from fast food to the growing minorities ... it is all but certain that the American melting pot works. But it is evident that it can never work here ... The risk of apartheid? It is real. It is more than a risk even, it is a misfortune already upon us (along with its logic of ghettos, racial confrontations, and, eventually, bloodbath).

— Guy Debord, 1985

We sometimes hear that "the Left won the culture war." But what exactly is it that's referred to by "the Left"? There have been many Lefts throughout history. During the 1800s Marx, the communist, struggled against Bakunin, the anarchist, for power over the workers movement. At the same time there were many local traditions of the Left, including followers of Lassalle, Blanqui, and Düring; many of which today would be labeled as Far Right and find themselves much more at home in our day's radical alliances than in any context determined by political correctness. The same holds for the early 1900s' German social democrats, with names like Plenge, Lensch, and Woltmann. Regardless of whether we refer to Blanqui, Lassalle, or Plenge, they were often nationalists; the connections between Lassalle and Bismarck are today well known. Also common were metaphysical and Christian elements, especially in the legacies of Fourier and Weitling. Fourier's utopian depiction of the *Phalanstères* was a chapter unto itself; when mankind would come forth to live according to his utopian template, men would evolve tails and the oceans would evolve a taste of lemonade. At the same time Fourier's work contained a scintillating civilizational critique, and sure enough, he has, to a great deal, inspired the situationists and that strain of anarchism that labels itself post-Left. Both Walter Benjamin and Louis Aragon appreciated Fourier—albeit not primarily, perhaps, for his statements about lemonade-tasting oceans.

At any rate, Marxism was the victor in the struggle among these alternatives, notwithstanding the fact that Marxism itself would undergo a foundational transformation in the process. Similarly, when we speak about "1968" we should keep in mind that we are dealing with a number of Lefts, three at least (and a strong element of libertarianism to boot). There were the classical Marxist workers parties, there were the 1968- and the student-Left, and there was also the New Left. The differences among these were significant, but the boundaries fluid.

The Marxist workers parties were often conservative on issues concerning immigration and sexual morality, and were, as such, quite skeptical of much of the assorted lunacies conjured up by students, bohemians, and academicians. It was unusual, however, that the student rebels found much interest in the workers parties; instead they would seek out the startup green and social democratic parties. These were easier to affect, and through them the society as a whole could be affected (something that the Islamist entrists in Sweden today have made use of; we find them more often than not in the Green Party and in the Left Party). The worker's parties maintained a skeptical stance towards mass immigration. For them the solution to the Third World's problems was internationalism and anti-imperialism, not anti-nationalism and immigration. As an example, we can quote the French communist leader Georges Marchais:

> ...this is a consequence of capitalism, materialism. Millions of people are forced into cruel exile in a foreign country, far away from their sky and their people, because they don't have any work at home.

The student Left was a heterogeneous movement; alongside orthodox Marxists, Maoists, and anarchists it also accommodated generic hippies. We should, however, make the distinction between what 1968 appeared to be and what it really was. 1968 was basically a revolt of one generation against the same society for which they would come to work, which explains the Janus face of the revolution. On the one hand, an earnest striving for a different world and different way of life was there; a striving that Klages would have approved of. Many of its elements can be traced back to anti-bourgeois movements in the early 20th century Germany, from nudism to vegetarianism; some other elements, however, were straight out pathological, like, for instance, the "chic" flirt with pedophilia as an element in the sexual revolution. On the other hand, a striving to advance the positions for that class to which one would come to belong was there too. This class was not the working class, but what Lasch among others have called the *New Class*. For reasons nostalgic as well as historical the New Class described their struggle as socialistic, but the reality was another. This explains why exponents of money-power to a large extent financed the whole thing, or why the French 1968 could be seen as an early "color revolution" directed against the eccentric—and, to the United Stated, insufficiently loyal—de Gaulle.

The New Left, in the sense that we now present it, seems to be difficult to distinguish from the student Left. In retrospect we see it as a lofty critique of the modern world and the society created by *Geist* and money-power. In fact, we can benefit greatly from their analysis, in particular of the consumer society. The two situationists Debord and Vaneigem's description of the so-called "Spectacle," for instance, is still valuable. Roland Barthes attempted to read the consumerism society as a *language*, from campaign posters to commercials and advertisements. In this way he was able to discern features in the consumerism society linked to the liberal conception-of-the-world, like universalism. Many movies that at a first glance appear exotic affirm a universalist bias:

> Herein we immediately find the equivocal myth of the "humanity as one," which serves as an alibi for the larger part of our humanism. This myth works in two time blocks: first the differences between the various human forms are exalted, outscoring each other in their exoticism … for entertainment's sake the world is portrayed as a kind of Babylon. And then—presto!—this diversity is made into a unity: men are born, engage in labor, laugh, and die in the same way all around and in all places; and if in these acts there still exists some ethnic particularity it is carefully pointed out that deep down in each of us there resides an identical "nature"…

A quite interesting and possibly fruitful project today would be a subversive use of Barthes to "read" pop culture. For example: What, for instance, is the *meaning* behind the representation of the masculine-feminine polarity in one song after another by the combination "African-rapper-European-female singer"? Which mythology and which conception-of-the-world lies behind such a thing? This could be successfully combined with Pasolini and his life-models.

For his part, Habermas analyzed the crisis of legitimacy and how the world of experience is invaded by the systemic world (state and economy). In addition, he described how traditionally bourgeois institutions like freedom of expression, civil society, and the bourgeois public sphere in our times have undergone significant transfigurations. Taking Habermas as a starting point we could describe our times as both post-liberal as well as "real-liberal." Marcuse, on the other hand, today comes across as a utopian, estranged from the real world; he did, however, coin some useful terms like *desublimation* and the *one-dimensional man*.

Another interesting figure was Cornelius Castoriadis—a pessimistic animating figure in *Socialisme ou Barbarie* (Socialism or Barbarism).

His usage of the term *autonomy*, for example, is of value for both an authentic Right and an authentic Left. Castoriadis proposed that the state is ultimately identical to the people; during the antiquity when someone spoke about "Athens" doing this and "Athens" doing that, what they were actually referring to was the Athenians. This entails a dilemma with respect to conquered territory and mass immigration, as state and people now, to some extent, are disjoint entities; "Sweden" and "the Swedes" no longer overlap. Here Castoriadis brought to mind Carl Schmitt's insight that democracy requires significant equality and significant homogeneity among the population. Many of the groups which we will visit in the subsequent chapters are attempts to deal with this.

Castoriadis also described how the capitalism of late modernity not only exploits the ecological environment, but also the social and cultural environment. What he meant is that it uses up cultural and social resources that have taken just as long to evolve as all the natural resources which are also rapidly depleted. He pointed out how the system has inherited a number of anthropological types, like incorruptible judges, honest civil servants, workers with professional integrity, and such. Types like this do not simply come into existence by themselves—they have been shaped for ages. Castoriadis' thesis was that these types and their values are undermined by the narcissism, hedonism, and egotistic self-interest fostered by late-modernity-capitalism; not least, he adds, does this also affect the entrepreneurial type that was molded by early capitalism. Work ethics, incorruptibility, et cetera are the very requirements of capitalism, and at the same time are destroyed by it.

Prevalent in many of the Left's representatives was also a pessimistic and politically incorrect undertone. Adorno's works are permeated with it, as is well known. He can often be characterized as reactionary in his cultural critique, his diffuse goals notwithstanding. The New Left often turned against the Americanization of Europe; not seldom was it critical towards the system that had emerged in the Eastern bloc. Neither Debord nor Castoriadis were unreservedly optimistic about the multicultural society as a project; but for them it wasn't that big of a question either. Castoriadis dispassionately noted that he didn't buy the rhetoric about "multiculturalism," and even managed in the same paragraph to formulate himself in a way that today would be labeled as Islamophobic:

> [Multiculturalism] might have been a possibility, but hardly anything more, in the past, in a completely different political context, when people who did not belong to the dominant culture had a limited set of rights, like Jews or Christians in Muslim countries.

The Marxist Fredric Jameson described postmodern man as deprived of the faculty to think historically, as well as the faculty to see depth and not just surface. With little regard for political correctness he spoke of both the "Gulag industry" as well as the "Holocaust industry"; he also described white activists who tried to participate in the struggles of other ethnic groups as *groupies*. They are attracted to the struggles of other groups by the notion that, somehow, these groups are more "authentic" than they are. Hence, there were plenty of promising elements in the New Left, although this potential was only realized in a very sparse number of groups and individuals. During the 1970s a deeply interesting New Left existed, today pretty much only political correctness remains. The Italian Marxist Costanzo Preve has accurately described what happened:

> In Europe the PC-phenomenon had the mission to turn the demographically large 1968-generation into full blown groupies of capitalism. Those who busied themselves with socialist and libertarian dreams in their 20s or 30s now have, in their 50s or 60s, completely reconciled themselves with the corporatist ideology. In universities and media they're playing a key role in creating consensus in favor of the continued subordination

of Europe under the new imperialistic American state. PC is in many ways a historical compromise between the system and the 1968 radicals.

At the same time, we should remember that the Left's most valuable insights often touch upon *aspects* of the system—"the repressive totality" as Marcuse called it. They could, for instance, analyze the culture-industry in a way that is still relevant and useful. As for certain other aspects, they often lacked the tools; as, for instance, when it came to ethnic relations or the *truly* one-dimensional society. In these cases they need to be combined with Evola, Günther, Jung, and others.

The Left and the Authentic Right

> Local communities are not only geographical places, but the results of aspirations undertaken by the citizens of previous generations in order to create social and political unities in particular ways, with specific characteristics. Even if it is true that all societies, to some extent, are demographically "porous," limits still exist as to the number of newcomers that can be successfully integrated without the emergence of some significant dysfunctionality.
>
> — PAUL PICCONE

In retrospect, it appears that the New Left of the 1970s was making good progress to develop itself from a new Left to something more—to a new Right, to something "beyond Left and Right," or to populism. Some of them lived long enough to carry on through the whole journey, like Christopher Lasch and the Genovese spouses; others, like Paul Piccone and the circle around the *Telos* journal, only in part. Interestingly enough these were often individuals linked to the Frankfurt School and Critical Theory, thus suggesting that this school contains elements with a rightish potential. It is fair to say that it is simpler to reconnect to those communal forms and dimensions that the "the world of systems" attacks, like family and local community, than it is to invent completely new ones.

The development of the Left in a populist direction often had an intellectually advanced logic to it; its deficits lay in its not having a sufficiently realistic strategy or vision. This trend was most obvious among its many pessimistic representatives; they could readily answer the question of "how" today's system works but seldom of "where" we should take it and how we would do so. The most refined representatives of the New Left became populists, and switched from class to *society* as the historical subject/group. Now, as soon as that switch occurs you will come close enough to the authentic Right to almost trip over it, populistic though it was, at least since the days of the Swedish Young Right. Lasch and Piccone, hardly surprisingly, became populists, while Preve became a communitarian and thought himself able to discern a similar change in the thinking of the older Marx (the same Marx that began to study the Iroquois and the Russian peasant communes). Jacques Camatte, too, moved in this direction, with focus on *Homo Gemeinwesen* combined with a perspective not too unlike that of Ludwig Klages' biocentrism. Large parts of the radical German Left later became radical nationalists, from Bernd Rabehl to Reinhold Oberlercher. Switching from class to society was a decisive step in terms of the history of ideas, something that is often overlooked in writings about the New Left. The focus is usually on another process—one that, practically, brought about the degeneration of the Left.

Indeed, the Left as a whole did not undertake the journey in the direction of the New Right or populism, but came to be dominated by the PC-phenomenon. Adorno was molested by topless feminists and threatened by student radicals. He never quite seemed to recover—he and his equals were in many ways strict conservatives. The development toward PC was, in part, caused by the Left itself; they opened up Pandora's box the moment they dragged rebellious egalitarian politics into the academic world. The result: a steady adaptation of the standards of education and, consequently, a steady decline. Subsequent generations of students have since lacked the necessary prerequisites to develop Adorno or Benjamin any further. It was easier to take up ideological production or moralism—in other words PC. Looking to Glubb, this was, in part, an unavoidable development. Adorno belonged to the era of intellect, but 1968 marked the beginning of the era of decadence. Therefore decadence and intellectual laxity were to be expected. Moreover, the student rebels weren't always that concerned with deeper knowledge.

A fascinating historical phenomenon is the relation of the Left to reactionaries and fascists like Carl Schmitt, Heidegger, Nietzsche, Spengler, and Klages. The critical theoreticians, not least, could achieve a kind of academic sex appeal by writing about these "dangerous" thinkers; few others have gotten away with it unpunished. As a consequence Critical Theory carried a deeper civilizational critique than the better part of the "Right." Spengler's legacy, for example, stood out in Adorno, according to whom one major merit of Spengler is the description of the second nomadism—of the giant cities and the houses that no longer are *homes* in any real sense. Spengler, wrote Adorno, with regard to his writing on the second nomadism, doesn't merely express a state of fear and estrangement, but also an increasing sense of historylessness. People oscillate between shock and amnesia, and view themselves as objects of opaque processes which they can neither understand nor influence. Here both Adorno and Spengler expressed a core insight about our times and the eternal "now" that historylessness has created—but a historylessness that is in itself created, as Adorno emphasized. He criticized Spengler for his contempt toward the kind of man that had emerged, the low-information, easily manipulated run-of-the-mill kind of person—Spengler's renowned *Fellaheen*, a unit of the masses. As an analyst of the masses and the society of the masses, however, Spengler was an important source, even for Adorno. With much approval he quoted Spengler's sober take on the press:

Democracy has evicted the book completely from the spiritual life of the masses and replaced it with the newspaper.

And furthermore:

Today a democrat of the old stock wouldn't call for freedom for the press, but freedom from the press.

He compared the press to an army, in which the journalists are officers and the readers soldiers. Also the party apparatus was described by Spengler in a way that brings Weil and Michels to mind. He wrote that *"the will to power is greater than all theories,"* which explains why we shouldn't be taken by surprise when career politicians "betray" their voters. Spengler identified an inner genealogy between liberalism, the bourgeoisie, and the party-based parliamentarism, a historical logic. He wrote:

When an aristocratic party takes place in the parliament it is every bit as spurious as when a proletarian party does so. Only the bourgeoisie belong here.

Adorno questioned why his friend Benjamin "admired his enemies," but with Walter Benjamin we find a fruitful combination of ideas both from the socialism and Fascism's mainstreams and margins, with names like Fourier, Blanqui, Baudelaire, Klages, Schmitt, and Adalbert Stifter. Ludwig Klages, in particular, played an important role for Benjamin; despite Klages being a theoretical antisemite and Benjamin of German-Jewish descent a friendship developed between them. Klages reasoned that from his science—characterology—everything from buildings to ethnicities could be understood, and this project reappears in Benjamin's attempt to "read" architecture and buildings. Klages also meant that it is through ecstasy, *Rausch*, that body and soul for a while could be reunited without *Geist* tearing them apart.

Benjamin's studies of intoxication and ecstasy reconnects to this. It is through an irony of history that Klages' ideas have been transmitted, first and foremost, by German-Jewish intellectuals like Benjamin and Wilhelm Reich during the latter half of the 1900s.

This phenomenon was not limited to Adorno, Horkheimer, and Benjamin. Foucault, more important for today's political correctness than Adorno, expressed his gratitude to Georges Dumézil both for his perspective and help with his own career. Derrida found himself compelled to step up and defend Paul de Man when it surfaced that he had written antisemitic articles in his youth; de Man's importance for postmodernism and deconstructivism could in no way be disregarded. Nietzsche was of paramount importance to Deleuze. Ideas have a tendency to move back and forth between camps in history; this is true, among other things, of eugenics, ecology, social criticism, diversity, colonialism, drugs, antisemitism, and pacifism. But that which we today call PC did originate intellectually with the Right, even though originally wholesome themes, as we have seen, have undergone perversion over time.

Saul Alinsky—Rules for Radicals

> True revolutionaries do not flaunt their radicalism. They cut their hair, put on suits, and infiltrate the system from within.
>
> — SAUL ALINSKY

In connection to our study of the ideological history of the Left it could very well be useful to take a closer look at some of its successful metapoliticians and strategists. The Left had several representatives who understood both politics and metapolitics. Adorno was primarily a theoretician, but the Left also had intelligent practitioners. One of them was Saul Alinsky, "community organizer" in many poor neighborhoods and the author of *Rules for Radicals*. The book is deeply interesting, both for those who want to understand politics and those who want to acquaint themselves further with the New Left and its transformation during the 1900s.

Alinsky was an interesting representative of the New Left with respect to his breaking away from Marx and becoming a leftist populist. He made ardent efforts to join with the political tradition, and put strong focus on the middle class rather than the working class as a political subject. (He also spoke about "the haves," "the have-nots" and groups in between.) Alinsky also reverberated an echo of Sun Tzu, Heraclitus, and the Nietzsche-influenced Deleuze when he emphasized the impermanence inherent in all phenomena. This, in turn, implies that dogmatism of every kind is harmful. At the same time we should be aware that for Alinsky "the ends justifies the means"; it appears almost sinful *not* to use the most effective means at hand since everything less would be a let down of "the many." Here, once more, we see one of the Left's deepest pitfalls—the connection between nihilism with regard to methods and utopism regarding the ends.

Alinsky was well aware of the significance of metapolitics, and that a change in people's consciousness must precede every political change. With reference to this he talked about "reformation" as a necessary step before a possible "revolution." Also interesting are Alinsky's thoughts on language and the politics of language; the choice of words we use is of critical importance. Some words remind us that there is an ongoing power struggle; these are the same words that the powers-that-be do not want us to use. But Alinsky insisted upon the use of the correct terms, such as interest, ego, compromise, and in particular *conflict and power*. Imbued in this lies a power-realistic and conflict-centered conception-of-the-world. The powers-that-be, however, want us to describe the world as if characterized by agreement and altruism, but Alinsky claimed that we must describe it as it is, not as we want it to be; for ourselves as well as for others.

Alinsky also described how to best organize groups and movements. He trained a number of organizers; some of them went out to

THE NEW LEFT — A FAILED ATTEMPT

organize poor black neighborhoods, others went to Indian reservations, et cetera. His experiences were mixed. Among other things he concluded that it is quite difficult to train someone into becoming a skillful organizer. But his advice on what to look for in terms of personal traits most fitting for a skillful organizer is still relevant. The organizer is inquisitive, curious, and respectful; he or she has a sense of humor and ingenuity, an organized personality, a massive ego, and a vision of social progress as a communal work in which everyone is making a small contribution. Ingenuity and compassionate understanding meant that the organizer could put himself in other people's shoes, base his motivation in compassion and goodwill, and be able to speak with people from a perspective anchored in his own experience. Alinsky put a great deal of emphasis on this last item. It entailed that radicals from the white middle class should not turn their back on the middle class, the flag, the United States, and so on, but rather should *use* these experiences and symbols. Everything else was useless virtue-signaling. Joined to all this was the courage to be oneself. Alinsky didn't pander to any minorities, but treated them like adults. Among other things this led a group of Canadian Indians to state that he was the first white man to tell them that they were clueless, that is, treating them as adults. All other white men before him had treated them like children.

As mentioned, Alinsky often summoned the ideas of Heraclitus and Sun Tzu; the same situation never occurs twice, hence the organizer needs a set of ground principles that can be applied in different situations. In this respect Alinsky stated a few ground rules. Power, for example, is not what you have, but what the opponent *thinks* you have; never move outside the experiences of your group, but do move outside the enemy's experiences whenever possible; force the enemy to live up to his own standards; ridicule is man's most powerful weapon; a good tactic is a tactic that your group likes; and never let off the pressure. In addition, we also recognize a tactic common nowadays: *"pick a target, freeze it, personalize and polarize it."* That the establishment was rather helpless against the onslaught of Alinsky and others like him doesn't seem surprising at all. His thinking focused, among other things, on the interplay between action and reaction; in short, how to gain an upper hand on the enemy by predicting and controlling his reactions. In our days, an example of someone deploying these tactics is Trump in his dealings with the media.

The goal was to build mass movements, and Alinsky showed how such a thing like picking and winning easy fights could have an empowering effect on a young and weak movement. He did, however, warn against becoming a single-issue movement as well as failing to network with churches and similar institutions. The dialectics between questions and organization, power and change, was recurring. He also brought up how conflicts among "the haves" can be exploited—*"the weak belly of the status quo."* In summary, *Rules for Radicals* stands out as worth reading. It offers a Heraclitian perspective on power and society, as well as a collection of valuable advice and epiphanies. In certain parts, Alinsky's populism also intersected with the New Right's focus on self-organizing local communities, while his nihilistic approach to methods is not ours.

Chapter 5

The New Right — Foundations

I had grown weary of slogans and pre-packaged ideas. Hence I broke with both politics and the Far Right to devote myself to the work of thought. It was then that I founded the journal *Nouvelle École*, right before the establishment of GRECE. The journal *Éléments* saw the light of day in 1972. I also started the journal *Krisis* in 1988, intended to be a "journal of ideas and debates." These three journals are still being published. Right from the get-go my intention has been to systematically inquire into all areas of knowledge so as to bring about a development of a new conception-of-the-world able to understand the historical time that we now live in. The examples I had in mind were the Frankfurt school, Action Francaise, and CNRS.

— ALAIN DE BENOIST

Most of the groups that we will bring up in the chapters ahead have, in one way or the other, a relation to the current of thought that has received the name "The New Right." This shouldn't come as a surprise, as the New Right plays the same role for our time's dissidents that the Frankfurt School previously played for the Left. It has developed a complete analysis and critique of the modern world; an analysis that has bode its time for decades, awaiting the right historical situation. Today the time has come and the ideas of the New Right will reach their concrete fruition and become a political force hitherto unseen.

Background

> Hard totalitarianism—the kind the Tibetan people have to endure. Soft
> totalitarianism—the kind that works by pushing the Western-American
> model down the throat of the whole world with the help of media.
>
>   — Pierre Vial

After the Second World War the public sphere was dominated by liberals and Marxists. The latter, given the ubiquitous incompetence among liberals in general, were able to advance their positions, although they changed beyond all recognition in the process. Nonetheless, attempts to challenge this state of affairs, to develop a future for Europe that was not an imitation of the United States or the Soviet, existed. A group of young activists gathered during the late 1960s in what would come to be *Groupement de Recherche et d'Études pour la Civilisation Européenne*, commonly known by the acronym GRECE. Some had a background in more classically political groups, others in the military; some were base-line pagans, others regionalists with their hearts in Normandie or Bretagne; many had a previous engagement in the defense of French Algeria and its inhabitants—a struggle they lost. Common to all was recognition that the earlier strategies had been insufficient; a new strategy was called for, something they termed *metapolitics*. Books and journals were published, conferences hosted, and networks built. GRECE, through names like Armin Mohler, also had a link to the Conservative Revolution, and promoted thinkers like Ernst Jünger and Carl Schmitt. At the same time they viewed the so-called life-sciences—sociology, ethnology, and others—as relevant in the critique of liberalism and egalitarianism.

Already during the 1970s they had reached a significant breakthrough; among other things, their representatives wrote for *Le Figaro* magazine, in response to which opponents and journalists launched an offensive against GRECE, accusing them of being both racists and fascists. It was through outsiders like this, through journalists, normally hostile towards GRECE, that they got the name the New Right. While the name stuck, it hasn't necessarily been seen as something positive by those involved. In fact, GRECE, in many ways, is neither Left nor Right, nor a political movement in any normal sense of the term. New Culture thus would have been a better term than New Right.

Similar groups also cropped up in the proximity of GRECE. During the 1970s a group consisting of Yvan Blot, among others, established the *Club de l'Horloge*, which regarded Catholicism and liberalism more favorably than GRECE had done. They are explicitly right-wing, anti-socialistic, and often described as national-liberal. Their perspective should be of interest to parts of today's Alt-Right, as it combines neoliberal economy with nationalism and attempts to free the Western world from the viruses of the mind which are currently afflicting it. For a while the club had contacts with GRECE.

The 1980s was a decade of fragmentation for the New Right during which Guillaume Faye, among others, left the circle around GRECE. There was a latent tension between a more sociobiological perspective and an increasingly sociological one. Schisms like this aren't necessarily negative, as it entailed a widening of perspective and hence availability to a larger number of milieus. If the New Right had been identical to the perspective of, say, de Benoist, it would have been unlikely that the Front National would have been partly shaped by the New Right; higher-ups in the former wouldn't have been interested enough in participating in the latter. If, however, the New Right's perspective had been identical with Faye's, it is equally unlikely that the New Right magazines *Krisis* and *Telos* would have influenced parts of the Left. In fact, there is a difference between GRECE and the New Right; GRECE is an organization, while the New Right is a broader scene for the exchange and development of ideas, in which many representatives are in disagreement with one or another on certain issues.

GRECE and, more generally speaking, the New Right, have over a period of years developed an alternative to the dominant ideologies.

Themes like communitarianism, the Conservative Revolution, geo-politics, IQ and sociobiology, the Indo-European tradition, and many others, were retrieved and reconnections were made with forgotten political traditions, such as the Conservative Revolutionaries like Schmitt, Jünger, and Spengler, but also to traditions on the Left, like the libertarian socialism that takes its departure from Proudhon.

The New Right included a critical mass of high quality members. Unfortunately the language barrier has made but a few of them known outside of France. First and foremost these are Alain de Benoist, Guillaume Faye, Dominique Venner, and the Belgian national Robert Steuckers. In addition Pierre Vial, Jean-Yves Le Gallou, Jean Mabire, Yvan Blot, Jean Haudry, among others, have also received some noto-riety abroad. Through the years the New Right maintained contacts with some of the most interesting thinkers and writers; either as fellows or else as recurrent interviewees or in other functions. This include the writers Richard Millet, Arthur Koestler, and Anthony Burgess. Burgess is primarily known for having written *A Clockwork Orange*; he described himself as monarchist. Even the homosexual writer Guy Hocquenghem orbited the New Right and is mentioned by de Benoist to this day as a welcome contrast to the politically correct LGBT-milieu of today. Connections to the Left have existed through Régis Debray, Baudrillard, Costanzo Preve, Alain Caillé, among others. The American Leftist journal *Telos* and its founder Paul Piccone worked together for years with de Benoist. The ecologist and anti-modern thinker Edward Goldsmith has lectured on GRECE conferences. Academic experts in comparative religion and archaeology like Georges Dumézil, Marija Gimbutas, Mircea Eliade, and Raymond Abellio have been more or less closely associated with GRECE. The same goes for representatives in the life-sciences like Konrad Lorenz, Hans Eysenck, Volkmar Weiss, and Swedish antropologist Bertil Lundman. In addition to these, we can also mention Armin Mohler, Julien Freund, Tariq Ramadan, and Michel Onfray. According to Pierre-André Taguieff, who has written extensively about "the Far Right," *Krisis* is ardently read by academicians, although many of them won't admit to it publicly.

Metapolitics

> According to my point of view, a revolution, or any kind of major political event for that matter, cannot occur within world history unless some change in the minds of the people—in the way they conduct their thought—precedes it. Hence, I maintain the view that a political revolution must always be preceded by a cultural revolution. This, however, does not mean that whenever we do something cultural we are also acting from some ulterior political motive. Culture and politics are done by different people.
>
> —ALAIN DE BENOIST

The New Right is often described as being engaged in metapolitics rather than party or day-to-day politics. The term *metapolitics* was originally coined by German liberals—Karl von Rotteck (1775-1840) was one of them—but was later appropriated by the French reactionary Joseph de Maistre. De Maistre used the term to describe "the metaphysics of politics"; values, myths, and fundamental principles that politics draw upon. For example, is a democratic order really what we consider to be most natural and sound in our society? Who, by the way, are these "we," and what exactly do we mean by "society"? These are metapolitical rather than day-to-day political questions. In relation to this, the Left, for all intents and purposes, must be said to have been victorious, metapolitically speaking, during the 20th century, in spite of a promising beginning for the Right with the alternative modernity. This is the case not least of all when it comes to views on family and gender, in which what was, just a century ago, a quite insignificant milieu around Otto Gross today rules the whole of society. The list goes on, but further explications thereof are rather black-pilling.

Already prior to the founding of GRECE, Dominique Venner had unsparingly analyzed the shortcomings of the nationalist environment in his book *For a Positive Critique*. This critique is worth a read even with today's immigration-critical movements in mind. In his book Venner delineates an environment marked by "*courageous acts and tragic failures*," and he brings up the conformist tendency of nationalists to sympathize with parts of the establishment as soon as these utter anything ever so slightly reasonable, instead of taking the time to elaborate a conception-of-the-world of their own. Venner also criticized nationalists who rage at symptoms rather than look to the deeper causes—such as anti-communists lacking any understanding of capitalism and liberalism. He introduces the useful notion *régime* to denote the establishment and the current system, and notes that "without revolutionary doctrine, no revolution." Venner also brings up alternatives—like virile humanism, organic economy, and European co-operation.

Thus, the New Right has realized since its founding days that those who aspire to influence current policy must first gain metapolitical influence—affect the public view on the notions and perspectives that most take for granted. The New Right doesn't ascribe to the more simplified historical materialism; instead, they assume that ideas possess actual significance in the shaping of history. De Benoist has noted that without Marx, there would be no Marxist Lenin. It might be argued that a Narodnikist or Saint-Simonist Lenin would have been an alternate possibility, and that such an ideological difference would have had significant influence on the course of history—ideas are more than a mere "superstructure." From a starting point in metapolitical analysis the New Right could show how and why the Old Right had failed. The Old Right had already been greatly influenced by the liberal and/or Leftist conception-of-the-world; instead of defending culture, nation, tradition and identity, this so-called "Right" put forward liberal policies, subordinated the state to the economy, and the nation to multinational corporations. At most they were "anti-communists," but to Hollywood's colonization of Europe they turned a blind eye.

The metapolitical strategies of the New Right depart to a great extent, but not exclusively, from the Italian Marxist Antonio Gramsci. In common with the young men who founded GRECE, Gramsci's Left had in the wake of WW1 suffered a decisive and bewildering defeat, a defeat which Gramsci saw a need to make sense of. Interest in metapolitical ideas seems often to follow historical defeats—an aspect which in no way devalues the matter. Gramsci developed a conceptual apparatus which facilitates metapolitical analysis. The apparatus fundamentally departs from Napoleon's observation that *"one can do many things with bayonets, but not sit on them."* Rulers ultimately rule by their monopoly on force—repressive functions, like police and military. However, an order based solely on the threat of force is mercurial and can neither unite the populace nor the different wings of the military and other elites. Rule is thus dependent on a certain measure of consent—that the people at large, on some fundamental level, adopt their rulers' conception-of-the-world. To describe this phenomenon, Gramsci used the term *hegemony*: in the 1910s, the Italian rulers still enjoyed hegemony in a way their Russian equivalents lacked, therefore the revolution of the Biennio Rosso failed, while the Russian revolution followed through.

Today, liberalism enjoys hegemony in the West, in the form of a not always frictionless alliance between a Left and a Right wing of liberals (from Gramsci's Marxist perspective these two wings are reflections of two respective social groups). Noam Chomsky speaks of "manufacturing of consent," which basically denotes the same phenomenon: hegemony. Gramsci described how that which is recognized as so-called *common sense* is predominantly a product of its concurrent hegemony. It is distinct from what he called *good sense*. Good sense originates, according to Gramsci, from things like a united struggle against injustice, and has a great deal in common with Orwell's notion of "common decency." The metapolitical Right has a lot to gain by identifying which areas of common sense in specific times and places overlap with their own conception-of-the-world, as well as which areas of the latter differ the most from the localized definition of common sense. Common sense is not a carbon copy of the hegemony's conception-of-the-world, but contains older artifacts. This fact could prove useful to those who wish to make conscious a conflict between the common sense of the people and the hegemonic conception-of-the-world, thus helping common sense to approach the likeness of good sense.

Gramsci's plan was to construct an alternative hegemony—a fundamentally counter-hegemonic project. He described the sections of the population that don't participate in the hegemonic institutions as *subaltern*, subordinated. These take no part in the production of ideas. This includes the working class, but also groups such as farmers, small business owners, and others yet. In Sweden today, many of those who vote for the less immigration-happy party, the Sweden Democrats, can be described as subaltern. The party itself, however, has an ambivalent relationship to its concurrent hegemony—conscious counter-hegemonic action is only taken in fits and starts. The pattern is repeated, as well as in other places, in the relations between Donald Trump, his supporters, and their concurrent hegemony. Regarding this emerging group, Sam Francis spoke of a post-bourgeois proletariat in a way reminiscent of Gramsci's subalterns. More about Sam Francis further on.

Gramsci distinguished between civil society and political society. Political society consists of the state and its governing bodies, while civil society contains a lot more complexity. In Gramsci's day it mainly consisted of the Church, the press, and the universities; today television, the entertainment industry, and, of course, the Internet play immense roles. It is through these institutions that our perception of common sense is construed; how we speak, what we consider as being normal, et cetera. Commonly, we remain unconscious of how our conception-of-the-world is shaped during the process—after all, it's only culture, entertainment, education, right? But as Andrew Breitbart has pointed out, "politics is downstream from culture." Accordingly, those who succeed in influencing culture will inescapably influence politics.

Setting out from the conclusions of Gramsci and his successors, as well as from those of Venner, one may construct a model of analysis of metapolitical strategies around the three categories ideas, personnel, and institutions. Every metapolitical strategy includes a profound analysis of its own as well as of hegemonic ideas (Venner used the term doctrine). A main point is to identify conflicts and contradictions within the hegemonic set of ideas—weak spots and visible absurdities toward which attacks can be successfully directed. Hegemonic tendencies which are, conversely, proximate to one's own can also be used against the hegemony. Constant self-criticism of one's own ideas is another necessity. Gramsci further spoke of the need for personnel, a cadre of counter-hegemonic intellectuals. He called these *organic intellectuals*, distinguishing them from the more traditional intellectuals of the Church, academia, and the like. Venner terms this category *militants*. The Left has historically been successful in molding, retaining, and educating personnel—lately not least by paying their salaries with funds originating either from the taxpayer or from "generous" oligarchs. This system, however, seems to have made the personnel corrupted and intellectually lethargic.

The analysis of the role of institutions was elaborated by the French Marxist Louis Althusser. He distinguished between the ideological and the repressive apparatuses of the state. This is where Napoleon's bayonets come in. The Repressive State Apparatus (RSA) is of deciding importance in every hegemony—if only to help it survive its neighbors. In common with Gramsci, however, Althusser additionally took interest in Ideological State Apparatuses (ISA). There exist several of these, and they need not be obvious or direct parts of the state. Church as well as school, press, and even family all constitute ISAs. Althusser described them as complex, and stressed that even within them conflict and class struggle are ongoing processes.

Related to Althusser's analysis of ISA is the German student revolt leader Rudi Dutschke's concept of the long march through the institutions. Dutschke posited that the Left should conquer society's institutions from within, and so far as universities and state media go, this strategy has delivered beyond all expectations. Gramsci's perspective was equally long. He spoke of a war of positions, in which the existing hegemonic conception-of-the-world could be undermined (or deconstructed, as it would later come to be called). The Left was also supposed to instate alternative institutions in every area from education to news media. It was also crucial to redefine prevailing values as well as foster organic intellectuals. This war of positions would later be followed by a war of maneuver, in which state power was to be conquered. In comparison, Gramsci put greater emphasis on creation of alternative institutions than Althusser did (Venner spoke instead of organization and of "bases" within the different sections of society—CasaPound is a good example of the latter). Further, Althusser reminds us that ISAs are in no way static. The emergence of the Internet is the prime example of this—an ISA which long since has been a refuge in which counter-hegemonic groups were able to create their own spheres and develop their own ideas. In the case of the Internet, we may note the latent conflict between conquered ISA and yet-to-be-conquered RSA, as well as between the widely differing personality types respectively populating them. The people of academia generally differ from the people of the military—Pareto spoke of foxes and lions. We will find reason to revisit Pareto further on in this book.

Gramsci's work can also act as a foundation for a model of the relationships between meta-, socio-, and geopolitics. Gramsci maintained that different groups within a country carry on relationships to other powers outside of it. In our time, this becomes obvious when one takes into account the myriad globalists and Atlanticists in power, who enjoy hegemony in so many countries around the world—Spengler spoke in his time of the "inner Englishman," von Lohausen of how snobs in every country are loyal to London. This hegemony is enhanced by ties to foreign powers. Similarly, a resistance movement can indeed have friends abroad—what Thiriart called "our Piedmont" after the region from which the unification of Italy was directed. Venner spoke instead of "external lungs." For many of Gramsci's comrades, this Piedmont, this refuge, was the Soviet Union. It is something we should all ask ourselves: what place, if any, constitutes our Piedmont?

The relationships between ideas and tangible social groups were also central to Gramsci: the ties between socio- and metapolitics. Some ideas, Gramsci posits, express the interests of the workers regardless of whether the workers themselves are conscious of this or not. Also of interest to Gramsci was the creation of a historic bloc—an alliance of several social groups. On this matter Gramsci spoke of a national-populist bloc, which by today's standards is far from politically correct. Centered around a core of workers, this alliance would also include other subaltern groups, such as the often impoverished peasants. Similar blocs can also be observed in current politics, like the Democratic Party in the United States which joins minorities and White working class in an anything but stable alliance. One important role of metapolitics is to contribute to the dissolution of hostile historic blocs. Another is to ponder what groups one represents, and whom else might find one's ideas appealing. Here too Sam Francis comes in useful. Considering his interest in one particular social group, "Middle America," as a starting point for the struggle, he may be viewed as a right-wing Gramscian. In our times Gramsci's sociopolitical perspective must however be complemented by an ethnopolitical one. Class is today but one of several central categories.

The New Right has influenced the Gramscian categories of ideas as well as those of personnel and institutions. De Benoist has pointed out enemies on the playing fields of meta-, socio-, and geopolitics alike—such as universalism, the bourgeoisie, and the United States respectively. The New Right has developed a coherent set of ideas which challenges the liberal hegemony without completely cutting loose from the prevailing perception of common sense. Through magazines, presence in academia, and conferences, the New Right has furthermore accrued institutions and personnel, often aimed at an elite. Struggling for decades during a disadvantageous period the New Right has still achieved metapolitical successes, including raising questions like IQ, Indo-European heritage, identity, and the right to "difference" (localized specificity).

The metapolitical focus of The New Right has varied through the years. When Faye made his comeback to politics in 1998 he criticized GRECE for misconstruing Gramsci's thoughts on metapolitics and cultural struggle. Faye noted that while the struggle for cultural influence mattered to Gramsci, it was also intimately linked to the social and political struggle of the Italian Communist Party. The struggles on these fronts each amplified the other; backed by a mass-movement the words of the intellectuals gained additional weight and attention, and the mass-movement correspondingly gained legitimacy through the analyses of the former. By contrast, the New Right avoided any ties to Le Pen and his mass-movement Front National. At the same time it's questionable whether the revolutionary and highly biological perspective Faye elaborates in books such as *Why We Fight* would be welcomed in the current Front National.

Opposing Liberalism

What is the greatest threat today? It is the progressive disappearance of diversity from the world. The leveling down of people, the reduction of all cultures to a world civilization made up of what is the most common . . . I believe that this diversity is the wealth of the world, and that egalitarianism is killing it. Because it is important not just to respect others but to keep alive everywhere the most legitimate desire there can

be: the desire to affirm a personality which is unlike any other, to defend
a heritage, to govern oneself in accordance with what one is.

— ALAIN DE BENOIST

The New Right has developed one of the most coherent alternatives
to liberalism, as well as a profound critique of it. Thus this critique is
often axiomatic: it questions not merely the "how?" of liberalism but
also the "why?" Axioms, first principles, matter. If, for example, one assumes the principle that "there are no Swedes, only individuals," there
comes no point at which one can say "that's enough" to immigration.
To fundamentally sort out the problems caused by liberalism one must
also analyze and oppose its axioms—and the New Right does so.

The New Right opposes liberalism because liberalism doesn't understand what a society is. Liberalism is individualist, meaning it maintains that the individual precedes society at large. Firstly, this assumption is factually wrong: society and nation precede the individual, for
example by endowing the individual with his language as well as other
tools used to make sense of the world. Secondly, the liberal assumption
leads to a vacuous anthropology in which the characteristics which
shape our very identities are viewed as mere accidents. According to
this view, it is only by shaving off layers of such characteristics that
the individual may be revealed. However, what all humans have in
common are solely biological characteristics, characteristics mostly
shared even with non-human animals. These are insufficient to give
us the sense of meaning necessary for the creation of identity. Humans
depend on identity, and liberalism offers identity only in the shape of
superficialities such as common habits of consumption or the posses-
sion of a particular passport.

That the New Right opposes a reductionist individualism does not
mean that it doesn't value freedoms; explicitly enough, de Benoist's critique of the ideology of so called human rights, *Beyond Human Rights*,
bears the subtitle *Defending Freedoms*; in practice, liberalism and
individualism lead to reduced freedom. The critique of Human Rights

is a good example of the New Right's critique of ideology. In his book de Benoist shows how the ideology of HR arose in a very specific historic context, and cannot be considered natural to most cultures or societies. Adopting the ideology of HR thus implies the imposition of liberalism on the remaining world. But the ideology is also founded upon a faulty anthropology, an anthropology by which the individual human organism is viewed as isolated from its society. It assumes that individuals, but not groups, may have rights. De Benoist also reconnects to Carl Schmitt by illustrating how HR and liberalism imply new ways to legitimate war. Every non-liberal state or group is subject to accusations of violation of human rights, thereby justifying armed intervention against them. Such intervention need not be construed as a political conflict between equals, however, but as an intervention against the enemies of Humanity. Politics are thus replaced by moralism, which furthermore entails that the usual rules don't apply. Such wars can become particularly brutal, as liberalism dehumanizes its enemies.

The same dehumanization is used for inner enemies; the New Right has convincingly delineated how liberalism leads to a kind of soft totalitarianism. This is not least true of the market society and consumerism. There exists within liberalism one model of how to live, described in de Benoist's *Manifesto for a European Renaissance* as productivist. De Benoist has also described aspects like intellectual terrorism, in which actual or perceived anti-liberals are decried as "racists," "sexists," and "Nazis." The liberal cannot handle recusants, but must construe them as enemies of Humanity. The concept of *pensée unique*, one-track thinking, is helpful to understanding the resulting echo-chamber.

The New Right also showed how liberalism's conception-of-the-world is closely related to that of socialism. The enemy of freedom is neither liberalism or Marxism, but egalitarianism. Whether this is a good choice of terms is disputable, since some find that the word anti-egalitarianism carries negative connotations. Renaud Camus' "replacism," emphasizing how liberalism views everything as being replaceable, might be a more conducive choice. Liberalism is the enemy of identity and of that which is particular. It is atomistic in its first principles, leading to atomistic societies wherever it is applied. By extension, it is doubtful whether the final result of liberalism even should be termed a society at all, rather than a mass of individuals each relating to state and capital instead of to one another. As early as 1835, de Tocqueville summarized this final result in his *Democracy in America*:

> I see an innumerable host of men, all alike and equal, endlessly hastening after petty and vulgar pleasures with which they fill their souls. Each of them, withdrawn into himself, is virtually a stranger to the fate of all the others.

Against liberalism, the New Right has proposed alternate ways to view society. Among these, we find ideas like the right to difference, and the insight that we only become human through our specific groups and communities. Several forms of populism, communitarianism, and participatory democracy naturally follow therefrom. De Benoist has developed a valuable synthesis of anti-liberal Right and anti-liberal Left, including his writings on Édouard Berth. Berth was a heroic syndicalist, reminiscent of Sorel, and not a stranger to Maurranian royalism: "A man of the *ancien régime* of the soul, a peasant soldier of Rome and Sparta."

Geopolitics

> Throughout history good causes have existed, causes worth struggling for. Whether the American Revolution was one of them I'm not so certain.
>
> —ALAIN DE BENOIST

Many of the early members of the New Right had a past in the struggle for French Algeria. The loss of Algeria was a hard blow, and it was be to followed by more. Among them decolonization and the demise of Rhodesia. It became obvious how Europe had become subordinated to the two non-European superpowers that came victorious out of WW2, and was now being subjected to Americanization as well as Sovietization. The New Right turned against this development.

A rich tradition of European geopolitics had always been available to the New Right. In 1988 Pierre Krebs released an anthology titled *Mut zur Identität* (The Courage of Identity), featuring Haudry, de Benoist and Faye as well as Krebs himself, but also Baron Heinrich Jordis von Lohausen. Jordis von Lohausen was an Austrian army officer and diplomat who took part in WW2 in Libya, Hungary, and Russia on the side of the Germans. After the war he came to champion Europe, "from Madrid to Vladivostok." According to his analysis the ideal situation for Europe would have been if North America following the Civil War had been ruled by three powers: the Union, the Confederacy, and Canada. This was not understood by European leaders of the time—except in Russia, which consequently supported the Union in an effort to weaken Western Europe. The result was the emergence of an immensely powerful non-European power, the United States, while the European powers kept fighting among themselves. Jordis von Lohausen quoted Churchill's alleged afterthought on WW2: "we butchered the wrong pig." The two brother wars that were the world wars not only cost the Europeans their empires, but also resulted in the occupation and molding of Europe by two external powers.

The New Right and geopolitical writers like Heinrich Jordis von Lohausen and Jean Thiriat opposed the post-war occupation, championing a Europe independent of foreign powers. From a geopolitical perspective, a Europe consisting of rival powers cannot stand a chance against the United States, which may also pit the rivals against one another. The chauvinistic small-state nationalism of yesteryear would thus need to be substituted by a European consciousness. The New Right has therefore been consistently Europeanist, if not always in the shape of the super-state nationalism associated with Thiriart, and has been cooperating actively with allies in several European countries. The New Right also distinguishes between Europe and "the West": "the West" is viewed as a nihilistic culture, distinct from Europe. Anti-American sentiments have been prevalent, particularly regarding geopolitics and the United States as an occupying power, but also regarding cultural and social Americanization.

Given the New Right's opposition to one-size-fits-all solutions, its opposition to globalization—in practice a form of Americanization—follows naturally. Proponents have therefore opposed globalist imperialism wherever it has reared its head, including in Iraq and Libya. The right of peoples and regions to decide their own direction and preferred models has been defended, opposing world-wide imposition of liberalism. Rather than a unipolar world dominated by the United States, the New Right champions a multipolar world. Today this entails an opposition by many within the New Right to the American efforts to demonize Russia. A central goal of United States foreign policy is the cordoning-off of Russia by a *cordon sanitaire*, mitigating any connections between Russia and Western Europe. De Benoist summarizes his position as follows:

> Today, two possible alternatives exist: one is either on the side of the American sea power, or one is on the side of the Eurasian land power. I stand with the latter.

As a future ideal, Guillaume Faye proposes the geopolitical space Eurosiberia, consisting of Europe and the Russian part of Asia. Faye emphasizes that the target of his anti-Americanism is in no way

European-descended Americans, but the power elite which attacks Europeans in America as well as in Europe and Russia.

Alain de Benoist has highlighted the importance of geopolitics in understanding our times. Geopolitics focus on "great constants" rather than on more ephemeral factors like ideologies. Jordis von Lohausen spoke of "thinking in continents" and "thinking in peoples," providing a shift of temporal perspective necessary to civilizational thought. De Benoist also notes that American and Russian leaders are all well aware of geopolitical conditions. In contrast, geopolitical awareness among European leaders lags behind, exposing them to manipulation by foreign powers—and the same is true of the geopolitical awareness of the European media class.

Economics

> *Le règne de l'argent* is the transformation of each thing into its monetary equivalent, in other words its price.
>
> —ALAIN DE BENOIST

The New Right does not stand to the right on economics, if right-wing economics is construed as being equal to economic liberalism. Nevertheless, the New Right's understanding of economics has much in common with older reactions to emerging capitalism and to what Alain de Benoist calls *le règne de l'argent*—literally "the reign of silver." For this reason it still may be considered as standing very much to the right. De Benoist directs a fundamental critique toward the conception-of-the-world and the anthropology which has emerged around the market, by which all values are reduced to price tags and all human behavior reduced to fit the model of *homo oeconomicus*. As demonstrated by Pierre Vial, this economic logic results in the demise of identities, but de Benoist notes how other aspects of humanity also meet the same fate. Historically, human action has been understood as driven by more forces than mere cost-benefit calculus, including honor and solidarity. The realms of the political, the social, and the sacral each contain their own set of logic, but under liberalism are all at risk of being completely supplanted by the logic of economics. The logic of the marketplace is but one possible economic logic; historically, gifting and sharing has been of equal or greater importance to buying and selling. The universal economization championed by liberalism leads to spiritual depletion and a one-dimensional society. Further, de Benoist mentions the link between capitalism and immigration, as well as the link between economic materialism and immigration. Economic materialism values material gain over culture and heritage; thus materialists often view migration as unproblematic as long as it might benefit their personal economy. The New Right opposes the economistic ideal as well as consumerism.

> The Right forgot that its one true enemy is money-power.
>   —ALAIN DE BENOIST

In no way does this mean that de Benoist goes to the opposite extreme, becoming a communist. De Benoist has described Communism as a totalitarianism, comparable to Hitlerism. De Benoist notes one difference between the two in his 1998 article *Nazism and Communism*: "*Communism killed many more people than Nazism, it killed over a longer period of time than Nazism, and it began doing so before Nazism.*" To de Benoist, totalitarianism is not an alternative. There exists, however, a greater range of alternatives than just neoliberalism and Stalinism. De Benoist refers repeatedly to non-conformist left-wing thinkers in his social critique, including mutualists such as Proudhon, Sorel, and Leroux. Likewise mentioned are Castoriadis, Polanyi, and Ivan Illich. This is in line with the focus on the local and on participatory democracy, which distinguishes de Benoist, as well as with his skepticism toward the nation state as the sole level of politics. He has said that he would happily live in a society with a market, but not in a market society.

Related to Benoist's perspective is that of Robert Steuckers. Steuckers critiques the three dominant schools of economics, including Marxism and the various existing crossovers, such as Keynesianism; the main characteristics for all of them are abstractions and universalism. The alternative is what in France is called heterodox economists—economists possessing a sense for the local and the historical; economists like Veblen and Schumpeter. Steuckers emphasizes that the culture of a nation includes its economic institutions, and indicates how it may be of value to a new Right to defend these institutions from neoliberalism. This regards not least of all the sectors which have been withheld from the logic of the marketplace, like medical care and education. Guillaume Faye by comparison looks like the more market-friendly of the two. Faye has said about Éric Zemmour that he is too Colbertist, putting too much faith in state direction of economy. A state-directed economy functions badly. Instead, Zemmour should look to the Pentagon as an instance of effective neo-Colbertism. Faye further maintains that our current system conjoins the worst aspects of capitalism and socialism.

What the proponents of the New Right all have in common is a favorable view of European protectionism, Europe as an economic space. Here we re-encounter ideas from the Conservative Revolutionaries, of autarky, and of Europe as *Grossraum*. De Benoist connects these ideas with environmentalism via the necessity of abandoning the neo-liberal order if we are to successfully protect the environment. This regards such issues as free trade, over-consumption, and never-ending economic growth. It is necessary to relocalize the economy, and relocalization implicates deglobalization. Speaking about people who want to save the environment and simultaneously keep global capitalism, De Benoist writes:

> On one hand they want to "save the planet", on the other they want to go on doing that which destroys it.

Anthropology, Identity, and Long Memories

> Modernity has given birth to the most empty civilization mankind has ever known.
>
> —ALAIN DE BENOIST

Central to the New Right's critique of the modern world and liberalism is the relation of these two to identity. Liberalism is an enemy to identity, partly because it has no regard for anything not individual. Liberalism is in practice a universalism, and it produces rootless "individuals" even where there were none previously.

In opposition to this, the New Right champions the right to difference, and groups possessing long memories. The way the New Right views culture is greatly influenced by the German philosophical anthropologist Arnold Gehlen. Gehlen held that mankind is different from other animal species in that we create for ourselves a "second nature": a culture. This is on account of the inadequacy of man's instincts in handling the world. Remove culture, and little will remain of the qualities we generally perceive as human. Culture is the sum of this second nature, which entails its being in a constant state of evolution. We constantly learn new things and re-evaluate things we learned before, causing our culture to evolve. However, this evolution always happens against the background of the current culture: anything novel that we encounter, we interpret using that very culture we've already obtained. This is an organic and metamorphic view of culture, distinct from the liberal's hatred of custom and tradition, as well as the unchanging, monolithic ideal culture of hypothetical arch-reactionaries.

The New Right, influenced by Heidegger, argues that we are authentic, true to ourselves, when we are living our culture. Our culture provides us with models for a good life, and it is when we incarnate these age-old role models in our own time, with our kin, that we are true to ourselves and that our lives become truly meaningful. Culture gives us meaning, and explains to us who we are and why we're here; our culture provides us an identity.

Connected to this emphasis on different cultures and identity is ethnopluralism, or "the right of peoples." This means that ideas like "the human race" and "human rights" are largely vacuous concepts, considering that the qualities that make us human are rooted in culture, and that humans don't have one single culture, but innumerable, each different from the other. This is where the concept of *bioculture* enters, which is not reducible either to biological race or the civic nationalist understanding of culture. The future envisioned by the New Right is one in which the European and European-descended peoples in the New World have regained their will-to-life and their long memories. The long memories are memories which have been preserved within the culture since time immemorial, and repeatedly have inspired great efforts throughout their history. This is not a case of nostalgic longing for anything outside reality or one's present time, but rather it is about living these memories like they are lived time and time again with each new generation. In this way, our long memories are always oriented toward the future, and they will live on as long as there are Europeans. This view is called *archeofuturism*—a useful concept that the ever-creative Guillaume Faye has further elaborated in his book of the same title. In this work Faye espouses a synthesis between archaic values and futuristic technology. It is not very reminiscent of Evola nor Klages, but more so of Nietzsche and Locchi. Faye explains his philosophical starting point as "vitalist constructivism," and delineates a fascinating future which includes high technology as well as small-scale organic farming.

The anthropology of the New Right is not monolithic, and has shifted over time. Originally it was influenced by the life sciences, including sociobiology, ethology, and human genetics (parts of the latter are now sometimes termed HBD, human biodiversity, but more on that later). This placed the views of the New Right in proximity to those of Hans Eysenck and Konrad Lorenz. Since then, de Benoist and others have gradually approached a more sociological anthropology, distancing themselves from the biological. De Benoist today opposes theories of race in which some groups are viewed as inherently inferior to others. Other parts of the New Right, however, have not shifted their focus in the same way de Benoist has, and have continued developing their anthropology in a sociobiological direction. The differences between the outlooks are gradual, and the most valuable contribution by the New Right to the field is the synthesis of biological and cultural sociology, termed *bioculture*. This is reminiscent of Klages' and Woltmann's insight that some human types are continually excluded from the gene pool of some societies in a self-increasing process. In a culture in which profit is valued over all else, dreamers and warriors aren't the ones to become the most successful. With time, genetics shape cultures, and vice versa. The New Right prefers to be described as ethno-differentialist rather than "racist," seeing as their views are in no way about hatred, but about recognizing and valuing differences of different groups. In comparison, so called anti-racists are most often unable or unwilling to recognize any such differences, and disregard even the most unambiguous scientific evidence.

A degree of disparity exist also among the New Right's views on the multi-ethnic Europe that is the result of the decades of mass immigration. De Benoist doesn't see out-and-out repatriation as being a realistic option, proposing instead a public policy marked by recognition of groups. His solution isn't Jacobinesque assimilation and homogenization but, conversely, a policy more reminiscent of the Hegelian concept of mutual recognition as well as German sociologist and historian Henning Eichberg's *Minderheit und Mehrheit*. The current state of affairs, in which the very existence of groups is denied and silenced, is bewildering and unsustainable. Others within the movement instead propose repatriation, considering that the multiethnic society otherwise will lead to civil war and, ultimately, to the demise of the European peoples.

The New Right and Feminism

The New Right isn't anti-feminist in any way one might associate with right-wing politics. In the pamphlet *Manifesto for a European Renaissance*, de Benoist and Charles Champetier make a case for recognizing the peculiarities of male and female, and a complementing case against the universalism which either views women as incomplete males or even insists on denying every difference between the sexes. The New Right is apparently *differential-feminist*, insofar it maintains that male and female differ, but that both are indispensable. The universalism that denies any differences is in practice a way to let male values invade the traditionally female sphere.

In his book *Sex and Deviance*, Guillaume Faye reminds us about this universalist view. His own view of feminism is multifaceted: Faye supports equal status for women in the workplace, and maintains that a civilization may be judged by how it treats its women. North Europeans have always set themselves apart positively in this regard. Faye is also well aware that there are women of many kinds. Departing from the work of Raymond Abellio, he speaks of three types of women: the original woman, the manly woman, and the ultimate woman (a synthesis of the other two types). Here, Faye's reasoning is reminiscent of that of Blüher, who also identified and distinguished female types. The majority of women, in Blüher's classification, are the *typical women*. Beside these there exists a minority of women that possesses a higher degree of masculine traits than the typical women; these Blüher describes as *hetaeric*, and as *free women*. They are less monogamous than women at large, and their femininity is less unquestionable to them. The psychoanalytic circles in which Blüher moved included several gifted women of this type, such as Marie Bonaparte and Lou Salomé, and Blüher evidently respected them too. Blüher claimed that "*the women's movement originates with the free woman; it is an explicitly hetaeric phenomenon.*" Nevertheless, this was in no way meant as an exculpation of the men concurrent to Blüher. Blüher wrote:

> It is furthermore not surprising that in our time, when regality and the will of men to rule have been displaced by the bourgeois type, women strive for equality.

In other words, mediocre and unmanly males seem to more or less force feminism into existence. Faye has a similar take: he maintains that many of the more recent waves of feminism consist of women who would much rather be men; they are women who highly value the historically male spheres. Also present is an element of misandry, and a paradoxical inability to protest the very actual oppression of women going on not only in the Muslim world but also in that world's innumerable enclaves in Europe. Faye further argues that when the males of a nation are feminized, women will usurp their roles, mentioning Margaret Thatcher and Joan of Arc as examples. The dilemma facing rulers of a society regards the difficulty to combine the freedom and careers of women with a sustainable birth rate. Today, most efforts to solve this dilemma consist of state benefit programs; in the future, technology might play a greater role. In any case, the process which Faye identifies and terms *devirilization* appears altogether obvious. European males aren't exactly becoming increasingly masculine, but quite conversely, they are being increasingly bereaved of such qualities that are necessary to protect their societies, their women, and their children. Faye also offers a slight correction to the creed of the manosphere, showing how capable women also have important roles to play.

The New Right and Democracy

> Democracy did not first appear with the Revolutions of 1776 and 1789.
> Rather, it has constituted a constant tradition in Europe since the
> existence of the ancient Greek city-state and since the time of ancient
> German "freedoms".
>
> — De Benoist and Champetier,
> *Manifesto for a European Renaissance*

Thanks to Julien Freund, the German Neue Rechte, the Conservative
Revolutionaries, and others, the New Right has had access to numerous valuable analyses of all things political. In contrast to many
historic Rights, the New Right is democratic, and not least of all opposes historical totalitarianisms. Likewise, it opposes more current
threats toward the rule of the masses, like the depoliticization in which
important spheres of society are increasingly exempted from democracy to instead come under the reign of "human rights," "core values,"
"experts," or "the market." In his book *The Problem of Democracy*
de Benoist traces the Indo-European roots of democracy—a subject
of which many republicans throughout history have been well aware
(Saint-Just and Rousseau were both pro-Spartans). Be that as it may,
the original democracies were organic, that is to say, they did not
spring forth from some mass of random "individuals." Before the idea
of *rule by the people* may be realized, there must first be a *people*.

The democracy of ancient Greece was a participatory democracy,
a concept de Benoist elaborates in *The Problem of Democracy*. On this
issue, de Benoist is largely in agreement with Castoriadis. People-rule
cannot be delegated to a gang of representatives, but needs some element of direct democracy and perhaps even appoints some positions
by lot. Naturally, the success of such a system relies on the overall
quality of the participants—a condition which might have been met
by the citizens of ancient Athens, but perhaps less so by the individuals
of late modernity.

The New Right has also questioned the modern attitude toward politics, centered around the nation state. This is an example of the centralizationist, Jacobin, attitude and, historically speaking, represents a change to the worse. The ideal of the New Right is instead a federalist model, with several levels of locality and regionality. Most decisions may be made on a local or regional level, while others must be made on the pan-European level. Here we can observe an attempt to unite geopolitical insights, like the need for a continental bloc, with a respectful concern for local communities and identities.

Paganism

> Pagan tolerance was born, as a principle, both from a recognition of human diversity and a denial of dualism.
>
> —ALAIN DE BENOIST

In stark contrast to most older right-wing traditions stands the New Right's break from Christianity. Several leading proponents have instead identified as pagans, including Pierre Vial, Dominique Venner, and Alain de Benoist. The paganism in question has not necessarily been faith-based or conventionally religious, but rather serves as an outlook and foundational philosophy. This kind of paganism melds very well with several aspects of the New Right's conception-of-the-world: the right to difference fits effortlessly into a polytheistic cosmos with room for several gods. Paganism is not universalistic; neither is the pagan understanding of history linear like that of the Abrahamic faiths, but it is rather cyclical, lacking a definite end goal. This understanding does not lend itself to utopian thinking.

Monotheistic faiths tend to emphasize time while paganism tends to emphasize space. Not only utopianism but also the linear view of human history and historicism can be traced to specific understandings of time. Particular spaces become of little interest when focusing on time, which leads the way toward a universalist tendency. In many ways ideologies like liberalism and socialism are nothing but secular *ersatz*-religions, with their roots deeply embedded in the monotheistic religions. De Benoist has also noted the anti-political tendency present in monotheism: in the Old Testament it is only with great reluctance that the Jews are allowed to appoint a king, the ideal being that they should be guided by the laws alone. Millennia later, this ideal mutated into the shape of classical liberalism, which, at its core, is likewise anti-political. Additionally, de Benoist has identified elements of critique of civilization in the Bible, in which Yahweh quite actively mitigates development toward large cities and other signs of civilization. Cain, furthermore, is not merely the very first murderer, but he is also the founder of the very first city.

Metapolitically speaking, de Benoist's pagan onset is interesting for linking some of the more fertile elements of postmodernism to paganism. His book *On Being a Pagan* has enjoyed longstanding appreciation among current pagans, although the paganism dealt with is of a more philosophical nature than it is a reconstruction of the cults of Odin and Thor. Connections between de Benoist and radical traditionalists and pagans are also to be found, including his contributions to the magazine *Tyr*. De Benoist has expressed that there were several different aspects of 1789, much of which he doesn't sympathize with, but he values the effort to revive the pagan and antique heritage. Many of the revolutionaries were inspired by antiquity, not least in the republican ideal.

One of the greatest instances of fruitful New Right metapolitics is its bringing into attention a conception-of-the-world pertaining to our Indo-European ancestors as an alternative to liberalism. The outlook of our forebears was a heroic one: Dominique Venner observed that the archetypal symbol of Europe is a warrior with drawn sword. Furthermore, this conception-of-the-world was an aristocratic worldview, balancing the quest for glory and the interests of the group. In short, a conception of life which joins freedom with solidarity.

In connection with the Conservative Revolution several research-ers delved into the Indo-European conception-of-the-world and religion. Here we may mention Stig Wikander from Sweden, as well as the German Otto Höfler, and the Frenchman Georges Dumézil. They touched on subjects like the cult of fire; the *Männerbunds*; the wolf as an Indo-European totem; and the commonalities in Indian and Scandinavian myths. This is largely fascinating reading and highly recommended. Dumézil also identified what he called an *idéologie tri-partite*, an ideology of separation of three societal functions. Dumézil proposes that our ancestors distinguished three fundamental categories into which every aspect of the divine as well as of society and nature were then arranged. In a 1978 interview by Alain de Benoist, Dumézil delineates his findings: the first things to catch his attention were the parallels between the three Roman gods Jupiter, Mars, and Quirinus, and the three Indian castes Brahmins, Kshatriyas, and Vaisyas. He later discovered corresponding elements in other Indo-European cultures. Medieval Europe had oratores, bellatores, and laboratores—those who prayed, those who waged war, and those who labored.

The first function is linked with sovereignty, judicial as well as supernatural, and has thus two foundational aspects. In the North European pantheon the god of the first aspect is Tyr, while the god of the second aspect is Odin. Their Indian counterparts are Mitra and Varuna, respectively. The second function is linked with strength and power, warfare and warriors, and correspondingly with gods like Thor and Indra. The third function is linked with fertility, vitality, youth, healing, and wealth. Recurringly, gods of the third function are twins, such as the Roman Dioscuri, Castor and Pollux, and the Scandinavian Freyr and Freyja.

Every society comprises by necessity all these three functions in some shape or form, but in order for the society to become and stay healthy the functions need to be properly arranged hierarchically. In a healthy society, the function of production is subordinated to the function of military power, and military power is in turn subordinated to the function of law, of earthly as well as divine nature. It follows, as the New Right maintains, that economy should be subordinated to politics, and that every instance of the third function ruling over the others is an instance of inversion—regardless of whether it's called socialism or capitalism. The values of the first and second function are superior, and should so remain. This constitutes a complete alternative to liberalism, and reminds us of how our ancestors would hold a person motivated by mere material gain in contempt. It is with societies as it is with men: those driven more by greed or lust than by wisdom or courage languish in tragedy.

As for the chances that the philosophical paganism of de Benoist and others might fill the post-religious void, this is difficult to assess. It is a paganism devoid of gods, reminiscent of a late pagan-era tendency: the "godless men" of which Hans F. K. Günther wrote in *Religious Attitudes of the Indo-Europeans*. Nevertheless, even these supposedly godless men had convictions beyond the merely material, which they expressed when they spoke of their trust in their own power and strength. Günther suggested that this sort of speech was distinguished from mere boasting and smug materialism, but could actually be linked to the circumstance that these late pagans spoke of the divine using the non-personal term *das Gott*. "The God" was nothing like a man, for he instead permeated all well-born men. For today's godless men who still look to a pagan renaissance to solve our spiritual deficit, the traditionalists at Gornohoor.net might offer some valuable insight: Christians can't completely turn their backs on their pagan heritage, and neither can pagans pretend that more than a millennium of Christianity never happened, or that it was altogether foreign and evil.

Influence

Nothing can stop the arrival of a Europe of study groups.
— MOTTO OF THE THULE-SEMINAR

Via Armin Mohler and others, the New Right has a link back to the Conservative Revolutionaries of the interwar period; in the form of perspectives and concepts, the New Right has cared for their valuable heritage and furthered it during a disadvantageous historical period. Along the way this heritage has been greatly elaborated and amended with everything from sociobiology to revolutionary syndicalism, ecology, and communitarianism, all in fruitful synthesis. The New Right has developed an impressive, broad perspective, complete with concepts by which we may make sense of our times. Liberalism is lacking such concepts, and the same goes for "immigration critics" and the like, who start from liberalism. Unlike many of the "Rights" which have come and gone during the 20th century, the New Right has been "an intelligent Right," and has treated issues of culture most seriously. Therefore, it hasn't been constantly adapted to increasingly radical forms of liberalism. Metapolitically the New Right is well positioned between the common sense of the people and a critique of liberalism. The New Right hasn't, for example, related to Hitlerism other than negatively. It has often managed to successfully reconstrue the latest fashionable ideas—as when postmodernism was linked to a pro-European pagan perspective, or when "anti-racism" has been critiqued for being a crypto-racism, unable to cope with human diversity (reducing the Other to the Same, as expressed by de Benoist).

Reliably assessing the amount of influence the New Right has had on European right-wing and populist parties is no easy task. An "anti-fascist" researcher like Tamir Bar-On asserts that the amount of influence has been great, but Bar-On has a clear agenda and little concrete evidence. Regarding Front National, on the other hand, it is known that Jean-Marie Le Pen partly adopted the perspectives of the New Right, although he was far from popular with de Benoist. Furthermore, people from the New Right and their vicinity have joined Front National, thus influencing the party.

Our current identitarian movement is obviously linked to the New Right, not least through Faye and Vial. One may compare the link between Marx and Lenin, between theory and practice. The New Right has purveyed an anti-liberal conception-of-the-world which has served as a foundation for a younger generation to successfully take action. The American Alt-Right has also in part been influenced by the New Right, not least Greg Johnson and Richard Spencer. A shared critique of culture is notable here, which focuses on critique of liberalism and its destructive effects on identities. Other parts of the Alt-Right can't be said to be influenced at all—the Alt-Right is a complex milieu. Another important result of the New Right's activities is their contribution to forwarding the heritage from the Conservative Revolutionaries, Evola, and other valuable sources—which is to say that some of its influence has been indirect. De Benoist has stated that many, particularly in the United States, who adopt his perspectives do so selectively.

Through the journals *Telos* and *Krisis* the ideas of the New Right also reached the Left. *Krisis* features many left-wing thinkers who are not afraid of being openly associated with the New Right. Through *Telos* and Paul Piccone, de Benoist could reach an American audience consisting of a non-conformist Left. In 2015, the hedonist-anarchist philosopher Michel Onfray appeared in *Éléments*; he is open that he prefers "an intelligent right-winger over an unintelligent left-winger." The impact of the ideas of the New Right on the Left has nevertheless been considerably less than their impact on the alternative and populist Rights emerging in Europe as well as in America.

The Swedish New Right

> . . .as a nationalist, one has access to a rich tradition of thinkers, ideolo-
> gies, and forerunners, easily comparable to that of liberals and socialists.
> This tradition includes the New Right.
>
> — I, THE AUTHOR, IN 2007, THE BEGINNING OF AN ACTIVE
> INTRODUCTION OF THE NEW RIGHT IN SWEDEN.

"New Rights" have appeared in several countries, often with close
connections to their French counterpart. The Italian movement
surrounding Marco Tarchi is noteworthy, as is the highly interesting German counterpart Neue Rechte. Within the latter we find
names like Karlheinz Weissmann and Pierre Krebs, formerly
also Henning Eichberg. The Russian New Right, centered around
Alexander Dugin, has also kept in regular contact with its French
counterpart.

A Swedish counterpart emerged around what was to become the
think-tank Motpol. Beginning in 2005 as a blog-portal featuring a
host of contributors, Motpol has continually included a wide range of
perspectives, from the New Right and elsewhere. For myself, the encounter with the New Right—in particular with de Benoist, Faye and
Steuckers—was of decisive importance. Here I finally found a solid
critique of the modern world, a critique combining the best elements
from other milieus, from the New Left to Old Right.

The alternatives available in Sweden at the time weren't as rewarding—rarely were they metapolitically oriented. Coming from the Left,
one easily experiences the Right as superficial and intellectually impoverished. "Free markets" and "NATO" are no solutions to the problems
of our times. The New Right seemed by contrast significantly more
relevant and intelligent. That de Benoist had stood in contact with
old Marxists like Paul Piccone and reconnected to syndicalists and to
the New Left was no drawback. Through the New Right, I discovered
ever more areas, such as the rich European geopolitical tradition and

Georges Dumézil. I view the diversity of focuses within the New Right fundamentally as an advantage—it can be likened to a toolbox from which each may retrieve the specific tools that best fit his own personality and the case at hand. To tackle the issue of liberalism contra identity, for instance, one may retrieve the sociological tools created by de Benoist as well as the more biological ones from the works of Faye.

Delineating a milieu in whose creation one has oneself partaken is somewhat risky, but my impression is that the Swedish New Right has played an important part, not least in furthering metapolitics as concept as well as viewpoint; it has also contributed to the interest in our Indo-European heritage, in a certain geopolitical perspective, as well as in the Conservative Revolutionaries. The Swedish New Right has also had its peculiarities compared to GRECE, including the exploration of the Swedish tradition. We have brought up central Swedish phenomena like Gothicism and the Young Right, but also the less known Finland-Swedish group unofficially called the Black Guard, centered around author Örnulf Tigerstedt. We have studied aspects of the historic Swedish Left, including names like August Strindberg and C. J. L. Almqvist, as well as the tradition of civilization-critical poets belonging to the Swedish 20th century, including names like Ekelund and Ekelöf. Furthermore, the Swedish New Right has kept a greater focus on Evola than have the French, not least of all regarding his view of history and Evola as an existential thinker. Contrastingly, the originally French ideas on the levels of identity haven't won the same popularity in Sweden as they have in France—in Sweden the Jacobin reformation into a homogeneous nation state is pretty much completed.

With time, Motpol has served as a starting point for several other projects. Some have been of primarily Swedish interest, while many others have achieved international impact. Here one may say that the circle is closed: what once began with our interest in the New Right has today resulted in Faye, de Benoist, and Venner being translated into English and thereby made available to a considerably greater audience. Projects like Right On, Metapedia, Identitär Idé, Arktos, and the AltRight Corporation all play central parts within our sphere, despite originating partly or completely in a small, North European people badly beset by liberalism. Motpol has been shaped by several high-quality writers and people; in particular, I want to mention Daniel Friberg. Besides being a good friend, Daniel has played a decisive part in the development of the Swedish New Right as well as in the internationalization of our effort, greatly contributing to all three areas central to metapolitics: ideas, institutions and people.

Chapter 6

Tidehverv and a Possible New Christianization

> Rather than a Christian, I might be a pagan believing in Christ.
>
> — Don Colacho

Jung showed in his time that without religion, Europe is living dangerously. This is probably something many would agree with. The connection between religion and *asabiyya* is strong, as is the connection between religion and meaning in existence. Atheism and science seem not to suffice as alternatives, no matter how useful they may be in other contexts. North American social thinker and immigration critic Lawrence Auster identified in this spiritual vacuum the root cause of the West's second problem:

> We must look inward and realize that the third worldization of our society is only the external symptom of a disease in our own soul—the rejection of the religious beliefs, moral truths, and the cultural loyalties that once made us a nation rather than just a collection of economic factors.

Nature despises a vacuum, and the void has therefore been filled with post-Christian *ersatz*-religions, such as liberalism and ethnomasochism. Prior to that, impossible long-term attempts to make race, "art for art's sake," or the class into *ersatz*-religions have also failed. Auster said that a society dies without its soul, and that its body then gets taken over by strangers. Whether we are believers or not, it is obvious that he has a point here. Atheists also do not conceive that many children, and their capacity for self-defense is small. Peter Turchin reminds us in *War, Peace and War*, about the link between *asabiyya*, meta-ethnic borders and religion. The groups on the various sides of the meta-ethnic border are often united by a shared religion; it is also shared religion that makes them fearless of death and urges them to gladly sacrifice their lives in the fight against the unfaithful. *"I lead those who love death as you love life,"* as Khalid ibn-Walid expressed it. History will reveal if strong *asabiyya* is possible without the religious factor; so far, it does not look too promising.

At this point, we encounter something that can be called the "Maurranian dilemma." Charles Maurras was one of the most historically significant French nationalists. He was Catholic but not Christian. In that way, he was a champion of the Church but could not believe himself. Many people today find themselves in a similar situation. Several attempts have been made to fill the spiritual void Jung described. Under other demographic conditions, parts of the radical Right converted to Islam, among them Guénon, Clauss, and Mutti. An interest in Hinduism and Buddhism has not rarely been combined with anti-liberalism. The pre-Christian traditions have experienced several renaissances in the 20th century, especially in the early 1900s and after the 1970s. Julius Evola explored both the Roman and the hermetic tradition, and, like Herman Wirth, sought "the light from the north" rather than "the light from the east." Since the 1970s, a second pagan renaissance has slowly emerged, including the Icelandic Ásatrúarfelagið, founded in 1972, and the Asatru Folk Assembly, founded by Stephen McNallen in 1972 (under the name the Viking Brotherhood). This was one of the best aspects of the motley legacy since 1968. The Pagan Renaissance still forwards its positions, even though it is now mostly quiet.

But even in Christian circles, valuable attempts to meet the modern world are ongoing, in spite of worrying starting points. During the 20th century, Christianity has largely degenerated and been influenced by liberalism, political correctness and 1968-ideas. This has, in particular, been facilitated by what is called *churchianism* in the United States, a term describing many believers' strong need to identify with a certain church even when it transforms. Their loyalty is to an organization rather than to God and Christ. But there have been examples of the opposite even in Lutheran circles. The Danish Tidehverv, founded in 1926 by theologians with inspiration from Kierkegaard and Karl Barth, later also from Grundtvig, is a good example. The Danish nation is shaped at least as much by the Church as by the state, largely thanks to the inheritance of Grundtvig, his joyful Christianity and his interest in the Danes' roots.

Grundtvig and Oehlenschläger are reminiscent of the Swedish *Göticisterna* in the sense that they were interested in the myths and tales of their own people, and successfully popularized them. But Grundtvig, in particular, is reminiscent of J.R.R. Tolkien and C.S. Lewis insofar as he created a synthesis of the pagan and the Christian, adding a homely and patriotic touch. Obviously, Grundtvig was more successful than his Swedish counterparts. Tidehverv has evolved into a think-tank, delivering a critique of the modern world in a style similar to the New Right and Evola. The intellectual level is often high, with references to Schopenhauer, Weber, and Ellul. The perspective combines the popular, the holy, the philosophical, and the political into a whole. In the vein of New Right, Tidehverv has developed a sharp critique against the ideology of human rights and the demonization of Russia, and like Evola, they have described the history of the modern world as a story of demonic humanism.

The Church and the People

Cult and culture have always been closely interconnected—a truth we will learn again in Denmark and in the Western world.

— CHRISTIAN LANGBALLE

In Christian thought, there has often been a focus on preaching the message to the "people"; and the people, subsequently, form *folk-churches*. In politically correct "Christianity," this is diminished or denied, but for Tidehverv it is still important. The definition of people is not linked to race, but at the same time it is not temporary or something you can change randomly. To assimilate into a people takes time—something which should be of importance for immigration policy. At Tidehverv, we find a significant interest in Islam, which is depicted as a potential threat; aside from a small secularized Muslim elite, the majority of Muslims cannot become Danish. Moreover, people, Church, and state are also not synonyms. Tidehverv has criticized the therapeutic State that is trying to force political correctness and other forms of politicization down the throat of the Church. Tidehverv is also strongly family-centered, and in Denmark, the EU resistance is largely a right-wing phenomenon, and includes Tidehverv representatives.

Grundtvig can be compared to Tolkien and Lewis in two ways: interest in our ancestors, and a deeper Christian faith. Here, Tidehverv also reminds us of the British professor and culture critic—as well as another Christian—Bruce Charlton. Charlton is a venerable civilization critic in his own right, and has, among other things, written on how the media makes us "addicted to amusement," and also on political correctness. He also writes with John Fitzgerald and William Wildblood on the blog *Albion Awakening*. The starting point is close to Tidehverv's: it is about rediscovering the British myth. C. S. Lewis described the history of the kingdom as the battle between Logres and Britain: "*After every Arthur, a Mordred; behind every Milton, a Cromwell.*" Charlton finds expressions for Deep Britain—Albion—for example, in William Blake—"Albion's only poet-prophet"—in the Arthur myth, and in the so called *Inklings* (Tolkien, Lewis, among others). Tolkien and Lewis mediated the myth in the form of, among other things, *The Lord of the Rings* and *Narnia* to generations of Brits. Each people has a similar myth, but there is also a struggle between the good sides of heritage, and the less good sides—a struggle between Milton and Cromwell. We are doing well to seek our own deeper Swedish heritage, the life-giving sources from which we can return to our contemporaries with new interpretations of the myths, truths and archetypes, so desperately needed among our people.

The War Against the Multidimensional Man

> Commerce has since the beginning appeared as the enemy of imagination.
>
>   — Brooks Adams

Tolkien's goal was a "mythology for England." Charlton emphasizes the role imagination played for the Inklings; Tolkien regarded it as something closely connected with divine creation. At the same time, the modern world, including all its distraction and entertainment, appears to be an enemy of imagination. This includes what social scientist Wright Mills described as sociological imagination, which also is lacking in the today's man: a human without imagination cannot imagine a world other than the late modern that he or she lives in, and therefore has difficulty criticizing it other than at a superficial level. Here Charlton joins a retinue of ancient civilization critique, with several representatives: Klages turned away from the fact that the modern world reduces the importance of dreams, of the oneiric, of fantasy and of magic; Lovecraft wrote his short stories about the *Dreamlands*; the narrative of Neil Gaiman's *Sandman* also touches the destiny of the oneiritic in the modern world; Brooks Adams believed that the modern world is characterized by a loss of imagination.

This is linked to a broader anthropological criticism of the modern world, where we lose touch with important aspects of our humanity. Marcuse talked about the fact that man becomes one-dimensional, and although the process was described better by others, it is an accurate concept. C. S. Lewis partially corroborated the loss of *thumos* when he set courage as the principal virtue. Courage is not just one virtue among others, but the form every virtue takes when tested in a trying situation. Without courage, we can neither be honest nor helpful when it really matters. *"Pilate was merciful until it became risky,"* as Lewis summarize it.

This reminds us of the loss of the *thumotic* dimension in our own society. German philosopher Peter Sloterdijk has developed this notion further in the book *Zorn und Zeit* (Fury and Time). Sloterdijk addresses the focus of psychoanalysis on desire and sexuality, but sees an equally central driving force in *thumos*. *Thumos* is what lies behind the pursuit of glory, the will to surround oneself with honorable friends, and the desire to avoid shame. But *thumos* is also what can make a man furious. At regular intervals, Achilles let loose his fury, to the great demise of cities and heroes. Sloterdijk is aware that there are negative forms of *thumos*, or "dark *thumos*" as he calls it. But politics that does not take *thumos* into account is based on a dangerously erroneous anthropology. Indeed, a person who experiences the violation of his dignity is driven more by *thumos* than by "desires"; he can not be bought; every attempt to bribe him will only exacerbate his fury. This is *one* aspect of the relationship between the ghettos and majority communities. But our society has forced *thumos* out—it even has difficulties in understanding the difference between positive *thumos* and "dark *thumos*." This permeates everything from politics and debate to popular culture and economics. When our society is described as "unmanly," it is often the lack of *thumos* that is referred to. Sloterdijk reminds us of how a *thumotic* policy and a *thumotic* economy can look like. Politically, it is based on the recognition of groups, similar to the thoughts of de Benoist and Eichberg. Economically, Sloterdijk connects *thumos* to Bataille and generous billionaires like Carnegie. A man driven by *thumos* can both pay off debts and donate to long-term projects and needs. But he or she also has *felix meritis*, pride in his success. In short, Lewis and Sloterdijk remind us that our society has lost a central dimension by demonizing *thumos*; it tries to reduce its citizens to children.

Overall, Tidehverv and Charlton remind us of the possibility of a deeper Lutheran criticism of the modern world. As such, this criticism cannot avoid the link between cult and culture, between people and Church. It should also pick up the link between the imagination and the divine, as well as the meaning of courage and *thumos*. In this sense, we are dealing with a genuine Deep Right, which means that the elements of Tidehverv's and Charlton's projects and perspectives should be able to inspire even pagans and others.

Chapter 7

The Identitarians

> To be identitarian is neither dogma nor an ideology, but rather a principle based on reality, on who we are.
>
> — Bloc Identitaire

In 2010, I interviewed Philippe Vardon, one of the front figures for the identitarian movement, and the leader of its offshoot in Nice, Nissa Rebela. The identitarians, through spectacular actions and compelling symbolism, had already made themselves known outside France at this point, even though the movement only started in 2002. Since its beginning, the identitarian movement has spread to many other countries, both in and outside of Europe. It is well worth taking a closer look at the movement, both in its theoretical and practical aspects.

Historical background

> Our position is simple. Neither "integration" nor "assimilation," which refers to the same thing—a multiracial society that the Gauls are supposed to accept as inevitable, something that means their submission to those that have invaded their land. The death of identity, identity for both Europeans and the invaders. Because the latter are doomed too, to become Westernized zombies even though they have all the right to live their identities ... in their homelands, that is.
>
> — Pierre Vial

The rise of the identitarian movement is connected to the peculiar history of France. France differs from Sweden in that France consists of many different historical countries (according to Adrian Molin, Scania and Dalarna in Sweden might have similar tendencies toward being countries of their own). There is the Celtic Bretagne, Corsica, Alsace, Nice, et cetera. Between these countries and Paris there has existed a more or less latent historical conflict, in which the government has tried numerous times to impose centralizing policies. There exists a Jacobin tradition that has been carried forward by both left- and right-wing parties. This means that a state nationalism does not appeal to a large part of the French people. Parts of France's historical Right have followed the trajectory of a Europe divided into regions, among them Saint-Loup. Many citizens of France identify more with their regions than the country as a whole. At the same time France is one of the countries where ethnic replacement has gone the furthest, which can be seen in Jihadi terrorism, racism against the native French, rioting in the *banlieues* and so on. This has become normal everyday life and a standard segment in the news. The ethnic French—the Gauls—are one of Europe's most jostled people. At least a third of newborns are of non-European descent; in the Paris region it is two-thirds. At this point, many feel that "integration" is out of the question, the ethnic problem is a reality. Immigration to France particularly from North Africa has brought Islamization as a problem.

France has many living right-wing positions like the New Right and GRECE, the Royalists Action Francaise, third position and Christian Bouchet, solidarism and Serge Ayoub, left-wing nationalistic Rebellion, et cetera. These traditions have many prominent representatives, both historically and today. The intellectual level has long been high and there is a tradition of activism. There is also a legacy of anti-Americanism in the various French rightist groups, often related to geopolitical and cultural reasoning; many French nationalists see a strong Europe as the necessary counterweight to American influence.

From our point of view there are few political groups that put forward really good questions: nationalists, anti-globalists, and some extreme Leftists and environmentalists. None of these provides the right answers though ... that is why we have to build our own organization born out of the meeting of different political sides that have reached the same conclusion: defense of our identities (against cultural globalization, mass immigration, Islamization, and the centralization of the state), the will to return the economy and the people to local level, the will for a participatory and direct democracy, the hope of a real political union of the people and nations of Europe.

— Philippe Vardon

The identitarian movement holds its founding to have been in 2002, when a number of activists got together and started it. Out of this, Bloc Identitaire was born. But there is also another, older organization that today calls itself identitarian: Pierre Vial's Terre et Peuple, founded 1994. Vial was one of the founders of GRECE and has also been active in Front National.

Fabrice Robert is one of the leading figures of the identitarian movement. He has a background in more orthodox-oriented nationalist milieus, including the kind that he describes as "white rebels with short hair." Among other things he has been chased by Africans wielding machetes, and has played in the band Fraction. Robert holds no regrets about his background; it has granted him important insights in, among other things, courage and comradeship. But today he has switched focus to metapolitics and networking.

Successful Actions

Words divide, actions connect.

— Bloc Identitaire

Fabrice Robert has said that among his inspirations are GRECE and Greenpeace. From GRECE and Gramsci he has learned about the importance of fighting with ideas, the need for a cultural revolution, and for metapolitics. From Greenpeace comes the inspiration for successful actions, something that has become the hallmark of the identitarians (so-called *agit-prop*, agitation propaganda). Robert points out that the identitarian movement belongs on the street, in the public. A recurring expression is *hic et nunc*, "here and now." The identitarians have long memories, but it is here and now that they act. Their actions often point to important political problems and to different forms of hypocrisy and conflicts in the official ideology. In 2004 the identitarians started handing out "identitarian soup" for the homeless. The soup contained pork, because it is cheap and because it is a traditional European staple. On the other hand, this meant that Muslims couldn't eat it. The action led to grieved, tiresomely predictable accusations of "racism," which put the finger on a derailed public debate in which "racism" is more important than helping the starving homeless. In the interview from 2010 Vardon described how many native homeless were especially vulnerable, as they ran the risk of being victimized by groups of immigrants. The action was both a practical and important act of solidarity and effective metapolitics.

Later on the identitarians planned a party at which meat and wine were served in the vicinity of a mosque—but it was banned to avoid conflicts. Even this was seen as a metapolitical victory: in what healthy European society do conflicts occur because of a barbecue? Is it possible to say that France is not experiencing Islamization when gatherings like this are banned for security reasons? Identitarians have also occupied construction sites of mosques and the Socialist Party's headquarter, and blocked bridges to the infamous migration camp, "The Jungle" in Calais. These actions have been very cost-efficient, if you compare how many people have been involved with their impact. Non-French identitarians have later made similarly successful actions in their countries, Germany and Austria for example.

Conception of the World

We don't call ourselves nationalists. Some of us have been that before and some of us haven't. Nationalism in France has been connected to Jacobinism and centralization of the state. Identitarians defend all levels of our identity, usually three: the local (your "small country"), the nation, and civilization. For myself, that means Nice, France, and Europe. We don't think that these levels are to be looked at as opposing each other—as many nationalists do—but rather as complementing each other. We claim that you can't know who you are if you ignore any of them. In accordance with this, we also think that each level should have a part of the political power.

— PHILIPPE VARDON

The identitarians are pragmatics, not dogmatists. They also see the situation as utterly serious, which means that the space for arguments over details in utopias is limited. There is a width in the movement when it comes to economic policies and religion. Some identitarians are Catholics, some pagans, and some atheists. Pierre Vial, for example, is more socialistic and pagan, and has a clear perspective about both money-power and monotheism. He writes about capitalism:

Capitalism exploits and kills people. It's foremost weapon today is globalism ... to better exploit people, all people, and to kill people, all people; immigration is a radical means to that end.

Terre et Peuple offers articles and videos with, among others, Georges Dumézil and Jean Haudry, both knowledgeable about our Indo-European ancestors and their trifunctional conception-of-the-world. Ethno-pluralism is prominent, as is the ecological approach. It is a movement that in many ways can be described as Deep Right. Fabrice Robert mentions among his influences the Catholic social teaching, Proudhon's and Sorel's French socialism, European federalists like Yann Fouéré, as well as the New Right. Guillaume Faye is a strong influence for the identitarian movement, but there are others from the old GRECE that are also important. Some of them, like Vial and Jean-Yves Le Gallou, can still be seen today in or around the identitarian movement. Others, like de Benoist, are seen as inspirations. Dominique Venner inspires many too; his symbolic value is great. An excellent paratrooper, he was jailed as an organizer for the terror-classed organization OAS. It was in large part from his organization Europe-Action that GRECE sprung. He faded out from political activism and became a respected historian for many decades. When Europe's crisis turned more acute, he decided to end his life in 2013 in the symbolic Notre Dame cathedral. The circle was now complete: what had started with action and continued with metapolitics could now enter a new phase in which decades of insights and theories turn into action once more. This is the role of the identitarians.

Today Renaud Camus is also an important influence. Camus is known as a homosexual writer, but has in later years dedicated his time to opposing current developments. He has, among other things, been fined for comparing immigration to conquest. It was Camus that coined the term *Le Grand Remplacement* (The Great Replacement) to describe the recent demographic changes in Europe. He has described the ideology to which the replacement is connected *as* an ideology, and a quest that is more extensive than just ethnic replacement. It includes for example the replacability of men, women, animals, and merchandise. Borrowing terms from Houellebecq and Marx, it is the logic of the market that is invading the entire world-conception—just as on the market, everything must be replaceable and universal, while the particular and unique is of no interest. When the process has gone far enough, the ability to see the uniqueness in disparate people is lost, they "see only people." For the great replacement to be successful it seems necessary to cut off ties to one's own culture. Camus has stated this about the situation:

> I don't want to live in a country without history, without borders, and without culture.

The very core of the identitarian conception-of-the-world is identity, which is threatened by a global model in which everything is replaceable. The identitarian view on identity has several layers, which all complement each other. Man on the one hand has a local identity, which is described as carnal; that is, a group of people who share ancestry, like Basques or Bretons. Here identitarianism is akin to tribalism or *völkisch* thinking. Then we have the national identity, the French for example. Above all this there is the civilizational identity—the European. In the Jacobin theory and practicality, the national identity has often been benefited at the expense of the other dimensions of identity, but the identitarians counter this by focusing on the importance of the local and civilizational identities.

This means that the identitarians are defenders of European civilization, and stand for European cooperation. They are not as critical of the concept of the EU as some other nationalists, although they do not approve of the EU in its current form. They argue for a common defense force of the European people, in order to throw off the yoke of being vassals to the United States. Out of this comes a skepticism towards the excessive nationalism that often creates brother-wars. Vial on National Socialism:

> National Socialism was anti-European since it was pan-Germanic…
> It was an excessive German nationalism that has caused the European
> ideal as much harm as an excessive French nationalism would.

The identitarian conception-of-the-world is described as "rooted," they talk about "long memories," and say that they don't devote themselves to politics but rather to defending a future for their descendants. There is a clear resistance towards consumerism and materialism and a connection to the Deep Right's cultural critique. At the same time they turn against European self-hatred and the ideology of European guilt. An identitarian anti-racism is often discussed: "0% hate, 100% identity." The thinking behind this is that the politically correct are wrong when they accuse identitarians of being driven by "hate"; identitarians are not driven by hate towards the other, but love of their own. They do not look down on other identities, but rather see them as belonging in their respective homelands. Because of this, the identitarians sometimes talk to Africans that are against the migration from Africa to Europe, like Emile Bomba and Kemi Seba.

Vial represents an identitarian socialism, and other identitarians strive for a European protectionism. This is supposed to bring about a more localized economy, something that is akin to ideas from the Green Movement; that which it is possible to produce locally should be produced locally, rather than being imported from half way around the globe. The identitarians bring to mind the federal and bioregional traditions.

Identitarians represent a popular democracy, often with aspects of direct democracy. A political interpretation of the three-dimensional identity means, in practice, that many decisions can be made on the local level rather than on the national. A natural consequence of their conception-of-the-world is a resistance to imperialism, no matter if it is an American imperialism that affects Iraqis and Tuaregs, or if it is an Islamic invasion of Europe. A strong Europe is seen as absolutely necessary to stand against imperialism and to have an independent, strong economy. This means that the opinion about Russia is often positive. Islam and Islamization plays a central role as an existential threat, and is often in the subject of identitarian articles and actions.

The Concept is Spreading

The identitarians are in contact with several similar parties and movements, like the Italian Lega Nord, the Belgian Vlaams Belang, the Spanish Plataforma per Catalunya, and the Swiss SVP. The movement has also spread through the formation of identitarian groups in other countries. It seems that the identitarian model works best in states that are composed of several historically distinct countries. France, Austria, and Germany are good examples of this; Belgium may never have been a kingdom in the traditional sense, but it is a state with two peoples. States that have been historically more homogeneous have not been as susceptible to the model, even if groups in such states have been inspired by elements in the identitarian strategy.

The circle around Richard Spencer has been inspired to such an extent by identitarianism that Spencer himself calls himself identitarian. However, it seems that for the most part it is the identitarian conception-of-the-world has been implemented; identitarian methods like *agit-prop* have not been adopted on the other side of the Atlantic to the same extent. Identitarianism has also been exported to South America. There it is represented by the people around Círculo de Investigaciones PanCriollistas, who have also been inspired by the New Right and by more modern North American phenomena like Jack Donovan and "the Dark Enlightenment." They put out the journal *Identitas* and have also published books.

Strategies

> By using new methods and a new message, we have been able to make entrance into the French political reality. We exist. And in many ways we are able to spread our words, our topics, and our point of view. We create the debate, we don't chase it.
>
> — Philippe Vardon

Robert has described himself as a "good student of Gramsci," and the movement as explicitly metapolitically aware. To take over political power the will of the people has to be conquered. The struggle needs to be total and must be fought on many fronts. The focus is on the street and on ideas, but Robert also speaks about networking, Internet, alternative media, and culture. Identitarians have created their own networks and charity organizations—a field in which the Left has hitherto been practically alone. They support the Serbian minority in

Kosovo, among other things. The identitarians have their own music label and their own media. They try to create "identitarian houses" in different cities. Vardon has described the strategy as "a tree with many branches."

The strategy has been a metapolitical success; they have been able to introduce concepts into mainstream consciousness. Identity is an important word that has been successfully introduced, but questions like racism against white Frenchmen, localism, self-defence, reconquista, remigration, halal, and Islamization have also been very successfully put forward, both through actions in the public space and through long term efforts in workshops and alternative media. Novopress and Polémia, in which Le Gallou is active, are examples of this. The identitarians have been successful with lobbying and creating protest storms against things like the rapper Sniper's French-hostile texts. They have created viral videos, in which the activists seem like any normal French youth. To use Vardon's words: they are characterized by the insight that you can be radical without being provocative or nostalgic.

There is a clear element of generation-politics in the identitarian movement. This is the betrayed generation, on many different levels. Their future has been sacrificed so that previous generations can feel good, their country has been degraded and given away. This kind of generational strife can also mean genuine potential, as indicated by a previous generation that turned away from the adults of their time: the famous 1968-generation. The difference is that the situation of the 68ers was rather idyllic compared to that which the identitarians are facing. They are, to quote a famous identitarian video, the generation for whom it is everyday life to *"be murdered for looking at the wrong person, not giving someone a cigarette, or for having an attitude that made someone angry."* Their generation is "the 68ers' victims." *"They wanted to break free from traditions, from knowledge and from authorities in education, but they only succeeded in getting rid of their responsibilities."* The Austrian identitarian Markus Willinger's book, *Generation Identity*, begins—logically—with the claim that *"this is not a manifesto, this is a declaration of war."* His declaration of war, in many ways, takes up the thoughts to the situationalist pamphlet *De la misère en milieu étudiant* (On the Misery in the Student Milieu) from the 1968-revolt. The similarity is in the personal angle; Willinger, too, describes different aspects of the life of the European youth. The difference is that it is turned against the generation that read *De la misère.* The 68ers were in large part successful in shaping Europe after their desires, and it is in that Europe that Willinger and his generation are growing up. There is a kind of "anti-misery" on account of this, full of ideals opposite that of 1968. It is against the 68ers that Willinger is turning, with a rhetorical onslaught that ends in a declaration of war. The 68ers wanted an endless freedom, freedom from family bonds, from collectives, from traditions, and from ideals. The result is a society in which nothing matters, in which the relationship between the sexes has lost its enchantment, in which parents neglect their children and in which millions and millions of babies are never born because of abortions. Willinger describes a society that is characterized by futility, isolation, and boredom, and proceeds to explain to the 68-generation why their children have such a hard time accepting their utopias and ideal.

All of this constitutes a factor of success, which means that the identitarians have the possibility of becoming spokesmen for the long-deferred youth-revolt against political correctness and betrayal of young Europeans. Flexibility, innovation, and pragmatism makes for a promising combination. They have had problems contending with Front National in party politics—meaning that so far, the concept is historically very new.

Chapter 8

CasaPound

> The road traveled feels lonely
> But you're not alone on this journey
> There's no burden, there's no pain
> Child of a desperate love
>
> — Zetazeroalfa, "Disperato amore"

2010 must have been an eventful year for me personally: I interviewed not only Philippe Vardon, but also representatives of CasaPound. CasaPound is an innovative Italian movement whose activists became famous for occupying empty buildings, thereby helping many homeless Italian families, among other things. They have in a relatively short time made a name for themselves far beyond the borders of Italy, and they are well worth a closer acquaintance.

Historical Background

> With usura hath no man a house of good stone.
>
> — Ezra Pound

The heritage from Fascism has been alive and breathing in Italy ever since 1945; many Italians view the era of Mussolini in a positive light and regard his political ideas as a solution to many contemporary problems. This often pertains to Mussolini's more socialist policies, although there have also been circles inspired by Julius Evola's more anti-socialist approach. For many, Mussolini's combination of socialism and nationalism appeared to be a better alternative than the corruption and subordination of money-power and foreign power that followed his reign. There has therefore been a continuity, with ever new generations of fascists who have carried and reevaluated the fascist legacy to fit their own situation.

From the 1960s to the early 1980s Italy was characterized by what has been called the Years of Lead. Back then, terrorists from both Right and Left fought each other as well as the state, and many innocent people were killed in bombings and attacks of various kind. In retrospect it has been revealed that foreign security services were involved, applying a tactic meant to cause social and political tension aimed at, among other things, destabilizing the country and making it impossible for the Eastern bloc to gain influence, while simultaneously preventing any nationalistic ambitions to reclaim sovereignty. One of those involved during this time, Gabriele Adinolfi, has in his analysis of the period linked it to the term *tertius gaudens*, "the laughing third party," to describe how both Right and Left radicals were used by the CIA and others. One effect of the era was that the tradition of a radical and passionate Right survived—although, according to the legacy of Mussolini, it would better be described as Right *and* Left. Here we find the *third position*, equally critical to capitalism and Marxism, sprung from, among others, Adinolfi's ideas. In the late 1900s, activists in several European countries were inspired by the third position.

In 2003, a group of young men occupied an empty building in Rome. What made the action unusual was that they were not Leftists, but activists from the Italian right-wing milieu. The action was therefore characterized by discipline and style, and weapons and drugs were forbidden in the building. From this moment CasaPound was born, and since then its members have occupied several buildings in Italy over the years. Many have been offered as homes for families regardless of political inclination, as housing shortage in Italy is high; others have been transformed into social and cultural centers. The name was chosen to honor Ezra Pound, "a poet, economist, artist, and fascist." The choice of the turtle as a symbol was also thought-out; it is a long-lived animal carrying its home on its back; this made the turtle suitable as a symbol for a movement occupying empty buildings and making them into homes. The turtle is also called Tortuga and Testudo. The first was a Caribbean island inhabited by pirates, the other a Roman military formation. Both were found to be suitable associations.

CasaPound was initially linked to the Fiamma Tricolore party, but has since 2008 been a separate entity. The movement has grown both in breadth and in depth, with constantly new organs in different cities and new activities. It has also made connections with groups in other countries, spanning from Spain to Ukraine. In 2016, the group was involved in the eviction of a camp of immigrants who were creating insecurity in Ostia, and also a march of 10,000 participants under the motto "defend Italy." In recent years, CasaPound has also cooperated with Lega Nord.

Activism and Activities

> You can found a party, but without great men it's just another name among countless others, a carbon-copy without originality.
>
> — GIANLUCA IANNONE

CasaPound is known for occupying empty buildings. Some are converted into housing: *occupazioni scopo abitativo*. Others are converted into social and cultural centers: *occupazioni non conformi*. With this as a starting point, the movement has built up a living network with many different branches. Metapolitically speaking, what has been achieved is a set of parallel and autonomous institutions, filled with staff of both quality and quantity; they simultaneously reconnect to a period in time that many Italians view as having been a good one; in the realm of ideas this creates new forms of a familiar past. Gianluca Iannone has stated that it is equally necessary to create one's own information channels as to claim physical space; CasaPound is present both in the realm of ideas and in physical space, and has effectively defended itself from attacks from the so-called Left. Many activists train in martial arts and can defend themselves against both anti-fascists and police; there is a significant feature of skinhead culture in and around CasaPound. On the other hand, they consciously avoid confrontations.

The network created by CasaPound includes bars, libraries, ice hockey teams, and gyms ("culture, solidarity, sports, and politics," as it was summed up in a 2010 interview). There is a conscious conception-of-the-world and an anthropology behind the many activities. For example, the gyms are cheap so that people can have alternatives to drugs and consumerism. CasaPound's various projects are often about gaining physical courage, through activities ranging from boxing and parachuting to mountaineering and diving. There is also an ecological aspect; many activities contribute to reducing the distance between man and nature that characterizes the modern world. The names are as imaginative as the aesthetics: the divers are called Diavoli di Mare (the devils of the sea) and the mountaineers La Muvra, after the great-horned sheep that inhabit the mountains. There is a significant focus on pirates, who symbolize the combination of life, freedom, adventure, and revolt that is CasaPound. Among other things, Jolly Roger banners have been waved at demonstrations. It is believed that one of the first house occupiers was a fascist named Gabriele d'Annunzio, who occupied a whole city (Fiume), unlike the left-wingers who could only manage to occupy a single house. If the focus on social justice and dignity is a legacy of Mussolini, one can see the focus on adventure and creativity as a legacy of d'Annunzio. The latter also had a connection to piracy.

CasaPound is pervaded by a will-to-life and authenticity; "life in a world of despair and plastic" is frequently discussed. In the old interview from 2010, the first occupiers where described as "visionary heretics." CasaPound is described tongue in cheek as neither Right nor Left but *estremo centro alto*, "extreme high center"; *alto* stands for altitude. CasaPound is both on the Right and Left, but above all, it is far beyond modern banality and consumer society. Their view of life and aesthetics is poetic and epic; it has been said that CasaPound is driven by a war ethos. The alternative culture that has arisen around CasaPound, with features such as the Bandera Negra radio station and the Zetazeroalfa band, is also characterized by optimism. It is doubtful that much can be understood of the movement without listening to Zetazeroalfa, whose frontman Gianluca Iannone is also a leading representative of CasaPound. He has been described as a tattooed and bearded giant, both biker and rock star. Zetazeroalfa is, for example, the only non-left-leaning band that has performed in an Italian prison. During the band's gigs, the phenomenon *la cinghia mattanza* has also emerged—a situation in which parts of the audience whip each other bloody with their belts. Later, fans often upload images of the results on social media. CasaPound is in many ways genuinely anti-bourgeois, and creates its own values.

In line with its social image, the movement strives to help people. When Abruzzo was hit by an earthquake in 2009, CasaPound had volunteers there earlier than the state to help the distressed. From that time the organization La Salamandra was formed, which swiftly aids people in need when even the Red Cross hesitates because the situation is considered too dangerous. The activists do not only operate within Italy, they also work through the Solidarity Identités organization and help with healthcare and other types of aid in Burma, Syria, and Palestine. Both the Serbian minority in Kosovo and the Karen people in Burma, two vulnerable but often forgotten minorities "adopted" by Europe's radical Right, get a share of the support. This Rightist support for the Karen people's struggle goes well back in time. CasaPound also has a student organization, Blocco Studentesco, which has grown fast and has given the movement a presence in the scholastic world. Among other things, this has granted them success in school elections.

Conception of the World

A nationalist not interested in environmental and social issues would
be an imitation.

— CASAPOUND

CasaPound sees itself as being neither Right or Left. To the extent that
it is Right, it is a social Right. The criticism of money-power, especially
in the form of Ezra Pound's *usura*, capital used for usury, is continuous
and clear. The dignity of humans and of a nation's people is superior to
the interests and logic of money. Ezra Pound established that a home is
not a simple commodity, but is something central to the family and the
people. A person can have a home, he can have two homes—but if he
has a third, it is capital. Similarly, parental leave is not just something
between an employee and an employer, but something that affects
both the family and the entire people. However, CasaPound is not
hostile toward private ownership itself, but only when it hurts the
whole. CasaPound has been described as fascists of the third millennium, an expression they have adopted, not without a hint of irony.
There is continuity with the Fascist legacy, but at the same time there
is something new and creative. You recognize the legacy of historical Fascism in their view of the state; they want a state that is ethical
and organic, a moral and spiritual fact. The state's responsibility is the
people, not the interests of money-power or globalist forces. The state
must be sovereign; it is not acceptable that it should be controlled by
money-power or by the United States.

CasaPound therefore wants the state to control the banks, as well
as necessary sectors such as water supply, defense, and energy. They
object to types of employment characterized by "flexibility," which lead
to the emergence of what de Benoist calls the *precariat*. Employment
should not be a temporary relationship solely governed by money.
CasaPound supports apprenticeship, as well as the ability to national-
ize companies in certain situations. They are for free health care and

support for single mothers. The Tempo di Essere Madri initiative calls for a system in which parents can reduce their working hours but maintain full pay by the state. This because, again, the family unit and children are too important to be dictated by money logic. Another well known initiative is Mutuo Sociale, a form of social credit whose effect would be to permit families to buy housing with advantageous loans. This concept has gained significant popularity in Italy.

The state is a useful tool in CasaPound's vision, although it is often envisioned as a benefit for families specifically. However, this does not imply a negative view of the rest of Europe or of European cooperation. The movement has contacts with many other groups, and takes a positive view of Europe as a separate bloc. They are against NATO and foreign military bases on Italian soil, and want to see more cooperation with Eastern Europe, including Russia, and the Mediterranean. Here is a link to geo-economic reasoning. European workers today compete with workers living under slave-like conditions in the Third World. CasaPound wants to see a ban on imports from such countries. Iannone has turned against Huntington's thesis about the clash of civilizations, noting that it is not an absolute but something that certain circles seem consciously to be working for. Italian geopolitics is in any case impossible when a line of conflict is drawn through the Mediterranean Sea.

Naturally linked to this is CasaPound's view of immigration. CasaPound realizes that this is about the interests of money-power: cheap labor, leading to misery and the "multi-racist" society. On the other hand, they do not turn against the migrants themselves, but see them as victims (as long as they do not violate the Italians). It is instead the modern slave traders who are viewed as the enemy, whose hunger for profit harms both migrants and the native Italians. There is an anecdote about an Egyptian pizza maker who had his restaurant destroyed by anti-fascists trying to attack Iannone. Iannone defended himself successfully, and then held a charity concert to fund the reconstruction. The neighborhood where CasaPound is located has been demographically taken over by Asians today, but when anti-fascists tried to interview them about their dangerous neighbor, these Asians only had good things to say about them. CasaPound believes that they are fighting for true diversity, while it is their opponent who "hates the other." They do not describe themselves as racists, nor as homophobes. They do not support marriage or adoption for gay couples, but they are for marriage-like contracts.

Other issues that concern CasaPound are more modern prisons to reduce the suicide rate behind bars—a question not normally associated with the political Right. They operate a telephone hotline which can be called when anyone needs advice about contact with authorities. CasaPound demands a qualitative participatory democracy, similar to the ideas of Castoriadis. The movement is also environmentally conscious. Their environmental department, La Foresta Che Avanza, works with issues such as the conditions in the meat industry and wild animals in the circus. Nor in these fields relating to nature and animals is the logic of money seen as a guarantee of dignity. CasaPound is against the banality of consumer culture, both in its own life and in politics. Among other things, they demand regulation of the advertisements in television shows, and the creation of a competitor to Hollywood.

Gabriele Adinolfi is a thinker often associated with CasaPound. He belongs to the survivors from the Years of Lead, when he co-founded Terza Posizione, third position. Adinolfi emphasizes the importance of a cultural revolution with heroic prophecies, as well as the creation of an elite. He is influenced by Julius Evola; he considers him quite disastrous as a political thinker, but valuable as an existential thinker. The Italian nationalists were one of relatively few milieus that gave Ukraine's radical nationalists support, including volunteers, during the conflict in Donbass. Adinolfi has explained this partly with respect for people who risk their lives for what they believe in, and partly through geopolitical reasoning. Putin and Russia are certainly valuable associates for Europe in the long term, but unlike the Ukrainian nationalists, Putin is completely uninterested in nationalist environments in Italy. The possibility of creating a radical base area in Ukraine has therefore contributed to the support. Regardless of how one might look at the conflict in Ukraine, Adinolfi is a worthwhile thinker.

Success Factors

> The political parties are stuck in bureaucracy. CasaPound is moving.
> The parties are dead and artificial. CasaPound is popular because it is
> alive, and because it doesn't give a damn.
>
> — CASAPOUND

CasaPound must be considered a successful movement. Its success is owed to a staff both of quality and quantity, and its metacultural work of creating an alternative culture. The CasaPound sphere is characterized by creativity, both in terms of aesthetics and world-conception. This approach was summarized during the 2010 interview:

> It is our opinion that we must renew the language, symbolism, aesthetics… If we cannot communicate with the others, it's not always their fault. We try to communicate radically and renew our dream.

This means that their aesthetics are not easy to connect to any historical period, but is new and appealing. They appropriate what is useful from popular culture, whether it is screenplays like *Fight Club*, *Fahrenheit 451*, or *300*. On wall murals and posters, we are as likely to find Ernst Jünger and Julius Evola as Ian Stuart or "Che" Guevara, Geronimo or Tolkien. Use of icons considered to the "Left" is viewed by CasaPound as unproblematic, if they are worthy of respect. CasaPound also invite outsiders for lectures and debates, including Nicolai Lilin, who wrote *Siberian Education*. At CasaPound, ideas, alternative institutions, and staff form an organic whole.

Another success factor is the will-to-life and social activities. One can compare this with Ludwig Klages and the requirement for a true life on one's own terms, a life that includes poetic, epic, and heroic elements. It is thus not surprising that these activists also cherish children and animals. CasaPound is not primarily a political party, but is characterized by action and community. The attitude of *me ne frego*, "I don't give a damn," against the establishment would also appeal to many. The combination of a war-ethos with social awareness is historically interesting. Warriors have often had a strained relationship with money-power, and have historically been able to liberate those who are indebted. This connection seems to be present in the sphere of CasaPound, sometimes described as a *Männerbund*, a League of Men. Hans Blüher wrote that the *Männerbund* has a non-bourgeois and non-liberal logic, *"in the Männerbund rules the revolution."* He also described them as the life-giving core that an Indo-European society is built around: *"A state is in the deepest corruption when power slips out of the hands of the Männerbund."* This means that a national rebirth, according to Blüher's view, requires the resurgence of the *Männerbund*, something CasaPound's development may seem to confirm. Blüher had many theories about the *Männerbund*, some of them less relevant, but he also believed that the presence in them of what he describes as heroes is central. Julius Evola's thoughts about loyalty and organic relationships of faithfulness springs to mind. Such elements appear to have been present in Italy.

It is not certain that the concept can be fully applied in other European countries; it depends on both history and national character. On the other hand, it has taken place in Spain, in which right-wing squatters created Hogar Social Madrid to offer housing and food to help the most vulnerable. What the Spanish experience shows is that such initiatives will be attacked by both police and anti-fascists, and that these attacks are facilitated by being geographically locked to a place that must be defended. This means that a fundamental capital of force must exist, while CasaPound's history shows that this can almost exclusively only be used defensively. Movements that have been inclined to use violence more aggressively have almost without exception received repression to an extent that they have ceased to exist. One might also suspect that few other European peoples have the same experience of a relatively popular fascist leader like the Italians; Ukraine may possibly be one of the few exceptions. The Italian national character also has a poetic element that some other people lack, which should be made clear if one plans to apply parts of Casa Pond's model. The social aspect is valuable regardless, as well as the affirmative and optimistic attitude.

Chapter 9

The Neoreactionaries

First of all, a reactionary is a gentleman (or a lady). A gentleman (or a lady) doesn't whine.

— MENCIUS MOLDBUG

Historically, classical liberalism not seldom played the role of a point of retreat for the defenders of a more aristocratic concept of freedom against an ever-expanding state. One could not take the state over, but one could mitigate its growth and preserve spheres of freedom. Among the most rewarding classical liberals we find Bertrand de Jouvenel and Erik von Kuehnelt-Leddihn, both with clear reactionary features. In particular, de Jouvenel is still interesting because of his historical perspective, and because of his recognition of the Indo-European and aristocratic roots of the notions of a specifically European freedom. He also described the state's ever-expanding power with the help of the parable of the *Minotaur*. Neither Mises nor Hayek appears to be consistent with today's politically correct liberalism; this is also true for Ayn Rand; her fictional attempt appears to be an assault on the reader, but she was much more a romantic Nietzschean than a politically correct liberal.

In taking the form of libertarianism, the classical liberal tradition also played an interesting role in the mid-20th century, when Murray Rothbard actively sought to create alliances beyond Right and Left; at first with parts of the more liberal and anti-war Left, later with the populist Right. During this voyage, he ended up on the same side as Karl Hess, Carl Oglesby, Pat Buchanan, and David Duke. He defended Duke's background with the notion that if it is acceptable to have been a communist in one's wild youth, then it should not be a problem that one was a member of the Ku Klux Klan either. The brand of libertarian-ism that we associate with Rothbard was not politically correct; among other things he described egalitarianism as a revolt against nature. His summation of the deficiencies of egalitarianism is still striking:

> Since egalitarians assume that all people, and thus all groups of people, are equal and the same, it follows logically for them that all differences in status, prestige or authority between groups must be the result of unfair repression and irrational discrimination.

Given the central place of freedom in the libertarian conception-of-the-world, this also means a high tolerance for politically incorrect views. Libertarianism at the same time has many shortcomings, including the anti-political and utopian element. We know histori-cally that a society with a small state and a modern economy is either conquered by its neighbors or torn apart by social conflicts. The latter indicates that some social reforms are usually cost-effective, making the nightwatchman state short-lived. But although libertarianism does share the shortcomings of "regular" liberalism, at least it has an ethos.

The Degeneration of Libertarianism

Libertarianism proved to be vulnerable to the *Zeitgeist*, and to its great deterioration. This is clear today with the libertarian presidential candidate Gary Johnson. He has described his party as *"liberal without socialism"* and *"conservative without nationalism and religion."* The liberties for which libertarians advocate today—such as marijuana and free immigration—are often irrelevant or harmful. Also one can ask what remains of human dignity without any socialism, national-ism, and religion. Rothbard's alliance with David Duke would be alien to most of today's libertarians. In terms of Carl Schmitt's friend-enemy distinction, David Duke's ideas are the *enemy* in a way that the Minotaur isn't. De Jouvenel and Rothbard's ability to think politically and historically, under the influence of popular culture, has been re-placed by a moralistic and emotional approach. To make a long story short, today's libertarians are often worse than yesterday's.

This development has not taken place without resistance. One of the most valuable libertarians today is Hans-Hermann Hoppe. Not surprisingly, he has a connection to the Frankfurt School, via Jürgen Habermas, and to Rothbard (whom he described as a fatherly friend). Hoppe has a historical perspective, and has portrayed how society moved from aristocracy through monarchy to democracy (with state officials abandoning the king during the journey). Like Evola, he de-scribes this as a change for the worse. Hoppe is culturally conservative and is an opponent of today's immigration policy. An important feature of his analysis is the notion of *time preference*. Low time preference imply a higher ability to postpone consumption and the satisfaction of needs to the future; in short, *"less now, but more later."* With support from Professor Philippe Rushton's research, Hoppe says, among other things, that whites have lower time preferences than blacks. Moreover, a hereditary monarch has lower time preferences than a democratic leadership which is replaced at short intervals. Several of Hoppe's texts have long been available on the Internet resource The Mises Institute, along with many of those by other more classically and historically conscious liberals. There they have been waiting for their time to come. Metapolitically speaking, they gained a huge importance when a new socioeconomic actor emerged, in a new historical situation.

Mencius Moldbug

> The other day I was tinkering around in my garage and I decided to build a new ideology.
>
> — Mencius Moldbug

In the same way that the bourgeoisie and the New Class gained confidence in the past and wanted to win not only economic but also political and cultural power, similar trends are to be found in the emerging layers of engineers, innovators, and computer programmers. Often these people are interested in such things as transhumanism, artificial intelligence, and cryogenics; frequently they are libertarians. A movement emerged from this environment that would be called *neoreaction*, in large part due to the intellectual work of Mencius Moldbug. Moldbug's real name is Curtis Yarvin and he is of Scottish and Jewish descent. He is a computer programmer, and a so-called geek. In 2007, he began to develop his political philosophy on the blog *Unqualified Reservations*. In 2013, he quit writing political philosophy almost entirely, because his other projects took up more of his time. But at that time there was already a sphere of blogs and websites that shared his perspective; this was the advent of so-called neoreaction.

The early neoreactionaries had usually read their libertarians, and often had a past in such circles themselves. But they also realized that modern libertarianism had limitations, in particular an inability to think politically and historically. Moldbug's choice of reading becomes clear from this perspective; most of the thinkers he used to supplement his reading were politically oriented. There were a large number of reactionary thinkers, such as Carlyle, Mosca, Movies, de Jouvenel, Don Colacho, von Kuehnelt-Leddihn, Burnham, Froude, and others. Moldbug was also inspired by ancient Rome's political theory and practice, as he believed that here one finds timeless truths about the political. In many ways, Moldbug was the logical consequence of Hoppe. This also explains why his thoughts were so attractive to many libertarians and old anarcho-capitalists. He introduced a valuable but mostly forgotten intellectual tradition that could explain our time; a tradition that for contemporary Westerners is completely unknown due to reforms of the common curriculum. Nonetheless, it is a tradition that offers a number of insights into the political. Mosca, for example, is *in the right* in a way that Nancy Pelosi can never be, and is more rewarding to read if you have a three-digit IQ. Moldbug also wrote in an entertaining way, mixing classical insights into a modern language; in his language, it was not strange to claim that Dawkins had been "pwned."

One could say that "libertarianism+modern society=neoreaction." Modern society was that which prompted many libertarians to doubt the feasibility of their utopia. The ideal—a society of free and independent people—was still realistic during the 19th century. But today, with demographic replacement, proletarianism and the Great Worsening, it is no longer possible. On Jim's blog, this was summarized accordingly: *"The Dark Enlightenment is libertarians mugged by reality, a libertarian who realizes that the eighteenth century was right about women, and Bull Conner right about blacks."* Libertarianism, for example, does not work in a multi-ethnic democracy, in which different ethnic groups can use the state as a sledgehammer against each other.

Moldbug's writing was stylistically appealing. His writing was characterized by a sober distance to the present, combined with large portions of higher learning and irony. He would describe the common white Americans as *Amerikaners*—a clear reference to the South African farmers, *Afrikaners*. He could compare the East Coast's politically correct population layer with H. G. Wells *Eloi*, engaged in the *"import of morlock voters,"* to shift the balance of power to the disadvantage of the Amerikaners.

The Neoreactional Analysis

> Let us define demotism as governance in the name of the people. The
> Eastern bloc was demotic, the same holds for the National Socialism.
>
> — MENCIUS MOLDBUG

Moldbug and the neoreactionaries ignored the obvious as much as possible in their analysis of society, and instead approached it with the same distance that a historian or an extraterrestrial alien would. Such a stance was partly facilitated by the introduction of a number of useful concepts. For example, in the idea of demotism, Moldbug's skepticism to democratic ideology was expressed. One of the "truths" more deeply embedded in the consciousness of contemporary man, is that democracy is better than any alternative; another is that we actually live in a democracy. Moldbug questioned both these assumptions by distinguishing between *demotism* and *legitimism*. Demotisms are political arrangements that claim regal power in the name of the people. These may include people's republics, National Socialism, or our own liberal-democratic variant. Against this, Moldbug posed legitimisms; in practice, monarchies. Approximating a libertarian conception-of-the-world he asserted that the royal house owned the state, and, like Hoppe, he meant that such arrangements work better than demotic ones. He also noted that we do not really live in a democracy, even though we are fooled into believing we do; we live in a non-democratic demotism that works badly, among other reasons because it pretends to be democratic.

The demo concept (demotism) was not as vigorous as some other of his innovations. Among them we find in particular the concept of *the Cathedral* and his caste analysis. Today these are part of a much broader sphere than the neoreactional, and have significant value in understanding our contemporary states of affairs.

The Cathedral

> The Left is the party of the educational organs, at whose head is the press and universities. This is our 20th-century version of the established church. Here at Unqualified Reservations, we sometimes call it the Cathedral—although it is essential to note that, unlike an ordinary organization, it has no central administrator. No, this will not make it easier to deal with.
>
> — MENCIUS MOLDBUG

The concept of the Cathedral has been widely disseminated. Moldbug showed that in the United States there is actually no separation between state and Church; the reason why Americans in general do not realize this is that their definition of "church" is outdated. A *church* is for Moldbug *"an organization or a movement that tells people what to think."* Here we recognize the legacy of Carlyle; the phenomenon of political correctness is a "church," in this sense. Moldbug noted that the Cathedral has the benefits of both the state and the Church, from its own perspective, combining the best of both worlds. Since it formulates the very items of policy, it can like a state be regarded as the ultimate governing body, but like a church it does not bear any responsibility for the policies it pursues. Parties can be elected to power back and forth, but the media and universities remains. The Cathedral has, to borrow an expression from Nassim Taleb, *"no skin in the game."* The consequences of bad politics are very indirect for the Cathedral representatives; instead, others pay the price—costs are externalized.

In this respect Moldbug, although perhaps unwittingly, brings attention to the metapolitics and Gramsci: the Cathedral and its constituents create "common sense" in our society. At the same time, Moldbug brings to mind Gottfried and Lasch's thoughts about the New Class; these can in many ways be regarded as the functionaries of the Cathedral. As for the presumably "private" educational system and big corporations—due to their lack of real boundaries against, among other things, the media, he included those in the state. This seems constructive—the Cathedral coincides largely with the establishment, and with Marx's "executive organ." It is worth emphasizing that the Cathedral is largely held together by informal connections. Like Gramsci, Moldbug was interested in institutions, functionaries, and world-conceptions.

Moldbug's analysis of the Left was also interesting. He identified its origin in a Christian sect (he shares this insight with others interested in political theology, from Donoso Cortés to Voegelin). His analysis of the sect's psychological aspects was often rewarding. He noted its similarities with the inquisition, not least of all in the fact that the group which de facto holds regal power, and which represses unallowable opinions with various forms of abuse, nevertheless regards itself as weak and threatened—in short, as the one who is inferior. As a post-Christian sect, it is obvious that this often makes its members dangerous to its surroundings. At the same time, he studied progressive ideology as a meme, that is, a thought spreading as it copies itself from person to person, and as a parasitic one at that. Still, this particular meme (or complex of memes) is effective; among other things, because it can make the one who agrees with the official ideology, but who demands *even more* of the same feel, like a rebel. In addition, he considered the illogical elements of the official ideology as its strengths rather than its weaknesses. It is when you agree with an opinion even though you really know better that you show that you belong in a group. He described today's "religion" as *universalism*.

Moldbug's historical relativization of Anglo-American liberalism is also interesting. He never tired of noting that in 1938 there were three competing ideologies, and if one of the other two had been victorious military-wise, we would today have learned this particular ideology's excellence in school. Moldbug considered both Hitler and Stalin as expressions of the modern era's demotic model, but thought that the same was true of Roosevelt and Obama. He held that the New Deal was in fact a *coup d'état*. Over all, there is a strong feature of historical revisionism in Moldbug, which is also the case with many other former libertarians. He did not regard history as a series of successes, but soberly regarded it rather as a series of more or less unfortunate events. For example, the American Loyalists were in the right; most victorious revolutionaries have been brutal maniacs; "diversity" actually means homogenization; the notion of "progress" is a lie; colonialism might not have been as catastrophic as we have learned. Moldbug departed from what is called Whig history; Whig historians assume that it has always been the correct side that won, and that this side then, fortunately, has been able to write history. Moldbug, in comparison, had a more pessimistic and tragic view of history.

The United States as a Caste Society

> In the Brahmin caste, status among both men and women is defined by scholarly achievement, success in an intellectual profession, or position of civic responsibility. The highest-status Brahmins are artists and scientists, but Brahmins can also be doctors or lawyers, although it is much better to be a doctor than a lawyer, and much better to be a lawyer than a dentist ... Entry into the Brahmin caste is conferred almost entirely by first-tier university admissions.
>
> — MENCIUS MOLDBUG

We live in an individualistic society characterized by mobility; anyone can become anything and all people are basically alike. This in any case is the official version. Moldbug departed even from this. He described the United States as a caste society, taking as his starting point the primate nature of the human being which instinctively recognizes group belonging and is always searching for status within the group. A society like the United States is accordingly divided into a number of groups with internal rules for how status is achieved and defined. Since the term "class" is not sufficient, and because he probably did not read Bourdieu, Moldbug used the notion of caste, but in a modified way. The neoreactional notion of caste combines culture, socioeconomics, personality, and ethnicity to distinguish the groups that are in play in today's United States. Moldbug spoke of *Brahmins*, *Dalits*, *Helots*, *Optimates*, and *Vaisyas*.

The Brahmins are in many ways the most interesting caste. It corresponds to some degree to Gottfried's New Class and to Carvalho's intelligentsia and bureaucrats. It is the dominant caste, and the members are characterized by the "progressive" conception-of-the-world. Through its grip of educational institutions and the press, it affects what is socially considered to be permissible opinion, and it constantly fosters new generations of Brahmins (including descendants from Vaisya background and old Optimate families). There is an intimate link between the Brahmins and the Cathedral; this is the caste that is the bearer of the Cathedral's ideas.

The typical Dalit is instead a gang member or "welfare mom." Most of them belong to one minority or the other. This caste is not to different from the Marxian *Lumpenproletariat*.

The typical Helot is a Mexican immigrant. It is an imported peasant caste. *"Status among Helot men is conferred primarily by hard work, money and power. Status among Helot women is conferred by attractiveness, motherhood, and association with successful men. The Helot value system does not seem to be sustainable in the US, and the children of Helots tend to grow up as Dalits. New Helots, however, can always be imported to replace them."* Moldbug identified an alliance between Brahmins, Dalits, and Helots, which explains a whole range of contemporary phenomena from affirmative action and the violence of Black Lives Matter to current immigration policy. This alliance is aimed at Vaisyas and the residues of the great Optimate caste.

The Vaisya caste largely corresponds to what Sam Francis called "Middle America." They are usually of European birth, and often vote Republican. Their most severe predicament is that they do not understand how modern America or modern politics work; they think that they can recreate a United States that has already disappeared. Moldbug had difficulty in identifying with them, as many of them are cretins. They speak about God and the Constitution and the Flag, and various other things that cannot really challenge the sway that the Brahmins hold over the country. In many ways Moldbug had more in common with the Brahmins, which meant that he could understand how they think. But at the same time, he had a distance to their conception-of-the-world and saw through its shortcomings.

The Optimates are the leftovers of the old American aristocracy. As they usually undergo higher education, they now are "Brahminized" at an early age. There has been a historical alliance between Optimates and Vaisyas—Moldbug described it in both Rhodesia and the United States. But there are also strong forces that drive Optimates to betray the Vaisya's natural self-interests.

Moldbug saw caste division and minority rule as basically natural. He turned—and tailored his message—to Brahmins rather than to Vaisyas, which is a subversive method, and it allowed him to avoid the elements of Vaisya conservatism that usually repel Brahmins (*"not all conservatives are cretins but most cretins are conservative"* as Moldbug expressed it). The approach therefore allows for a subversive Brahmin ideology to take form.

Other neoreactionaries have later supplemented Moldbug's castes, and introduced among others *Antyajas* (rednecks) and *Frontines* (*"Frontiers in Technology and Frontiers in the Financial World"*) in the analysis. The imaginative choice of concepts might bring Dungeons and Dragons to mind, but it is an interesting and valuable project to map out the groups that compose our society as a whole. In order to apply these perspectives to Sweden, the division and corresponding concepts need to undergo certain modifications, but here too we can identify Brahmins, Vaisyas, and Dalits. However, our Brahmins are subordinated to American Brahmins, and receive their conception-of-the-world from them. The alliance between Brahmins, Dalits, and Helots is the same, as is the conflict between them and the Vaisyas. As in the United States, the Brahmin caste actively uses migration policy to increase the number of Dalits and Helots. They also use the Cathedral in the form of, among other things, state television, media, and the educational system to create new generations of Brahmins. In both the United States and Sweden it has been difficult for Vaisyas, Antyajas, and Frontines to gather together on a project or even to describe what's going on.

Moldbug's own project often appeared to be directed to Brahmins and Frontines who had seen through the system, and realized that the

Cathedral's policy is directly dangerous to all. There is a latent conflict between Frontines and the ideologically and culturally dominant Brahmins; in this context neoreaction can then be regarded as the ideology that the former develops in their opposition to the cultural Marxism and political correctness of the latter. Given that Frontines often are young and have significant financial and intellectual resources, there are good reasons for the Brahmins to worry. At the same time, there are signs that the Frontines have been bad at deflecting the Cathedral's intrusion into their sphere. The hacktivist Weev said that *"programming, considered as an industry, has no will to power."* Many Frontines avoid conflicts altogether, something that has consequences.

After Moldbug

> The Right represents peace, order and security, the Left represents war, anarchy and crime … Whatever you make of the Left-Right axis, you have to admit that there exists some force which has been pulling the Anglo-American political system leftward for at least the last three centuries. Whatever this unfathomable stellar emanation may be, it has gotten us from the Stuarts to Barack Obama.
>
> — MENCIUS MOLDBUG

Neoreaction was not a one-man project, there have always been other neoreactionaries who helped formulate the perspective. After Moldbug switched focus to his Frontine business, these have developed the project in somewhat different directions. This is not surprising, as there are several threads in Moldbug's work. One can develop it in a techno-commercial direction, and interest oneself in the possibilities of technology; here we find the philosopher Nick Land, with the blog *Outside In*. One can do a deeper reading of the various reactionaries that Moldbug recommended, and develop a pure reactionary philosophy (*Heroic Reaction*, as it is called on *Froude Society*). One can discover Julius Evola and/or become more critical of capitalism. A recurring concern, also raised by Moldbug, are ethnic relations. Radish and Theden focused on this, among other things, thus foreshadowing the Alt-Right. One can also, like Henry Dampier, focus on what makes a civilized society possible, and how it is threatened today. Some projects well worth a visit, besides Land's, are *Social Matters* and *West Coast Reactionaries*. Today there is a wide reactionary environment—a *reaction sphere*, in which the legacy of Moldbug, Evola, Hoppe, purebred reactionaries, de Jouvenel, and several others gather.

Some neoreactionaries have taken on Moldbug's *passivist* approach, focusing on working metapolitically rather than politically. These maintain the view that political work today only triggers the Cathedral and that it is better to work on becoming *worthy*—develop the necessary qualities for leadership within oneself and one's local community, in preparation for the day that the sway of the Cathedral reaches its end. Others have in practice become parts of the Alt-Right. This is natural, given the built-in conflict in Moldbug's thinking: on the one hand, he outlined a possible alliance, a historical bloc consisting of Vaisyas, Optimates, Antyajas, and Frontines; on the other hand, he fixed a political ideal—privatized governments, which are far from the interests of most Vaisyas and Antyajas. Some kind of populism would have been more logical; this demand is supplied by the Alt-Right.

Success Factors and Limitations

The fact that royal authority derives from itself produces a much higher degree of social justice in a monarchy than in any known form of republic. Republics are less likely to be fair because all governments are necessarily party governments.

— Von Treitschke

Metapolitically, neoreaction is an interesting project. If we use Gramsci's and Althusser's concepts, we find that the Internet, considered as ISA, was a necessary prerequisite. The Internet was not yet an anti-market, but was characterized by significant freedom, and taboo subjects could be discussed anonymously. Other necessary conditions were the participation of highly intelligent individuals from the Frontine and/or Brahmin castes. American conservatism does not usually appeal to these layers, but the neoreactionaries formed a conception-of-the-world suitable for an avant garde. Neoreaction also became part of an environment of several overlapping spheres, the so-called Dark Enlightenment. A rich, and for our time very relevant legacy was discovered through Moldbug. Neoreactionaries transformed the term *reaction* from being a simple invective and pejorative and made it cool again. They coined their own concepts and abbreviations, from GNON to NRx. Things like appealing pictures of neoreactionary cats with several well-selected quotations also contributed to the attractiveness of reaction.

Hence, it is not surprising that neoreaction influenced the Alt-Right—among other things through the analysis of the Cathedral and the term *Amerikaner*. Moldbug was a fruitful metapolitician, and explained key aspects of how power and politics work. He also described a present state of affairs characterized by deterioration. The criminal classes are allowed to advance their positions, the debate is infantilized, the system has become sclerotic and it *will* collapse. This reality is partly hidden by technological advancements, but it is still very much a reality.

For the neoreactionary, the quest for order and security is at the center. It pointed out how *bad politics* had become widespread through demotism and the Cathedral. This correlated with an inquiry for a better political order. Moldbug described the goal as the privatization of the political, with states practically being companies with boards. In such a state there is no voting, but each has an interest in keeping itself in good stead with its capable citizens, who can otherwise vote with their feet. Sources of inspiration here include small states like Dubai and Singapore. With states largely managed as companies, everyone is not necessarily desirable as resident. Moldbug had a number of suggestions for how to resolve this, including a form of neo-feudalism in which individuals who cannot support themselves are not ordinary citizens but "wards" to other citizens or the state. He also sketched a solution in which dangerous individuals can live the rest of their lives in a kind of virtual existence. This system has similarities to feudal Europe, and Burckhardt's and Don Colacho's *Old Europe*—both in terms of the amount of small states and the distinction between free and unfree. One might assume that many such small states would in practice be ethnocracies.

At the same time, this means that politics is subject to the logic of economics, so the heavily politically centered conception-of-the-world is paradoxically not at all political. Nonetheless it is one of the great values of the neoreactionaries that they remind us that civilization and liberalism are not the same, and that liberalism can even undermine civilization. Moldbug also quoted Metternich when he stated that freedom is not the starting point but the goal, and that order must therefore be the starting point.

Moldbug's neoreaction is in its foundation a materialistic and reductive conception-of-the-world, and a child of the historical Left. What is missing in comparison with a classic Right is therefore a transcendent aspect, and partly a more organic view of what a society is (in short, more *Gemeinschaft*). To vote with your feet, to "exit," is, for example, not an alternative for those who have long memories and roots. Relations of loyalty also become difficult to understand given the confusion of the economical and the political. Moldbug also did not focus on the historical role played by money-power in the emergence of universalism and the Cathedral. Here, his shortcomings become clear in comparison with, for example, the New Right or CasaPound.

Neoreaction is lacking even a strategic aspect in addition to passivism, and beyond the unwillingness to create the above-described historical bloc. The lack of *kshatriyas*, the warrior caste, is an important shortcoming of the neoreactional analysis of the United States.

The military is an important factor in the country, and in the long term, a military coup is not an impossibility as the system fails more deeply. It is worth noting that the military is largely recruited from Vaisya circles, but to a growing extent also among Dalits and Helots. The strength of the neoreaction—its attractiveness to a highly intelligent circle—could at the same time have been a weakness. It has been characterized by anonymity and lacks the prospect of becoming a mass movement. Metapolitically, however, its significance has been remarkable, and seems to continue to be so. There is a lot of value for an emerging Right, both in Moldbug and the others.

Chapter 10

The Right in the Non-Western World

A leader must be terrible for the few that are evil, to protect the many that are good.

— RODRIGO DUTERTE

The American world order can be divided into two aspects. One aspect is geopolitical, in which countries are subordinated under a system through entities like NATO, NAFTA, and the several hundred active military bases around the world. Another is the sociopolitical and metapolitical aspect in which the liberal ideology is disseminated to other countries with the assistance from NGOs and Hollywood, as well as media and human rights organizations. There is a connection between the geo-, meta- and sociopolitical spheres. The middle class is often liberal-minded and friendly to American values, what Spengler called "the inner Englishman" and what Dugin describes as the fifth column. De Benoist's description of the enemy circles back to these three areas: geopolitically it is Atlanticism, sociopolitically it is the uprooted bourgeoisie, and metapolitically it is liberalism. The latter two are the Trojan horse or "the England within," which equates modernization with Westernization—beginning with economical growth but ending in cultural and social degeneration and a breakup of structure. In the last few years a growing number of countries have broken with this logic. It is now possible to identify alternatives with respect to the geo-, socio- and metapolitical areas.

Geopolitically Atlanticism is being replaced in several countries with an independent and alternative foreign policy, not seldom with elements of cooperation between nations in the same situation or position. One such formation particularly worth noting is BRICS, an alliance between Brazil, Russia, India, China, and South Africa. It is based on the idea of creating and developing alternatives to counter-weight the American world order and its institutions, such as the International Monetary Fund or the World Bank, but also to include countries like Egypt and Iran into the fold. Aside from BRICS there are collaborative projects between China, Russia, and other regional players such as the Eurasian Shanghai Cooperation Organization. The American hegemony and its destructive actions in (but in no way limited to) the Middle East, along with the exposure of espionage against its own allies, have contributed to the image around the world of an empire engulfed and engaged in chaos. The conception-of-the-world that this empire represents is not any longer what it was during the Cold War, but is now one in which the methods used seem short-sighted and destructive.

Sociopolitically the uprooted bourgeoisie is being replaced by other social and historical groups. This could mean an alliance between the nationalist middle class and other groups such as farmers and military personnel, or it can include more ordinary people—the little man—in general; or as an example, alliances between people from different Hindu castes in India. Chávez in Venezuela built his idea of Bolivarism, to no small degree, on an alliance between military and people of lesser means. Erdoğan builds his popular support to a high degree on the more religious and rural populous in Turkey. Both of these historical groups go against the logic stemming from an Americanized middle class that has ruled the nation's narratives in the past. These other groups can often be described as populist in their mindset.

Liberalism is thus being replaced by several different alternatives that have their roots in the nation's own history and identity. Currently this contributes to the notion of the Western model as being less attractive and harder to integrate in local traditions and customs. This creates a need for alternatives. In Turkey this means a combination of Islam and nationalism with some Ottoman influence, the end result being authoritarian populism. In Venezuela this means furthering and developing the legacy of Bolivarism with an added Leftist theme. These developments are challenging the liberal universalism that de Benoist, among others, criticized. The kind of policy that a country like Sweden follows might not be deemed suitable or even desirable in other countries like the Philippines or India, as these have a different culture and another set of issues to deal with.

A Self-Chosen Path—India and the BJP

The nation, just like the individual, becomes the victim of many accidents whenever it's natural instincts are neglected.

— PANDIT DEENDAYAL UPADHYAYA

India is an ancient civilization but also a modern state. For a long period India was governed by the Congress Party, but since 2014 a shift of regal power occurred to the benefit of the Bharatiya Janata Party or the BJP. This party is conservative and Hindu-nationalist and has its roots in the paramilitary group Rashtriya Swayamsevak Sangh, RSS. The party has suffered accusations of Fascism and involvement with violence targeting Muslims, although the party itself denounces these accusations as lies.

The BJP is interesting because their program is based on the fact that different nations have their unique characters, and should abide by them. Colonialism meant that India's, or Bharat's, natural identity was repressed and oppressed. This brought a challenge for BJP and the Hindu-nationalists. Pandit Deendayal delves into the European history of ideas in his significantly important article "Integral Humanism" from 1965. In this article he identifies socialism, nationalism, and democracy as the predominant ideologies in more recent European history. At the same time he notes that these ideas are not universal and are not always suited for other nations—especially since they didn't work even in Europe. Nationalism led to war between nations, and the conflict between democracy and socialism seem unsolvable (in this instance he seems to view democracy and liberalism as synonymous, and individualism as the force binding them together). India therefore has to find its own way, adapted to the nation's own identity and issues. This does not mean a return to the situation prior to British rule, nor does it mean that India could ignore the three ideologies the European continent is struggling with. It does mean, however, that one has to start analyzing that which is truly one's own and search for a solution by looking inward.

Deendayal describes Indian culture as integral and holistic, with a single cultural core and a diversity that thrives through unity. In comparison, Europeans tend to focus on differences, which often results in conflict, or even idealistic views of struggle and conflict as reflected in the ideas of Social Darwinism and its "fight for survival." Deendayal describes this as degeneration; civilization has not evolved according to this logic, but in quite the opposite direction, by striving to minimize it. These integral views do not only concern society but also the individual itself. As the individual has both physical and spiritual needs, neglect of these needs has led to high suicide rates and poor mental health in rich countries such as the United States. Deendayal uses the Indian terms *dharma* and *artha* to describe what the ideal for society and life is. Here he breaks with Western individualism, that emphasizes the individual parts of society. Society and the group within it are not something that is created by individuals, it is rather an entity in itself with its own character, its own life and emotions. A nation has a soul, called *chiti*. Whatever conforms with *chiti* can be embraced and accepted as a cultural form by the nation. *Chiti* resembles the soul and character of an individual. When a nation acts in accordance with *chiti* it grows strong and potent. In this we can also see a partial explanation for the problems facing the peoples on the European continent: they have abandoned their *chiti* in favor of abstract ideas. The country according to Indian social doctrine has a number of institutions to solve different tasks. The state is one of them; it is important but not as important as the nation. Deendayal thinks that *chiti* stands superior to temporary political majority, that there are things no majority can legislate on. This is the nation's *dharma*—the expression of its *chiti* and its *virat*, the potent energy that saturates it. This perspective is useful for understanding the BJP's will to find both its own way, as well as understanding some aspects of the crisis now facing Western civilization.

The BJP has seen changes in its political stances; when in power it has implemented a more conservative economic stance and drawn back on financial support for environmental causes. It also opposes immigration to India from Bangladesh, in particular of Muslim refugees rather than Hindu refugees. But it provides an interesting example of an ancient civilization trying to find political paths most fitting to its own identity. The reasoning behind *chiti*, *dharma*, institutions, and *virat* could be an interesting example for Westerners. It is also a sign of a new world emerging, when a party of the so called "extreme Right" now rules one of the most populous countries in the world.

Thumos and Populism—Erdogan and Duterte

> We will not leave this nation in the hands of Youtube and Facebook.
>
> — ERDOĞAN

In his day Carl Schmitt described the root-conflict between democracy and liberalism, between the will of the people and the rule of law. This conflict becomes clear in both Turkey and the Philippines, where charismatic leaders rule their nations with little or no respect for the liberal laws in their respective countries. Their political views or personalities are not identical, but seen from Schmitt's viewpoint they have many similarities.

Rodrigo Duterte, the leader of the Philippines, is a fascinating example of a leader with *thumos* and a politically incorrect sense of humor. For instance his bragging about shooting rapists during his time as mayor of Davao, or calling a foreign leader "a son of a whore"; he once made an unruly tourist swallow his own cigarette. These things have given him notoriety in the world and popularity within certain segments of the Alt-Right, and have made him a totem of hate in the eyes of the media. But if this is the extent of one's knowledge, the popularity of this man among his countrymen seems preposterous—unless one deems the Philippine population outright stupid. During Duterte's long reign as mayor of Davao the city became a safe place in comparison to most other cities in a country ravaged by violence, though his methods might have been considered brutal. He has declared an outright war on drug dealers and drug users, but treads lightly on practical matters of policy. Duterte supports the idea of a federalized political system in the Philippines and believes this might be the solution to the conflict with the Muslim minorities in the south. He has halted the escalation of the conflict with China over islands in the South China Sea, and instead uses diplomacy to solve the conflict. At the same time he is building closer ties with Russia and China, and has reacted with anger when American leaders expressed worry over his use of language and policy. Duterte, in short, is the typical populist and nationalist, even if his federalist views do not fall in line with the views of a typical nationalist.

Turkish president Erdoğan does a better job than Duterte at illustrating the difference between democracy and liberalism as Carl Schmitt described it. His view is that democracy is not solely based in parliamentarism, and views his role as a leader as being more than just administrating a system. Erdoğan is a good example of someone who embodies what Goldman called *theopolitics*. During most of the 20th century Turkey was a secular republic backed up by the military. But demographic changes eventually made military coups hard to organize. The Westernized middle class that supported the secular republic produced fewer offspring, while the opposite was true for people of faith. This reminds us of the situation in many other countries in which religious people produce more children and change the political landscape and electoral base. This is also true in Israel and Europe. Turkey has had an interesting political landscape for decades, not only in a positive sense, with several ultra-nationalist groups operating in the country. Turkey's scattered political map includes a group internationally known as the Grey Wolves, that through its activity in the diaspora in Germany is Germany's largest "extreme right wing" group; also included is the left-wing and Eurasian-emphasized Doğu Perinçek's Workers Party.

Erdoğan has skillfully mastered the world of metapolitics. He has combined Islamic conservatism with a nationalism that could be said to embody the heritage of both Kemalism and the Ottoman empire, initially without challenging the military powers of Turkey. In this he reminds us of Günther's emphasis on the fact that you cannot conquer a thought if you cannot *fulfill* it at the same time. Erdoğan both fulfills and repeals the heritage of Kemal Atatürk. He has expressly said that Turks should have more children and has taken a clear stance against smoking and abortion. If Erdoğan had been a Christian European leader he would most likely have gained as much popularity as Orbán or Putin within groups critical to the system in many European countries. At the same time it is obvious that Erdoğan has made some significant mistakes similar to other national populists, by gaining too many enemies at the same time and by turning against both the Kurds and the Russians. The two principles that guide his policy—the religious and the national—might also be hard to combine. Historically,

Turkish nationalists in exile have been on good terms with European nationalists, but in a situation in which Turkey is contributing to the Islamization of Europe this is becoming more difficult. This could also be applied to a possible Eurasian project, in which the heritage from Atatürk is Jacobin rather than federative. Paradoxically, Duterte's approach might be a more effective method to create a rock-solid and mature populist order with a basis in federalism domestically, while having "no issues with the neighbors" regionally.

Both Duterte and Erdoğan simply reminds us that a move away from liberalism and toward populism is a process, with all that it entails, both good and bad. It can certainly take unfortunate forms. Historical peculiarities like misogyny and chauvinism can find their place in a populism by and for the people. A populist movement can also be colored by certain traits of its leaders, again taking the good with the bad.

The Generals—Thailand and Egypt

> I am a soldier, so I can be somewhat temperamental, but I am not a politician. Don't expect me to speak politely. I will not speak politely and then lie.
>
> — GENERAL PRAYUT

Erdoğan and Duterte are populists, or demotists according to Moldbug's terminology: their nations break with liberal logic. But there are also nations that chose their own path, in part due to the threat of said demotism. These nations often have a strong military presence that sees itself as the carrier and protector of certain national values. If the negative political trend in Europe and the United States continues, the risk of military coups, with the intent to stabilize and stifle increasingly common ethnic and social conflict, might become a reality in the near future.

In Thailand politics is, traditionally, heavily influenced by a strong military presence and the popularity of the king. This stalemate was recently challenged by billionaire and populist Thaksin Shinawatra and his "red movement." Thaksin has been accused of both corruption and buying votes of poor people by taking from the rich. Nonetheless the policy was focused on the rural communities and their situation; it was these people who voted Thaksin into power. Growing conflict eventually led to a military coup. This military junta was characterized by nationalism and royalism. It also promised that illegal immigrants would be "arrested and deported." This led to hundreds of thousands of Cambodians and Burmese leaving the country in a short time span.

The military junta combines royalism and nationalism. General Prayut has emphasized that a nation is only strong if the nation's inhabitants are strong. He therefore issued twelve values that are to be taught to children in school. The main characteristics of these values, which aim to uphold the nation, are based in religion, monarchy, and preservation of Thai tradition. Values on a more individual and personal level including discipline, physical strength, and mental health, are also indicated, as well as respect for elders, honesty, self-sacrifice, and patience. There is also a conversation about *sufficiency economy*. Which brings our thoughts to Almqvist's *Den svenska fattigdomen* (On Swedish Poverty) or autharchism. King Bhumibol Adulyadej coined the approach and concept, inspired by economist E. F. Schumacher's *Small is Beautiful*. Schumacher himself was inspired by what he called Buddhist and Christian economic theory, like distributism. He had also read Guénon. King Bhumibol translated *Small is Beautiful* into the Thai language and popularized the approach. The theory is focused on localism, endurance, and moderation. Inequality, on the other hand, is to a large extent not seen as problematic.

In Egypt the people's support fell on an Islamic leader, the Muslim Brotherhood's Morsi, and the military acted against the rule of the majority. Morsi had won the election that followed the previous military leader's fall, but he was seen as a threat to Egypt's security. Especially since the Muslim Brotherhood is an international movement with radical contacts around the world. The suppression of Morsi's followers was extensive—swift as well as brutal. The new president and military man, Abel Fattah al-Sisi, has been well received despite painful economic reforms. He is also trying to take control over religious practices by working with the Sufis, who are the main rivals of the Muslim Brotherhood. Sisi was also the first Egyptian leader to attend a Christian mass. This gesture of goodwill was received well in the country's Coptic minority.

Historically, military coups of this sort have often received support from the United States, as long as they have been seen as authoritarian rather than totalitarian. The current situation is different, as the United States today is a postmodern empire, or even an "empire of chaos." Neither Prayut nor Sisi are, or have been, satisfied with their respective relationship with the United States, especially not with president Obama. These military leaders have instead been defined by their approach to Russia and China. These examples imply that the military leaderships of Turkey, Thailand, and Egypt struggle metapolitically. Sisi to some extent seems to be the exception.

Eastern Europe and Visegrad

> Our experience under Communism was long enough that we now judge the EU through this lens.
>
> — VÁCLAV KLAUS

After the wall fell Eastern Europe was characterized by a rather naïve attitude towards Western Europe and the liberalism it now had access to. But the political model it associated with the West was fading. It was being rapidly replaced by political correctness, self-hate, globalism, and neoconservatism. However, many Eastern European leaders realized this fairly quickly. As a result, a bloc of nations in old central Europe has formed; these nations include Poland, Hungary, the Czech Republic and Slovakia. This bloc is called the *Visegrad Group*. Hungary's president Orbán has been very visible as one of the most important critics of today's derailment and dangerous policies on issues like immigration and Russophobia. But he is not alone. In the Czech Republic Václav Klaus is seen as a good example of "normalization from the East," in which central and Eastern European leaders and peoples turn their backs against the irresponsibility promoted by the West, in a wide range of areas spanning from foreign to cultural policy. Also worth noting is the recent development in both Hungary and Slovakia, with its leaders Orbán, Fico, and Vona. Poland is another example, as well as the Baltic states, and partly the Ukraine. Experiences from the atrocities of the Soviet Union contribute to a difference in geopolitical analysis within these countries, but they are aware of the dangers with respect to areas like multiculturalism and liberalism

Klaus was the president in the Czech Republic between 2003 and 2013. He represents the Old Right, and is seen as politically incorrect because of the bourgeoisie's sharp turn to the left in Western Europe. At the same time he exemplifies how the older strain of anti-Communism that was common during the Cold War has been able to update itself, and to understand the current situation, which has been brought on by a new political landscape in Europe. Klaus has written that people like him fear every path that leans towards socialism. The current European path is so far the most dangerous of these. Indeed, regular people tend to underestimate its power, while intellectuals tend to support it. He rejects the democratic legislative body of the EU, and points out the relationship between the nation-state and democracy. The peoples in central and Eastern Europe had hopes of becoming "normalized" when they joined the EU, but according to Klaus it is obvious that they joined neither a prosperous, well managed, nor fast-growing economic zone, nor a genuine democratic phenomenon. Klaus discerns the greatest threat of today in the development toward transnationalism and globalism. This affects Europe in no small way—Europe, a continent that is on the forefront of post-democratic, post-national, and post-political development.

According to Klaus the experience of the Czech people during the reality of Communism has made them keener to pay attention to these tendencies; support for the EU in the nation is relatively low. He puts strong emphasis on how the economic policy of the EU leads to a less effective economy. Klaus concludes that the nation state as a concept has become politically incorrect. He also states that the attack on the nation state is built on a simplified and inaccurate interpretation of it. For Klaus there is an important intimacy between nation state, freedom, and democracy. Focusing on the aspects of the nation state and its citizenship, he maintains that we need responsible citizens with ties to the nation, not cosmopolitan, selfish individuals. The development toward transnationalism is thus a significant threat to democracy and freedom. Hence it is not surprising that these ideologies take root in nations that are anti-democratic, anti-European, and anti-freedom. As opposed to other anti-communists Klaus is not resigned to this. Instead he identifies the new ideologies that now threaten Europe and its freedom, despite the fact that this results in his being labeled "politically incorrect." The ideologies is question to wit are the -isms: multiculturalism, aggressive feminism, and homosexualism. These are the new collectivist ideologies that threaten to devirilize Europe and threaten the freedom of her peoples. Collectivism carries new names, but is very similar to its predecessor. Klaus' analysis of what led to this development is certainly interesting; it is an analysis in which WW1 is seen as a fundamentally catastrophic event, leading naturally to both Bolshevism and National Socialism, and in which the injuries in social, moral, and cultural capital had a more profound impact than what appearances show. What was historically considered safe was now replaced with uncertainty. He connects this to 1968. The catastrophic effects of the First World War led the people to the cultural revolution of 1968. He also notes that the world war was an "attack on Europe". It was also a situation in which the lines between good and evil were blurred. He likens this to the current situation and believes that a war between the West and Russia is not an unlikely event. Klaus is not an uncritical proponent and supporter of Putin, but he has often criticized American policy, especially with respect to the treatment of Serbia and the recognition of Kosovo as a state, as well as the invasion in Iraq. Klaus is critical of the official version of what actually happened. He considers the coup in Ukraine to be a result of American manipulation, intended to turn the Ukraine against Russia and to start a conflict with the latter—naïve and risky behavior.

On the whole Václav Klaus is an interesting personality. He has obvious connections to more classically-liberal-minded groups and people, such as Mont Pelerin and Hayek, but also reminds us of Hoppe and Janusz Korwin-Mikke. Here we find Euro-skepticism and defense of the nation state from a classic liberal perspective, but also an analysis of political correctness and policy in the East that could be of great value. Not least, what we see in the old *Mitteleuropa* is that from their point of view, the West stands out as a warning of what not to do, which renders the slow transfiguration of societies and values, that could occur in the West, impossible. There is a consensus in countries like Poland, where nationalist demonstrations easily gather tens, sometimes hundreds of thousands of people. At the same time Poland is well aware of what the neoreactionaries call the Cathedral, and Dutschke calls the long march through the institutions. Control over media therefore becomes as important as the control of public space. When the conservative president Andrzej Duda took control of the state-run TV outlet the reactions were strongly against this, especially from liberals outside of Poland; but given the historical context it was anything but surprising. The alternative would have been a gradual indoctrination of the population through a media outlet that they have no democratic control over. This is something that many Polish citizens realized. The people who have lived behind the Iron Curtain may play an important role in the future. As the New Right realized, the reality of socialism is capable of killing the body, but Western liberalism can kill the soul and spirituality. This is why we see the more spiritually healthy peoples now reacting to degeneration and oligarchy. They have seen what Western liberalism and its projects lead to, and are not in the slightest interested in experiencing something similar. These people can to different degrees become what Venner called "external lungs" for groups in Western and Northern Europe.

Chapter 11

The Street and the Public Space

> Without action, words are just words. Without violence, laws are just words. Violence isn't the only answer, but it is the final answer.
>
> — JACK DONOVAN

Control of the public space is crucial, both for political and civil life. To be able to have a public presence is central to humans. The public space has shrunk for the European peoples in the last couple of decades, as growing portions of their homelands have been lost. In Europe, this started with suburbs such as the French *banlieues* and similar areas, to which native Europeans avoid going; but it has spread into the city centers where gangs of street kids now roam. In America violent trends such as "polar-bear hunting" and "happy slapping" have emerged and are almost exclusively aimed at whites. The author and martial arts expert James LaFond accurately describes *"The Hunt For Whitey."* "Whitey" is an easy target—he seldom defends himself, either verbally or physically. The phenomenon is hardly mentioned in public debate.

This is a consequence of atomization, but also of the most deliberate ongoing demasculinization of white men. In the politically correct public sphere, the combination of the white male with masculinity is associated with Fascism, and is often even the definition of Fascism. The white man is simultaneously accused of lacking authenticity, depth, and humor, and in addition is called a coward. This can be described as a catch-22: "Damned if you do, damned if you don't," as Bart Simpson expressed it. Behind the construction of this unsolvable dilemma a particular sentiment can be discerned: hatred of the white man. The psychology of ethnic relations is today a neglected field, but it is clear that among many groups, hatred for white people flourishes, and in particular hatred for white men. This hostile attitude often combines *ressentiment* with narcissistic hubris—the intoxicating sense of power when you as a group show "whitey" who's in charge. The relation to power in these contexts is schizophrenic in nature; these groups are economically insignificant and provided for by "whitey's" tax money. Symbolically, however, they are everything but insignificant and play an important role in pop culture as well as in anti-racist rhetoric. The other side of the relation consists in "whitey" frequently embracing the idea of himself as bearer of historical guilt. Modern anti-racism has many faces but one can often identify a strain of fear in it. Some anti-racists are essentially afraid of certain groups of immigrants or minorities, but twist this into wrath towards those who criticize them. When I studied postcolonial theory in the past, this was called *"identifying with the aggressor."* In that context it was about relations with old colonial powers, but the term fits well in this context too. When an uncomfortable development is perceived as unavoidable, some people choose to identify with it rather than confronting their own fear and compromises.

The result of these processes is demasculinization. There are Afro-American thinkers who deem that their collective will be next, but so far only men of European descent are targeted. In order to reverse this process, we must acquaint ourselves with the concept *Männerbund*.

Männerbund

> This country is dying because of a lack of men, not a lack of programs.
> — CORNELIU CODREANU

Inability to handle ethnic relations and ethnic competition is just one example of lack of proper function in our liberal order. The party system creates an establishment separated from the people, and atomization makes collective action impossible. An alternative lies in our history, the so-called *Männerbund*, coalitions of men with cultic, social, and military functions. Such coalitions of men taken in their broad sense have been the lifeblood of Europe, and have kept together church, military, universities, and guilds. When spiritual death looms, the *Männerbund* in the shape of everything from Gothic federations and monastic orders to knightly orders and *Freikorps* has intervened and sparked new life in society. The *Männerbund* is the natural organizational form of the genuine Right, and well worth further acquaintance. The study of the *Männerbund* commenced with Heinrich Schurtz and his *Altersklassen und Männerbünde* in 1902. Schurtz was a member of a patriotic connection centered around Friedrich Ratzel, one of the fathers of continental European geopolitics, who early realized the political importance of the *Männerbund*. Schurtz wrote his influential work as a historian and ethnographer. While it was Schurtz who introduced the term *Männerbund*, the term was later picked up by Hans Blüher, by National Socialists, by homosexual masculinists, and by scientists such as Höfler and Wikander.

Through his study, Schurtz could identify different approaches towards society between men and women. Where women historically were engaged in family matters and the regrowth of mankind, men had a somewhat different focus. Men with focus on society and state congregate with their peers. These foci follow from different logics— the logic of the family and the logic of society, between which conflicts often arise. Schurtz separated two different forms of communities, those based on *choice*, and those based on *blood*. He discussed the conquest- and reaver-coalition Dschagga as an extreme example of the former. They kidnapped foreign children but could kill their own. He described the *age classes* which occur in most populations, whose function is to handle the latent conflict between generations, the fighting spirit among the young men, and to administer initiation into manhood through rites of passage. Confirmation, the baccalaureate, and military conscription used to serve such functions in our society. But rites and trials that would confirm that boys become men, and would make it possible for adult men to accept new members into their sphere, are almost entirely lacking today. Painful and distinguishable elements in the trials, such as tattoos and piercings, have returned in the youth cultures of the modern world. Schurtz described a myriad of phenomena in the *Männerbund*, such as the link to the ancestors, animal symbolism, group marriages, *Männerhause*, the dance and the significance of intoxication for the fellowship, and how the young man in the *Männerbund* ritually dies and is resurrected. His description of the configurations of the European *Männerbund* is also interesting. He wrote about the Germans:

> During Tacitus' time, the Germanic tribes were subordinated in part under kings and in part under dukes. The king is the prince of peace whose regulating and mediating efforts are directed toward the interior and supported by the patriarchal authority, while the duke represents an expansive desire toward aggression, which can be destructive, but also state-building, and depends on the young warriors of the entire tribe.

According to Dumézil's trifunctional system, the king and the duke are thus each linked to a separate aspect of the first function, to Tyr and to Odin respectively. Like Jack Donovan, Schurtz also described blood brotherhoods, which among Germans involved mixing blood and among Albanians involved drinking blood. Schurtz had a historic perspective on the *Männerbunds'* various fates. In the case of certain feared secret African associations, dark homicidal elements occurred. Researchers have described how a feudal development comes into existence in the case in which the *Männerbund* was subordinated under a chief or a prince. Schurtz also discussed how the *Männerbunds* face the growing class divisions. He describes the *Geheimbund*, a more advanced form of *Männerbund*, and how the *Männerbund* at times could gain political power. We recall how scholars of Indo-European cultures believes that *Männerbunds* rather than families are the creators of the state. Schurtz proposed that the formation of secret associations is natural given the male will to solve the mysteries of existence. Associations such as Freemasonry, the Ku Klux Klan, The Vehmic Courts, or Carbonari were no different in this regard. Thus, in various forms, the *Männerbund* emerges again and again throughout history. Schurtz also describes how the *Männerbund* can challenge and defend power.

Our society has lost the age classes, and with them the rites of passage that made transition from boyhood to manhood possible. This can give rise to confused attempts to solve such transitions individually through harmful subcultures, or it could lead to some people remaining children for their entire life. What is even graver is the fact that the latent conflict between the generations has become manifest, a situation which since 1968 has been exploited by groups hostile to Europeans. In short, we need something similar to the age classes and their symbolic initiation rituals in the fellowship of men once again. There have been numerous attempts to achieve this, from the German Wandervogel to Boy Scouts, from student fraternities to Burschenschaft. Schurtz reminds us of the *Männerbunds'* cultic, military and political implications. A society consisting solely of individuals, bureaucrats, and political parties dies from within. Schurtz, not particularly bourgeois himself, neither moralized over male use of intoxicants nor the free man's contempt for physical labor. Schurtz reminded us about the conflict between the logic of the *Männerbund* and the logic of individualism. Paradoxically, the latter emanates from the logic of the non-masculine sphere. While this sphere is an important part of society, it becomes destructive if it takes precedence. The male logic from which the *Männerbund* emanates is needed as well, and with it a sort of aristocratic freedom along with its duties. Here is a clear connection between Schurtz and the *völkisch* thoughts.

This perspective was later transmitted through antiquity scholars such as Otto Höfler, and paradoxically by the female anti-Nazi Lily Weiser who wrote the influential *Altgermanische Jünglingsweihen und Männerbünde*. Höfler later wrote the classic *Kultische Geheimbünde der Germanen*, in which he described our ancestors' cultic *Männerbund*, with ingredients such as death cults, demon masks and ecstasy. He also described the Wild Hunt. Höfler studied the Germanic sacred kingdom. During the Second World War, he wrote numerous articles about the Scandinavians which still give us insight into our national characters. He assumed a historical Germanic continuity, which involves forms and archetypes among our ancestors that can still be identified today. Höfler wrote excitingly about wolf-warriors, werewolves, and how the wild hunt advances through the country in its search for witches and demonic beings. He pointed out that the *Männerbund* is an archetype, not an economic class or a family. His conception of the cryptic sources of power that exist in the primal, in the numinous (the collective), is *völkisch*. However, Höfler's description of our ancestors differs from Günther's. While Günther perceived Wotan as an atypical god, and not distinctly Nordic, Höfler described death cults, animal warriors, and ecstasy as central Germanic phenomena. His work makes for a fascinating read, and persists in the many studies inspired by him. This is true for example of Speidel's *Ancient Germanic Warriors*. This work declares that *"Nordic Úlfhéðnar were Wotan's men, so he who joined a band of wolves did not become wolf, but a mythical being, who relived the time when the gods walked the earth. Any courageous warrior could be a 'wolf' but a true wolf warrior wore a wolf pelt and howled like a wolf to become one with the beast."* Höfler's version of the *Männerbund* is dark at times but always fascinating. He reminds us that *"every normal man must sometimes be tempted to spit in his palms, take on the wolf pelt and start cutting the throat of his enemies,"* to paraphrase Mencken. When the northern Europeans rediscover their identity, *"become who we are"* as Richard Spencer expressed it, their ancient totemic animals will follow, together with *thumos*, Dumézil's first function, and not least of all the *Männerbund*. These are all parts of an ancient mythical and philosophical complex.

Another scholar to reintroduce the interest for the *Männerbund* during the early 20th century was Hans Blüher (1888-1955). Blüher was complex, both as an individual and as a scholar. He dwelt in the border-land between psychoanalysis, Conservative Revolution, sexology, and individual anarchism; he was influenced by Freud and Nietzsche, de-picted Fleiss' theories about biorhythms with approval, and described with empathy the tragedies of Weininger and Mainländer. Blüher was not a feminist and viewed men and women essentially as differ-ent entities. According to Blüher, the woman is closer to Eros, which he regarded as something positive. This implies that woman's goal is *"belonging"*—to completely belong to someone else. This deep relation to Eros also means that women can develop great insight and wisdom. He gave examples of this, gathered both from German history and his own time. In comparison with Klages, it is clear that Blüher described woman in a way that Klages called pathic. But this also means that "woman cannot understand spiritual or political matters" according to Blüher. He regarded man, on the other hand, as being characterized by *Geist*, active creativity.

Blüher was influenced by Schurtz, but while Schurtz focused on *Männerbunds* in different parts of the world, Blüher had a more psycho-logical focus. He claimed that a *Männerbund* is held together by ethos, community, and loyalty, which he named *Eros*. A true *Männerbund* is permeated by an idea; in this sense it brings to mind Evola's interest in orders and Dugin's ideocracies. It has more in common with a brother-hood than with an economic association. Blüher also raised the virtues that permeate a genuine *Männerbund*: *"tradition, faithfulness, tough-ness, discipline, and a certain skepticism towards the rapidly changing age and Zeitgeist."* Siding with other intellectuals, he claimed that it was out of the *Männerbunds* that the state had emerged. At the same time, he linked his theory to his reasoning about different types of gay men. He saw some as a result of *pathogenesis*, others as simply unmanly. There was also a particularly masculine group, which he described as *Männerhelden*, male heroes. Blüher said that types like the SA leader Röhm often played an important role in the *Männerbund*. This feature made the dissemination of his work somewhat limited. Nonetheless, it can be used to understand Jack Donovan's androphile approach.

In recent years, Jack Donovan has revived the *Männerbund* as an idea through his book *The Way of Men*. It gained significant traction both in the manosphere as well as in the early Alt-Right, and reminded the reader that being a man does not mean being solitary. Indeed, the only way to be a man is among other men, according to Donovan. Men are generally bigger, stronger, and more aggressive. Their task has therefore been to defend the tribe, to hunt, and perform similar more or less dangerous tasks. Moreover, these tasks have been group tasks. Donovan concludes that masculinity is about being a part of a group of other men (Blüher's ethos). He has also developed a critique of civilization, wherein the modern world is described as anti-masculine. Donovan notes regarding the modern welfare state that it *"makes us all into beggars and children, and as such it derides and hampers adult masculinity. … Male resistance towards being dependent on others is a stronghold against the therapeutic nanny-state."* He also describes how *the way of men* today is undermined. There are fewer and fewer spheres in which groups of men compete with other groups of men, in which risk-taking and masculinity fulfill a function. Male values are depicted by globalists and feminists as threatening, obsolete, and negative in general. Some men can handle this, either by not having any of these qualities themselves to any high degree, or by substituting the struggle of life and death for example by sports (either by direct participation or by proxy). Donovan has also written about modern attempts to create *Männerbunds* with cultic elements, like the *Wolves of Vinland*.

English Defence League

We have risen from the English working class to act, lead, and inspire in the struggle against global Islamisation.

— THE EDL

The realm of supporter culture and hooliganism has historical ties to radical ethno-nationalism, including Chelsea Headhunters and Combat 18 as well as the Danish firm White Pride. This is not surprising seeing the significant commonalities shared by supporter gangs and the *Männerbund*—both consist of groups of men with their own, localized rules and codes of conduct. Additionally, supporters have a certain feeling for who owns the streets, in a way the *thumos*-lacking average Joe can't even begin to imagine. This entails potential conflict with other groups that aspire to masculinity, territory, and the public space. There is also a growing dissent among supporters toward what they call *modern football,* which in practice means the entrance of money power and the New Class into the sphere. It should be noted that this is true regardless of political color—the entrance of money power is ill-seen on the Left as much as it is on the Right. Political affiliations are common among supporter's groups on every continent.

Popularizing radical nationalism appeared somewhat more difficult though, in particular in a society increasingly marked by liberalism and political correctness. Meanwhile, the problems caused by liberalism and political correctness steadily grew—most obviously Islamization and the Jihadism following in its wake. There thus appeared a possibility of defending nation, neighborhood, and society. Among the first to realize this were a group of supporters in Luton. In 2009, Islamists had demonstrated against the war in Afghanistan and the involved British armed forces, while simultaneously trying to recruit terrorists for the Taliban. Many supporters opposed the unpatriotic display, not least of all because most had friends who were soldiers. In Tommy Robinson they found a representative at a time when supporters from several associations were all in agreement that the issue was of such gravity that any possible conflicts between the associations must be set aside.

This is when and where the *English Defence League* emerged—a concept that became relatively successful, uniting people from rivaling associations, attracting members in the tens of thousands. Several manifestations have been carried out in which the EDL has established *de facto* control of the streets, drawing considerable media coverage. Clashes with so called anti-fascists and immigrant street gangs have been recurrent, but neither have been able to win any significant victories against the EDL in the streets. The media aftermath has been a different story, the media having the agenda it does. In any event, the question of how one converts street-rep and media coverage into political capital has remained unsolved (the EDL possesses considerable RSA, while having a harder time mustering ISA, to reconnect with Althusser). After the EDL advised their members to vote for UKIP, for instance, UKIP decided to distance themselves from the EDL. Exporting the concept to other countries has, likewise, proved to be difficult.

The ideological leanings of the EDL are worthy of note, as well as the different tendencies identifiable within the milieu. While it might not be acceptable in today's political climate to criticize immigrants as a group, or specific religions, *extremism* is fair game. Well aware of this, the EDL walks a tightrope in their public announcements, skillfully using the rules of political correctness for their own ends, and simultaneously criticizing these rules for leniency toward Islamists. On the other hand, one can also identify elements that have little to do with a liberal critique of extremism, for instance when the EDL condemn the use of the burka and the niqab, or point out how the Muslim demonstrators mooch off the taxpayers. The EDL have also tried approaching Zionist critics of Islamization, including making contact with the Kahanists *Jewish Defense League*, and flying Israeli flags. But several differing tendencies exist within the organization. Many demonstrators on the street level express dislike toward "Pakis" and Muslims during confrontations, and while black and colored members do exist, most participants are white Britons. Another element has been composed of people linked to the British National Party and what is called the "Far Right," sometimes at leading positions. The EDL has also called attention to phenomena like *grooming gangs* by publishing a compilation of data which shows how no less than 300 out of Rotherham's mere 3000 Muslim men were suspected of systematic rape and abuse of English girls. Pointing out such truths is indeed a breach of the rules of liberal discourse.

Also notable is the choice of the name EDL over BDL, "British Defense League"—displaying an element of specifically English nationalism or an identitarianism-light. The EDL have taken good care not to break too definitely with the liberal hegemony—which was probably sensible metapolitics back in 2009. Muslims in general are not the target of the EDL, but Islamists. Thus the League appear as defenders of liberal values—such as freedom of religion—against those who menace them. Efforts have also been made to recruit Jewish, Pakistani Christian, and LGBT members, but with limited success. It is interesting to watch the balancing act involving abstract, liberal values as well as traditional English culture. Many liberal freedoms are construed as parts of English culture, a metapolitically sly move not least of all considering the ties between liberal and Anglo-Saxon history. In conclusion, the EDL clearly have managed to aptly combine several success factors. They chose an issue with broad appeal, neither irreconcilable with the liberal hegemony nor the common sense of the people: defense against Islamists, who are not rarely terrorists. This enabled larger numbers of people to join forces with the EDL, without having to conform to some more profound political consensus. Their great numbers, in turn, allowed supporters to reclaim the public space—regardless of their individual level of radicalism.

Ideas similar to those of the EDL are identifiable among the Swedish supporters in Stockholm who have made efforts to reclaim parts of the city center from the mostly North African groups of so-called street children who have been linked to rapes and robberies even by the mainstream media. Here, too, the issue is one of broad appeal, an appeal able to unite people regardless of differing politics and backgrounds. Given the more brazenly biased public milieu, actions taken by the Swedish supporters have by necessity been of a more clandestine nature than those of the EDL.

Soldiers of Odin

How can we hope that migrants will stop their rush into the European "paradise" if it is undefended and inhabited by old men?

—BERNARD LUGAN

The primary task of the state is to provide security: protection against threats, domestic and foreign. The moment the state neglects to fulfill this task, the so-called *social contract* can be said to have been breached, rendered void. In the wake of decades of mass immigration, largely consisting of young males, such a breach has been made reality in several countries across Europe. In an effort to make sense of the countless transgressions this development has entailed, a sociobiological perspective comes in handy. Humans are social animals, and groups of men compete for resources, respect, and women. The transgressions committed by migrant males is therefore a way of probing the terrain, of surveying the limits of what one may get away with in Europe. The answer revealed was that one may get away with almost anything without significant repercussions. This can be contrasted with what would happen if some men from one ethnic group were to beat up the men and sexually assault the women from another ethnic group in, say, Syria or Afghanistan. The repercussions following such an affront would be brutal, which explains why such attacks are relatively rare in most multi-ethnic societies: in most societies of this kind, collective declarations of war are recognized as such, and responded to accordingly.

The situation in Europe, on the other hand, is pathological. The necessary reaction is conspicuously absent, since the government as well as the media and the establishment at large are more concerned over "growing racism" than they are with seeing to it that the primary task of the state is fulfilled. They are likewise incapable of grasping ethnic relations, but obstinately cling to an obsolete, moralistic, one-track thinking according to which "racism and xenophobia" are the only permissible explanations. Combined with the advanced stages of demasculinization and atomization, this thinking all but halts any natural human reaction to violent transgressions. In many environments within European societies groups of young, immigrant, non-European males exert dominion over the public space, while men native to the land huddle in the shadows. In the Swedish town Ronneby, for instance, hundreds of Arab and Afghani men violently clashed at a high school in 2016. Further inquiries into the matter reveal how gangs of "youths" have pestered the town for years, unprovokedly assaulting passers-by, extorting business owners, and much more. The transgressions would have kept on going if the mainstream media had not called them to attention. In Ronneby, as in towns such as Rotherham and Malmo, the native men are no longer in control of their streets.

Reactions to this development are often delayed, but when they finally materialize, they often do so in the shape of vigilante-guards. Founded in Finland in 2015, *Soldiers of Odin* have spread to Sweden as well as Norway, Estonia, and other places in the region. That the initiative was first taken in Finland is not surprising, considering how immigration to Finland has been comparably moderate, and an organic society still remains somewhat intact. Similar conditions seem to be in place on the Swedish island Gotland, in the Baltic Sea, where another vigilante-guard was formed in reaction to a string of sexual assaults in 2016. That guards of this kind would be formed in places like Rotherham is less likely; they are more likely to form in countries like Poland and Finland. The mainstream media has construed Soldiers of Odin as a band of ruffians and "right-wing extremists"; the members themselves emphasize that the organization is an initiative by local citizens taken purely as a measure against rampant violence, and have stated that they don't tolerate racism among their ranks. Soldiers of Odin are now established in several Swedish towns and cities, and not merely have they patrolled the streets, but they have also handed out coffee and snacks to the homeless. Still, they have recurringly been made targets for attacks by self-proclaimed "anti-fascists," with varying outcomes.

Establishment reactions to the emergence of Soldiers of Odin and similar initiatives have consequently been of a negative, often downright hostile nature. In part, this is due to political correctness, but not entirely. Another reason for the frowning faces and public denigration is the fact that coalitions of this kind have a dynamic of their own, and might, like the Squadristi of post-WW1 Italy, quickly grow to become serious contenders to a detested establishment. Having attained such a position, the group may utilize the combined powers of Althusser's state apparatuses, ideological as well as repressive. On the other hand, one must keep in mind the risks associated with this particular strategy. A vigilante-group on patrol is subject to coordinated attacks from armed assailants, while in many jurisdictions guard members are prohibited by law from carrying even the smallest non-lethal weapon. Their adversaries may also choose the time and place for the confrontation—a circumstance which is far from decisive, but nevertheless gives a significant advantage to the attacker. Conditions like these make patrolling vigilante guards more demanding than the mass manifestations of the EDL, though with possible payoffs much greater than those of the latter, locally as well as temporally. The likelihood of a vigilante-group gaining recognition among the broader public is, at any rate, considerably greater today than it used to be a couple of decades ago, a dubious advantage provided by our current historical situation. Back then, vigilantes were commonly perceived as men who chose violence for its own sake; henceforth, they will, quite conversely, be increasingly perceived as men who choose violence as a means to protect others against those who *do* choose violence for its own sake. CasaPound urges us to heed the importance of discipline, and to use force strictly for defensive purposes. Should this fail, the repression tends to grow overbearing—and public support becomes sparse.

PEGIDA

> A peaceful co-operation of sovereign nations worldwide must be the basis of a safe future for all of us.
>
> —The Dresdner Theses

Control of public space has multiple aspects. One is the simply *physical*, the aspect support groups and vigilante-guards both pertain to. Also of importance is which groups are *visible* there. Regarding the latter, the Left have longstanding traditions of taking to the streets to demonstrate—demonstrate their sheer *numbers*, if nothing else, as much to themselves and to one another as to outsiders. "*We are the 99%!*" they assert, cocksure in congregation. For *actual* critics of the political status quo, the very same act has proved considerably more difficult to pull off. This has not least of all been a result of the unabashed violence that rioting Leftist counter-demonstrators recurrently have directed against any attempt to demonstrate in critique of immigration in particular. Such violent attacks have not rarely been committed with the silent consent of the government and the mainstream media, and have, at times, even been directed or otherwise facilitated by the police. In recent years, nonetheless, the situation has begun to change. One notable example is the German association *PEGIDA*, acronym for *Patriotic Europeans Against the Islamization of the West*. The association was founded in Dresden in 2014 by Lutz Bachmann, after he had witnessed a rally by the Kurdish left-wing party PKK being attacked by Salafist Muslims. Dresden, once part of the GDR, had been one of the cities where masses had gathered to demonstrate during the time of the fall of the Berlin Wall, chanting *We are the people!* It follows that Dresdner relations to their public spaces are qualitatively different from those of their Western countrymen. The initial PEGIDA rallies gathered but a few handfuls of participants, but numbers quickly increased. Soon, thousands showed up for the events, numbers peaking at around 25,000 participants. Surveys show that they're often men, often well educated, and that they display considerable ideological diversity. Also frequenting the events in Dresden are, according to local police, a few hundred "violent hooligans."

In a one-page, ten-point manifesto titled *Dresdner Thesen,* or *the Dresdner Theses,* PEGIDA summarize their positions. The manifesto expresses the demand that native German culture and language be respected and protected—partly against Islamization and fanaticism, but also against premature sex education in schools, a practice the authors claim leads to sexualization of young children. PEGIDA further demand a fundamentally revised immigration policy, as well as a family policy that reverses the trend of diminishing nativity. Regarding foreign policy, PEGIDA opposes the demonizing of Russia, as well as supranational trade agreements such as TTIP, CETA, and TiSA. Thus, the conception-of-the-world they convey can be said to be a mature and multifaceted one; a conception-of-the-world with the potential to unite great numbers of ordinary people. The PEGIDA rallies have served a valuable purpose in making it clear how the opposition to the political status quo consists of people who are in every respect normal—"we are the people," as the old slogan goes. Similar phenomena are Folkets demonstration in Sweden and La Manif pour tous in France. At PEGIDA events, the invited speakers have not rarely been of a more radical, less politically correct constitution than the establishment can stomach. Thus, Akif Pirinçci as well as Jürgen Elsässer and the German identitarians have made appearances at PEGIDA and its Leipzig counterpart LEGIDA. The concept has been exported to other countries, though without great success.

To anyone harboring plans of taking the leap into the public arena, the English Defence League, Soldiers of Odin, and PEGIDA all may serve as sources of knowledge and inspiration. In addition, one should analyze the resources available—each strategy has its drawbacks as well as its virtues, the effects of which all depend on the conditions at hand. A lesson to be learned from all three organizations is the value of *positioning*. This means identifying and assuming a position which has a broad enough *appeal* to amass discontented people in great numbers, while simultaneously being *radical* enough relative to the hegemony to *mobilize* these amassed discontented. Regardless of the exact nature of one's plans, one should acquaint oneself with the term *Männerbund* and the phenomenon it denotes, which in turn is closely linked to the resurgence of *thumos*. Even so, *Männerbunds* come in innumerable shapes and forms. The clique of Christian authors around Tolkien and Lewis can be construed as a successful association of men, a property shared with the *Männerbunds* that favor a more hands-on approach. Making sense of who we *are*, and consequently in which kind of environment we may be of greatest *use*, is incumbent on each of us.

Chapter 12

The Alternative Right

> Equality is bullshit, hierarchy is necessary. The races and sexes differ.
> Morality counts and degeneration is real. All cultures are not equally
> good and we have no obligation to believe so. Man is a fallen creature
> and life is more than vapid materialism. Finally, the White Race is of im-
> portance, and our civilization is a precious thing. This is the Alt-Right.
>
> — ALTERNATIVE RIGHT

In 2015, the term *Alt-Right* spread like wild-fire across the web. Up
until then the term had existed in obscurity since it was coined, probably by the paleoconservative thinker and author Paul Gottfried in
2008. The term Alt-Right was embraced and adopted by the circle
around Richard Spencer, who ran a website by that name in 2010–2013.
Spencer and Gottfried were initially closely connected. Today Spencer
labels himself an identitarian, and among other things he is a leading character in the think-tank the National Policy Institute and the
publishing imprint Radix, as well as being a respected figure in many
American anti-liberal circles. Prior to 2015 the term Alt-Right appeared less commonly than *the Dark Enlightenment*—a collective term
for bloggers critical of different aspects of the established ideology regardless of whether their focus was set on economy, gender relations,
or race issues. The term *the Dissident Right* was also seen, and still is.

There is a connection between the European *New Right* and what
was to become the American *Alt-Right*. Spencer and his projects are
prime examples of attempts to apply the perspectives and metapolitics of the New Right to American conditions: both Guillaume Faye
and Alain de Benoist of the New Right have been invited to speak at

Spencer's conferences. Spencer's projects keep a high standard, not least intellectually. Outlining the reasons why he favors the term Alt-Right over "conservatism," Spencer has stated that he saw American mainstream conservatism as stuck in its stated ideals of "freedom" and "free markets"—concepts Spencer considers anti-ideals: freedom to what? Freedom for whom? Freedom for a capitalist to destroy the environment or for Miley Cyrus to twerk? From early on American conservatives were also war hawks, making for little actual difference between them and current neoconservatives. The average IQ of neo-cons is possibly slightly higher, Spencer speculates. In opposition to such "conservatism," he offered the ideas of the European New Right; the Conservative Revolutionary movement of post-WW1 Germany; Nietzsche, and others. In contrast to these ideas the intellectual poverty of American mainstream conservatism became clear, and Spencer saw the need for a new, alternative Right, although initially he was unsure as to what such a movement would look like. He later stated that the Alt-Right had not become exactly what he envisioned when he first started using the term. Spencer's project originally called attention to several alternative Right movements. European anti-liberals such as Alex Kurtagić wrote articles for *Alternative Right*, as did traditionalists like Jim Kalb. One could read Stephen McNallen of Asatru Folk Assembly, as well as Jack Donovan, Jared Taylor and Paul Gottfried. A few of the main figures of the original *Alternative Right* project are currently running the blog *Alternative Right* (alternative-right.blogspot.com), among them Colin Liddell.

Apart from the circles around Spencer and Liddell there is Greg Johnson, who with the website and book publishing company Counter-Currents has established what he calls *the North American New Right*. Counter-Currents has mustered an impressive band of intellectual writers, not least of all within philosophy and cultural criticism, expressly directing themselves to readers with an IQ above 120. Johnson himself is a skillful writer, as is James O'Meara,

Eugene Montsalvat, Margot Metroland, and Guillaume Derocher. A strong connection to the Conservative Revolution runs throughout the articles on Counter-Currents, with texts ranging from Evola and Pound to Hamsun and Schmitt.

While Spencer was one of the first to use the term Alt-Right, its initial diffusion was moderate. In 2015, however, interest exploded, to the point that the term came to be used in a much wider sense, as an attempt by the establishment to associate Donald Trump with "Nazis" during his presidential campaign. To understand the background of this we need to turn our focus to the degenerative tendencies that coincided in the creation of a new political landscape. Wall Street and other special interests had long since seized power in the country, populations were being replaced, and year by year the intolerance of the *ersatz*-religions grew harsher. The established "Right" proved as useless as in Europe, and if possible an even more obvious servant of money-power. Simultaneously the foot soldiers of the *ersatz*-religions worsened—a change which represented an opportunity as well as a nuisance.

The Great Worsening, and the Internet as a Refuge

> Uneasy and fractional people, having no center
> But in the eyes and mouths that surround them
> Having no function but to serve and support
> Civilization, the enemy of man,
> No wonder they live insanely, and desire
> With their tongues progress; with their eyes pleasure; with their hearts death.
>
> — ROBINSON JEFFERS

The late 1900s witnessed the intensification of what we have called the *Great Worsening*, and the degeneration to accompany it, which among other things meant the emergence of a new human material, shaped almost entirely by *ersatz*-religions and the pop-culture industries. Each year the universities continue to mass produce new hordes of easily offended, intolerant and ignorant individuals ready to infiltrate and co-opt everything from environmentalist organizations and Wikipedia, to atheism and role-playing games—often to the great chagrin of the original members of these groups, but with the whole choir to back them up in event of any conflict. This human type has been characterized with several different designations, the favorite of many being the *SJW*, for "*Social Justice Warrior.*" Most often this is used in an ironic, derogatory manner, as the individuals to which it refers are neither warriors nor do they care about any genuine justice. Quite the opposite, they are rather motivated by a diffuse sense of *ressentiment*: underneath their veil of "anti-racism", one usually finds a profound hatred of, for example, "white cis-males" ("cis-males" referring to actual males, in contrast to "trans-males", who have "transitioned" from their native male form).

Marxist metapolitical thinkers such as Antonio Gramsci in the 1930s and later Louis Althusser emphasized the importance of controlling non-governmental as well as governmental institutions, to shape the conception-of-the-world and "common sense" of a society. In the late 1960s German student activist Rudi Dutschke, inspired by these thinkers, formulated a revolutionary strategy which he called *the long march through the institutions.* Thousands upon thousands of Leftist baby-boomers emerging out of the various counter-cultural movements of 1968 later made their careers within said institutions, fulfilling Dutschke's plan. Recruiting the SJWs from the younger generation to gradually replace them, the marchers consolidated their power. By the end of the century these conquerors were dug in deep in the mainstream media as well as academia, and they had no intention of tolerating any challengers to this position. Another long march to counter the one completed by the Leftists was thus not an option. Simultaneously however, a new institution had without much notice by those in power rapidly grown in importance: the Internet. The Internet was becoming, to speak with Althusser, a crucial *ISA,* an *"Ideological State Apparatus"*; and moreover one which the Right had an actual chance to conquer. Right from the start discussion forums and trolling played a major part: Internet-based environments sprung up where people freely discussed every thinkable aspect of reality in a manner elsewhere considered far too politically incorrect.

The HBD-sphere

> ...Imagine for a moment that creationists ran the government, academia, and the media ... only instead of denying evolution completely, they deny that it applies to humans, especially within the last 50,000 years...
>   — JAYMAN, DESCRIBING THE CURRENT SITUATION
>   AND THE SO-CALLED *LIBERAL CREATIONISTS*

Some participants in these Internet-based environments were interested in the differences between groups of people, differences of which our egalitarian age speaks very reluctantly and immediately associates with notions of "superiority"—particularly when it comes to differences in intelligence. Many of these people were interested in much more than intelligence, and a relatively large number were women or non-White. The sphere they came to compose was named HBD, Human Bio-Diversity, taking as its common interest the biological diversity within the human species. The sphere to some degree overlapped with the more politically minded *race-realists,* but not fully. Some HBD bloggers and writers were, and are, Steve Sailer, HBD Chick, Peter Frost (Evo and Proud), JayMan, and Greg Cochran (West Hunter). Regardless of its possible political relevance, the connections made by the HBD crowd are often intriguing, at least to an inquisitive mind. Among other things they have presented studies indicating that Europeans are on average more empathic than people from other continents, that White America is really several historical nations (such as New France, Yankeedom, and Greater Appalachia), and that there are connections between alcoholism and how long a history of agriculture a society has. Within the HBD-sphere we also encounter fascinating studies of the so-called Hajnal line showing significant connections between family patterns and things like high intelligence as well as economic and political success. West of the Hajnal Line, which divides Europe in an Eastern and a Western part running roughly from Trieste to St. Petersburg, people married comparatively late or even not at all, and consanguineous marriages were avoided. West of this line was also where, e. g., the modern state and general prosperity first developed. As Günther already understood in his time, family patterns do matter.

One cannot draw conclusions about who is ultimately "superior" or "inferior" from findings on human biodiversity—no such universal standard exists. Indigenous Australians, for example, have an average IQ significantly lower than that of indigenous Europeans, but in the long run their biocultures might very well be shown more sustainable and may possess a deeper spirituality than that of European peoples. Conversely, one may also draw some less liberal conclusions from HBD. For example, that human populations are in no way identical but rather unique and thus, just like the polar bear, the indigenous Andamanese as well as the typical Northern European peoples all are worth protecting from extinction. HBD also reminds us of how political models which have worked in Europe won't necessarily be successful if exported to radically different biocultures. Furthermore, HBD reminds us of the practical and ethical complications of subjecting multiple, differing groups of people to the same political and economical systems, such as "the market" or "democracy."

Roosh and Neomasculinity

> When you live below your means, you begin to see that most people are
> unnecessarily living above theirs. That leads to the conclusion that they
> were trained to live a life of excess by corporations with the complicit
> help of a government that wants to keep society in a never-ending state
> of indebtedness and distraction, so that they ignore everyday injustices
> while losing any will or desire to fight the establishment.
>
> — ROOSH VALIZADEH ON ADOPTING A MINIMALIST LIFESTYLE

Another important sphere consisted of men who were fed up with the
recommendations of the official ideology to "be themselves" and with
the promise that "women like nice guys." Their conclusion was that
none of it worked, that they felt confused, and they needed new, useful
advice. Ultimately this was caused by the generational conflict: youths
no longer received advice from their parents but were forced to try to
explore the world on their own. The advice they got from their teachers and television was too rooted in politically correct feminism and
was part of the process of demasculinization.

The sphere created by these men was termed the *manosphere*. The
men within the manosphere discussed the ways in which men and
women function. It was initially largely focused on how to bed women,
but gradually developed a more obvious interest in politics, culture
and ideology, as well as a natural opposition to feminism. Several
sub-spheres emerged—some consisting of men who turn their back
on women completely, like MGTOW, *Men Going Their Own Way*, and
the zealous virgins at *Wizardchan* (it is, of course, widely known that
a male who is still a virgin at thirty turns into a wizard). Among the
more familiar figures of the manosphere are Roosh Valizadeh and the
more secretive talent behind the blog *Chateau Heartiste*; with time,
both became increasingly politicized.

Bit by bit at, with Roosh's project *Return of Kings*, a conception-
of-the-world crystallized, and was given the name *Neomasculinity*.
What had begun with juvenile travel guides like *Bang Poland—How to*

Make Love to Polish Girls in Poland, developed into interests in traditional gender roles, spirituality, anti-socialism, and defending of our civilization against the looming cultural collapse, feminism, and mass immigration. Roosh explains his concept of cultural collapse:

> ... the decline, decay, or disappearance of a native population's rituals, habits, interpersonal communication, relationships, art, and language... Cultural collapse is not to be confused with economic or state collapse. A nation that suffers from a cultural collapse can still be economically productive and have a working government.

The phases of cultural collapse Roosh identifies as the loss of religion, the elimination of traditional gender roles, decline in family formation, decreasing nativity, mass immigration, and natives becoming marginalized within their own country. Consequently, it is reminiscent of our civilizational perspective. Roosh has also developed a minimalist philosophy, in which he for instance expresses the view that full-time employment, college education and "entertainment" are hindrances to the discovery of truth, reminding us of earlier critiques of proletarianization and culture-industry; Roosh is not seldom an interesting cultural critic himself. Further, Roosh has adopted the traditionalist concept of *inversion* to describe modern society: all old values have been turned upside-down. What was once looked upon as beauty is now seen as ugliness, what was once seen as desirable is now considered harmful, and so on. This inversion affects every aspect of human life—from family formation to art.

Roosh and the RoK collective are not necessarily part of the Alt-Right, but multiple aspects of the neomasculinist project overlap with the views of the Alt-Right—possibly with greater emphasis on self-improvement and less on ethno-nationalism. One writer from the manosphere who today *is* part of the Alt-Right is the man, or men, behind *Chateau Heartiste*. The blog now combines advice on how to attract women with political commentary. The language used is far from politically correct but rather quite vulgar—*globohomos* and *shitlibs* are derided, and *mudshark psychology* explained. The page has many visitors and, along with much else, has provided an analysis of how Donald Trump won the presidential election. From *Chateau Heartiste* also stem pithy expressions like *"Diversity + Proximity = War"* and *"Physiognomy is real,"* often in conjunction with scientific studies which confirm their veracity, demonstrating that Lombroso and L. F. Clauss were right all along.

The manosphere is a phenomenon which often conjoins analyses of psychology and society with vulgar commentary on and scantily veiled *ressentiment* toward the female sex. It is reminiscent of Don Colacho's observation that while "feminists are ridiculous, the anti-feminists are vulgar." As Roosh exemplifies, though, there is a tendency among its better participants to mature with time. This tendency may be facilitated by the study of Jung, Illich, Ludwig Klages, and others, all of whom offer a more nuanced picture of the sexes and the differing shapes they take. These can be valuable to explore for those who want to avoid imitating a non-Nordic misogyny. Such misogyny is, to reconnect with Günther, as *artfremd* as pop culture and its hatred of European masculinity.

The Trolls

> If hackers were an ethnic group, the UN would be declaring a humanitarian crisis.
>
> — WEEV, ON THE REPRESSION OF HACKERS

It is doubtful whether the anti-feminist environment that is the manosphere would have been able to sprout without the Internet. However, HBD geeks and pick-up artists were in no way alone in finding their asylum online. On the web forum 4chan a distinct environment also sprouted, particularly on the sub-forum */pol/, Politically Incorrect*. On

4chan free and anonymous debate flourished, and countless images of varying entertainment value were created and posted as an integral part of the discourse. Many users felt sick to death of the SJW types and their grasp on society, and took to ridiculing them and their conception-of-the-world. Some of these users were trolls, and they carried out veritable raids on the surrounding web. A distinct, irreverent attitude emerged, as did a do-it-yourself culture permeated by memes and obscure jargon.

Within this sphere of trolls and hackers we find Andrew Auernheimer, known online as *Weev*. Auernheimer started out as an inventive hacktivist, but following a fundamentally questionable prison sentence he came out as a pagan and a National Socialist. His interests include "computing's lack of will to power" and the treatment of hackers by the United States government. *The Right Stuff* as well as the *Daily Stormer* trace much of their roots back to Chan culture. Both are highly visited initiatives employing irreverent humor in the service of undermining hegemonic ideas and taboos. The mercurial boundaries between irony and gravity, person and persona pose something of a problem. For instance, *The Right Stuff* found themselves in a massive quarrel about betrayal when it was revealed that one of the headmen was married to a Jewess. Evidently, many participants equated the Alt-Right with National Socialism rather than utilizing the latter as a tool to ridicule and troll politically correct power-holders.

The troll mindset was also prevalent within the manosphere, in which bloggers caught attention with articles that crossed ethically as well as politically correct boundaries by, for instance, arguing for the legalization of rape and the how and why of slapping women. While patently distasteful, such bait attracted droves of readers and, to much delight, successfully enraged the despised politically correct crowd. These spheres often overlapped with each other as well as neighboring spheres: some within the HBD sphere were attracted by the realistic view of the men-women-relations promised by the manosphere, and some combined their interest in HBD with a more politically inclined race realism. Commonly, seeing through one part of the official ideology, such as feminism or the myth of no significant genetic differences between races, naturally leads to the questioning of other parts. With reference to the Matrix movies, this process of questioning and discovery is often called *taking the red pill*. The choice of whether to take or not to take a certain red pill is not necessarily an easy one to make, as leaving a world of cozy lies and convenient illusions comes at its cost. To seekers of inner freedom, however, it is difficult to abstain from the taking of red pills.

Older Spheres Critical of Immigration

> Race is a biological fact... Human races have been evolving separately for perhaps as long as 100,000 years, and evolution has marked their temperaments and mental abilities just as it has their physical characteristics.
> — JARED TAYLOR

For quite some time, a number of organizations criticizing immigration and advocating race realism have been present on the web. Among these were *VDARE* and *American Renaissance*. *VDARE* is named after Virginia Dare, the first English child to be born in the New World, and champions what it calls the *Historical American Nation*. Several well-known writers have contributed to their website, among them Richard Lynn and Ann Coulter. At VDARE.com, one can find articles on anything from HBD to immigration policy. Founder Peter Brimelow has advised the GOP to go for the White vote, a strategy seemingly proven effective by the Trump victory. *American Renaissance* is run by Jared Taylor, who is seen by some as the grand old man of the Alt-Right. *American Renaissance* is reminiscent of *VDARE*, and focuses on the Historical American Nation and the race question. Taylor does not see it as a positive or necessary development that White Americans become a minority in the country they once founded. Both *American*

Renaissance and *VDARE* are reminiscent of the European New Right insofar as they've been actively practicing metapolitics for decades, by every means from the organizing of conferences to book publishing. It was within this environment that Sam Francis, with whom we will soon familiarize ourselves, could be encountered and where he published his work. The environment is a solid one, ethically as well as intellectually; the age of the participants is generally higher than that of Alt-Right trolls; rarely are they anonymous.

Among the older influences, there were also a number of lifestyle bloggers, fantasy writers, black metal circles and so-called conspiracy theorists who with time were to become parts of the Alt-Right, and the same goes for what Americans call *White Nationalism*. Other notable influences trace back to certain libertarian and neo-reactionary circles.

Shaped by Victory

Become who we are.

— Richard Spencer

The very motley milieu which in time was to give birth to today's Alt-Right long gathered its strength online. A series of victories came to define it. Firstly, the so-called Gamergate—a complex conflict which developed into a protest against what was seen as corruption and infiltration of the gaming world by SJWs, beginning in 2014. The background is too complicated to narrate here, but a broad alliance of gamers refused to bend in spite of the usual accusations of "sexism", "racism" and the like. They had identified the infiltration of the gaming world by SJWs, and they were sick of it. They were likewise sick of the corruption within the gaming industry, in which critics not rarely carried on relationships with game developers, and so on. As in so many other spheres, political correctness was a brand of rhetoric which could be used to veil more conventional kinds of corruption. Similar conflicts had erupted in the 1980s, when SJW types infiltrated and co-opted environmentalist organizations, leading to the item of policy regarding negative consequences following mass immigration to the United States getting taken off the agenda. This time, however, the pattern was broken: Gamergate enjoyed success. Several of their opponents lost their source of income, lost ad revenue, or even went belly up.

The achievements of Gamergate revealed successful strategies that can be employed, such as a diffuse and leaderless resistance in which a multitude of different groups fight a common enemy, each in their own way (it is likely against this background that the maxim *Pas d'ennemis a Droit*—no enemies to the Right—first gained strength). Attacks were aimed toward the enemy's most vulnerable point: his economy. And the full force of the Internet was utilized. Gamergate meant that a generation of more or less conscious activists had now gotten a taste of blood and caught a whiff of victory. Closely related to Gamergate were the phenomena *Sad Puppies* and *Rabid Puppies*, in which the infiltration of the sci-fi and fantasy genres by SJWs was met with similar methods. There too many had grown tired of political correctness and corruption.

The second breakthrough for the Alt-Right was the virality of the *cuckservative* meme. The year was 2015, and the increasingly numerous Alt-Right viewed the American establishment "conservatism" with contempt. Establishment conservatives were compared with "cucks"—unmanly cuckolds—for their refusal to stand up against the liberals, and *for* their core constituency. The meme caught the attention of the mainstream media, which predictably enough tried to paint the whole thing as racist—which it sometimes was, and other times wasn't. That the association was well founded is proven by the widespread reactions it provoked from representatives of the derided establishment. Predictably, in accordance with the Streisand Effect, these reactions only added to the popularity and viral proliferation of the cuckservative-meme.

The third breakthrough was the United States presidential election of 2016. The Alt-Right generally supported Trump, for multiple reasons: he broke with Cuckservatism, and stood up against political correctness and SJW outrage. Trump's promises to erect a wall along the Mexican border and to "make America great again" was also attractive to many on the Alt-Right. The Alt-Right was in fact one of very few groups that wholeheartedly gave Trump their support—most established groups were hesitant at best. These hesitant included the very party Trump was running for, the Republicans. To the Alt-Right the Trump victory was another victory of their own, and they got a fair bit of attention from Hillary Clinton and others prior to as well as following the election. Meanwhile, the Trump victory demonstrated itself not only one of the Alt-Right's successes, but also one of its threats.

What is the Alt-Right?

The Alt-Right contends that identity > culture > politics.

— Vox Day

There exists more than one definition of the "Alt-Right." To the politically correct the Alt-Right are no more than a bunch of hateful Nazis having their go on the Internet. But the politically correct are, as is nowadays well known, seriously misinformed. Turning to the most familiar proponents of the Alt-Right one finds somewhat different aims, but also much overlap. Colin Liddell of *Alternative Right* rates *American Renaissance*, *Occidental Observer*, Radix, Counter-Currents, *VDARE*, Traditional Youth Network, vloggers Millennial Woes and RamZPaul, *Right On* (nowadays merged into AltRight.com), and Amerika.org among the core of the Alt-Right, along with his own project, *Alternative Right*. The situation is in flux: it is, for example, not certain that RamZPaul considers himself Alt-Right even as this text goes to print. Richard Spencer does not count *Taki's Mag* as belonging to the Alt-Right, as Taylor does, et cetera. Currently, one should add

The Right Stuff among others to Liddell's list, along with Red Ice Radio and the multitude of tweeters and vloggers contained within the sphere. Many would also consider the *Daily Stormer* part of the Alt-Right, along with the forum My Posting Career. Many would—but far from all.

Clearly defining the Alt-Right is easier said than done—not least of all due to its motley lineage. Another reason is that there exist two alternately used, contending definitions. One may construe these as one loosely defined *big tent* Alt-Right and another, more narrowly defined, *small tent* Alt-Right. The wider definition starts with the assumption that the Alt-Right is *alternative* as well as *to the Right*. That is, the Alt-Right is neither established conservatism nor is it *to the Left*. Davis Aurini views the Alt-Right more as an *anti-label* than a label *per se*. Viewed like this, the Alt-Right consists of everything from traditionalists and nationalists to nihilists and trolls, united by the common sentiment of being fed up with establishment lies. The Christian Orthosphere has a similar definition, which includes her own perspective within the Alt-Right.

Using the looser definition, we get the Alt-Right as a broad alliance, a huge tent which may contain widely differing groups and perspectives—united as they are by a common enemy. This huge tent contains what is sometimes referred to as the *Alt-Lite*. Ideas as well as symbols have spread from the more strictly defined Alt-Right to circles that are not actually Alt-Right, but which rather criticize the Left from a classically liberal standpoint. Not rarely these have large audiences and numerous supporters, and, like the Alt-Right, they too stood with Trump during the election. Examples are Gavin McInnes of *Taki's Magazine* and The Rebel Media; Milo Yiannopoulos, former tech editor at Breitbart; Paul Joseph Watson of Infowars; and independent vlogger Styxhexenhammer666. Spencer's take on the Alt-Lite is that they have a need to live somewhat close to the edge to be perceived as novel and exciting, something they achieve by flirting with the

Alt-Right. One may compare this to how Adorno et al. increased their intellectual sex appeal by using Ludwig Klages and H. S. Chamberlain. Yiannopoulos gave the Alt-Right a fair bit of promotion with his text *An Establishment Conservative's Guide to the Alt-Right* (Breitbart, March 2016). The *Guide* is a portrayal that tones down some of the less easily digested components, such as antisemitism, and instead emphasizes that the Alt-Right mostly consists of fun-loving young men who happen to have grown tired of the establishment. The Guide is still worth a read; Milo and co-writer Allum Bokhari are hip to the Alt-Right's roots in Spengler as well as in the New Right and Sam Francis. They also emphasize that the Alt-Right has come to stay.

There is, however, a stricter definition of the Alt-Right. Jared Taylor of *American Renaissance*, for example, defines the Alt-Right as a broad movement in which views on economical matters greatly vary. What it has in common is the view that the idea of human equality as a dangerous lie. This pertains in particular to races—races exist, and they do matter. Richard Spencer too sees this as the core idea of the Alt-Right. The Alt-Right is *not* egalitarian. Joined with this view is often an ethno-nationalist position and/or what in the United States is called *White Nationalism.* Greg Johnson of Counter-Currents emphasizes for instance how *"either the Alternative Right means White Nationalism— or it means nothing at all."* One who removes the connection to the European peoples, in the United States frequently summed up under the racial term *Whites,* has in Johnson's view no longer anything to do with the Alt-Right—the *"we"* of the Alt-Right are White people of European descent. A consensus on how to view other ethnic groups is lacking.

The anti-egalitarian and ethnocentric perspectives of the Alt-Right are connected to a drive to speak frankly. Most challengers to the establishment adapt greatly to what Foucault called the *rules of discourse*—what one is allowed to say, and what is forbidden. Such behavior is included by the Alt-Right within the concept of *cuckservatism*—it is a sign of weakness, and one of the main reasons as to why these "challengers" fail to achieve anything of value. The Alt-Right strives toward realism, even regarding political minefields like race relations and differences. If Black-on-White violent crime is significantly more common than White-on-Black, this is not something about which the Alt-Right stays silent. If pop culture is contemptible and permeated by hatred of White men, the Alt-Right duly reacts with contempt. If feminism leads to women making choices that make them unhappy, the Alt-Right is not hesitant to say so, et cetera. The Alt-Right is aggressive in form as well as in content, and staunchly unapologetic.

Brett Stevens at Amerika.org has a definition of the Alt-Right which is in several ways reminiscent of Julius Evola. As Stevens bluntly puts it: "We hate modernity. It's nothing but lies." Amerika.org also brings up the need for spirituality and a deep ecological outlook. There is obviously an enormous difference between such a position and an Alt-Lite which is fundamentally liberalism of a somewhat older, more *thumotic*, passionate breed. Stevens' Alt-Right is in many ways a *Deep Right*—a trait that makes it somewhat of an exception in the context. One could if one so wishes identify three levels of Alt-Right: from the comparatively liberal *Alt-Lite* via the more ethno-nationalist *Alt-Right* to the alternative Deep Right which includes spirituality and deep ecology. All three levels are needed, but a correct balance between the three is also needed. A reduction to ethno-nationalism or other group interests might be historically sound in a situation in which one's back is against the wall, but it does not come without its pitfalls. A weft of *Deep Right* might mitigate the danger of such pitfalls.

No Enemies to the Right

Whichever way we decide to define the Alt-Right, we can identify some of its key success factors. One of these is the capacity for creating coalitions of people from relatively diverse environments, for the purpose of combating common enemies. The big tent of the Alt-Right is one in which multiple, differing groups find the space to coexist. Not rarely has the Alt-Right been able to successfully co-operate with its neighboring environments. Particularly Vox Day (real name Theodore Beale) is skilled at this. He is often seen with libertarian Stefan Molyneux, he publishes books by Israeli military historian Martin van Creveld, and by Christian fantasy writer John C Wright, he co-operates with Greg Johnson as well as the Trump-supporting lifestyle blogger Mike Cernovich, et cetera. The Alt-Right was also brought to the attention of many by Milo Yiannopoulos and Breitbart. Richard Spencer has collaborated closely with Jewish-American paleoconservative Paul Gottfried, and has been an effective initiator of partnerships and networks since the start with Alternative Right. Parts of the Alt-Right also find allies among the other ethnic groups in America. Davis Aurini has proposed that the African-American community has disintegrated by fault of the Democratic Party and the novelties of '68, and that they very well might be future allies of the Alt-Right. More conservative Black Americans, mainly men, have also lately approached the Alt-Right. Jared Taylor has invited Jewish critics of immigration to his conferences, and so on. The coalitions have thus had ideological as well as ethnic components

This view of the Alt-Right as a big tent is in no way uncontroversial; it seems to be the more or less National Socialist groups, described by RamZPaul as "1488ers," that in particular turn against coalitions with Jews and homosexuals and want to define the Alt-Right in a way centered around a more National Socialist conception-of-the-world. Between the 1488ers and several other branches of the Alt-Right there lies a latent conflict. This would seem to be in part an issue of differing backgrounds: many within parts of the Alt-Right come straight out of Chan culture. In many cases they have little to no knowledge of Richard Spencer, Jared Taylor, or other members of preceding generations, but a great deal of experience trolling "normies" with, for instance, Hitler-memes. More than a few people within the Alt-Right would like to draw a line between themselves and National Socialists like the *Daily Stormer*, but given the lack of centralized leadership, drawing such a line is practically impossible.

Another threat to the big tent is the rift between on one side the more respectable, more liberal Alt-Lite, and on the other the more ethno-nationalist core. In many ways this is hard to avoid, given that what holds the tent together is its enemies, and that these by way of Trump's victory suffered a defeat. The more liberal subscribers of the Alt-Lite might make do with Trump, as they see no need for pure-bred *White Nationalism.* Under such circumstances, a breakup with the "antisemites" and "racists" might start to look tempting. Add to this the tendencies toward purity spiraling prevalent within parts of the Alt-Right, in which adherents zealously value National Socialist doctrine over allies. Such rifts are in any case lamentable, and compare well with the rift dividing the bourgeoisie and the nationalist movement in Sweden nearly a century ago. They could be bridged, but not without difficulties.

What Does the Alt-Right Want?

This is not a Jeffersonian revolt, but a Nietzschean one.

— Brett Stevens

When Richard Spencer was to define the Alt-Right before an audience of college students in Texas he opened by establishing *identity* as the core. He noted that the African-American students already had an identity—*"You are a people."* Many White students refuse to be a people, refuse a more profound identity. "I'm just an individual, just an American," they would say. According to Spencer, this is *precisely* what Soros and Zuckerberg strive for: the United States as a market, and nothing but a market. The elite would much prefer a world without roots, a world devoid of meaning. The world they want would be a world dominated by passive nihilism.

The Alt-Right take off from the value of identity, with regard to their own as well as other groups. Spencer is an ethnopluralist and clearly influenced by the European New Right; he addresses not only Whites but also African-Americans and Jews, reminding them that their identities too are under threat. When Vox Day defines the Alt-Right he lands near Spencer. He defines it as nationalist, anti-globalist, anti-egalitarian, and influenced by a scientific outlook. He also asserts that the Alt-Right is seeking peace, and that all peoples have a right to their nation and their culture.

The Alt-Right are less emotionally bound to the United States as a polity than many other Americans. One may speak of an unsentimental, rather instrumental attitude toward the United States. It has little inclination toward flag-waving or the cult of "the Constitution." Quite the contrary, they contend that a multi-ethnic United States is unstable, and unfavorable for the White population. More favorable would be, in the words of Greg Johnson, *"a nice White country,"* even though such a country would hardly encompass the entire current United States territory. The penchant for ethnic separatism is strong and explicit. It is hoped that Trump will manage to solve the situation through reform, but should this fail the United States will come apart, likely with violence. The attitude toward Trump is often, similarly, instrumental; it is recognized that his victory meant a weakening of the enemy's positions; that the risk of nuclear war with Russia has diminished; that a border wall might postpone by a few years the day White Americans become a minority in the United States; and that the Trump presidency means it is now possible to speak frankly about things previously considered taboo. It is not believed, however, that president Trump will enact the policies one might wish for, nor that he will redeem and restore the glory of the Historical American Nation.

Otherwise the Alt-Right is highly diverse. Some have a more conventionally nationalistic view, others long to see more transnational co-operation or even supranational organizations consisting of European-descended peoples and their respective states. Vox Day opposes free trade, and he is not alone within the Alt-Right in favoring some kind of protectionism. Most also oppose the current foreign policy, with its wars of aggression and provocations against states like Syria and Russia. The Alt-Right realizes the impossibility of simultaneously *attacking the world* and *inviting the world*. There is also the political realization that as cultures and peoples differ, believing that the American system could be exported and implemented anywhere else in the world is nothing but folly. The Alt-Right also tends to be anti-feminist, but the assessed importance of that question varies greatly.

Concurrently, there is a populist aspect of the Alt-Right, which seemed to be exacerbated during the Trump presidential campaign. It coexists with a more Nietzschean aspect, which esteems hierarchies. This partly coincides with what Vox Day has described as the *Alt-West* and the *Alt-White*—two discernible tendencies within the broader movement. The Alt-West and the Alt-White differ somewhat regarding their respective focuses: is it first and foremost Western civilization which is to be protected, or is it the White race? In practice the two often overlap; not rarely do those who champion Western civilization set forth how said civilization hardly could be imagined bereft White majority populations, while those who primarily champion the White race greatly value central aspects of the civilization that members of said race have created. To Vox Day the core of the Alt-Right is our civilization, and what he rates as its three foundational pillars: Christianity, the European peoples, and the Greco-Roman legacy. Vox Day argues that these three pillars are inseparable, and emphasizes that White people built and maintain our civilization: decreasing their numbers will have its repercussions, replacing them will mean the end of the West. In no way does this mean that Vox Day hates non-Whites—he is himself of partly Native-American descent. However, he does assert that *we must secure the existence of our people and a future for White children* (a statement known as the *14 words,* tracing its origin to the American White Nationalist environment).

Juxtaposing the Alt-Right and the New-Right, differences as well as similarities appear. Both are anti-liberal and skeptical to the United States' republic. The Alt-Right is an American phenomenon, to a greater degree influenced by American categories such as White, Black, et cetera, than the European New-Right, which rather focuses on ethnic groups or nations. Thus separation and a state of their own becomes an aim for large portions of the Alt-Right, instead of the European *Imperium* of kindred tribes. Simultaneously, there are parts of the Alt-Right which do not view complete separation as a goal, and Guillaume Faye of the European New-Right stands relatively close to the more biological conception-of-the-world. The differences are in no way absolute. The Alt-Right might give a less anti-capitalist impression than the New Right, but this too varies. One should however ask oneself whether the American Alt-Right is possible and desirable for Europeans to import as it is. Previous imports have not always been fortunate, and parts of the Alt-Right still combat obvious teething troubles.

The Alt-Right and the Jews

> I am often dismayed by how some people associated with the Alt-Right express their views on Jewish issues. I have often thought that anyone who hasn't read a lot in the area and has an IQ of less than 120 should not be allowed to discuss Jewish issues in public.
>
> — KEVIN MACDONALD

The greatest division between the Alt-Right and establishment conservatives might be their respective relations to the American Jewry. Many within the Alt-Right describe the roles Jewish minorities have played in Europe and the United States as detrimental. Kevin MacDonald ranks among the central proponents of the Alt-Right, and his book series *The Culture of Critique* explores the subject of Jewish influence at length. In his books he deals with psychoanalysis, Bolshevism, and the shift in United States immigration policy away from the prior, Nordicist policy—all as examples of how small but tightly knit Jewish groups have affected the situation of European-descended peoples for the worse. Historically Anglo-Saxon elites within the news industry, Hollywood, academics, and other areas were to a great extent replaced by Jewish elites. These were not always amicably disposed toward the culture and religion associated with the historical majority. Historically considered, the existence of such hostile attitudes since 1945 would be unsurprising; however, many within the Alt-Right contend that the phenomenon is far older than that.

Pointing out what has just been mentioned is normally considered *very* politically incorrect, but within the Alt-Right it is mostly agreed upon. Conversely, the conclusions drawn therefrom are manifold. There are explicit anti-Semites, who oppose any collaboration with Jews. Regardless of their irony, most outsiders likely find oven jokes distasteful and insensitive, yet such jokes occur on the margins of the Alt-Right. Jewish names are sometimes placed within triple parentheses—so called (((*echoes*)))—when the Alt-Right writes about various subjects, partly to illustrate how ubiquitous Jews are within power elites. The more common attitude is represented by Spencer, Taylor, and MacDonald. Spencer has carried on a lengthy collaboration with Paul Gottfried, and even described him as his mentor. This is in line with Spencer's ethnopluralist approach. Taylor has collaborated with Jewish critics of immigration for many years, among them Edwin Rubenstein who is the author of the report *The Color of Crime*. MacDonald himself has a more nuanced view than one might believe; he has written that he would love to see an alternative Right movement with significant Jewish support, and that Jews who do support the defense of Europeans should focus on influencing the attitudes of other Jews—organized Jews in particular. At the same time MacDonald emphasizes the danger that movements which include Jewish members might avoid the question of Jewish influence altogether, which would mean that they could not possibly grasp the origins of the current state of affairs. Or else they might adopt such a vehemently pro-Israeli position that they would altogether deny the interests of the Palestinians. Yet another pitfall would be the formulation of an abstract *"Judeo-Christian civilization,"* and a concurrent dodging of the issue of the different peoples within it.

In several ways, the current situation is reminiscent of the situation in Germany a century ago. While growing parts of the German Jewry had begun to assimilate and considered themselves as German nationalists, there was also a backlash. One cause of this might have been that the assimilation as well as the reaction by the German majority to Jewish influence occurred with a certain delay. In any case, many Jews in Germany were patriots. Rathenau described the Jews as being one of the tribes making up the German people, Kantorowicz risked his life participating in the *Freikorps* and later authored important works such as *Friedrich der Zweite*. Within the radical right-wing circles around Stefan George were many Jews. Analogously, most American Jews these days identify as White; one finds frequent warnings that the group might cease to exist through intermarriage with gentiles. My own assessment is that it is possible to speak of the historical relations between Jews and non-Jews in ways that are not one-sided, and that doing so in no way implies antisemitism. Metapolitically as well as humanly there are still some major questions regarding the consensus and modes of expression that have developed in parts of the Alt-Right—not least of all when these are stacked up against the European situation of a century ago, in which Jewish intellectuals comprised a natural and valuable component of the alternative modernity. The danger of (((*echoes*))) and the like is, metapolitically speaking, that the large number of Jews who are neutrally or favorably minded regarding the ideas of the Alt-Right might shift toward feeling intimidated or challenged. "Many enemies, much honor" might alliterate attractively, but turning potential allies against oneself is no recipe for successful metapolitics. This not least of all taking into account that significant segments of the Alt-Lite are Jews, and a division of the Alt-Right and the Alt-Lite would be comparable to the rift which ruptured the Right of the early 20th century. Here looms one weakness of a movement that lacks leadership: the inability to control counterproductive and subhuman behavior on its margins.

The Alt-Left

> For many Whites—Democrat and Republican—the embrace of immigration and multiculturalism is an expression of class interests.
>
> — BAY AREA GUY

One development of interest—partially a reaction to the Alt-Right and partially a reaction to the same factors that gave rise to the Alt-Right—is the *Alt-Left*. Here we encounter people like Robert Lindsay, Ryan England, Anatoly Karlin, and the website AltLeft.com. The Alt-Left is as heterogeneous as the Alt-Right, but has a greater interest in economy and a more progressive attitude regarding issues like feminism and homosexuality. Lindsay opposes racism and sexism, and describes his version of the Alt-Left as a kind of liberalism or Leftism that perceives the establishment Left as having gone too far on cultural issues. Lindsay combines this with race realism as well as sex realism, but not chauvinism. Bay Area Guy from *Alternative Right* is ideologically relatively close to the Alt-Left. His pet subject is that the Alt-Right should concern themselves more with economic matters, and realize that class interests are what lay behind policies of multiculturalism and mass immigration. He mentions Matt Forney as one of the few exceptions. Greg Johnson, too, has actively called attention to economic theory fitting a new or alternative Right; Bay Area Guy has mentioned the need for a *"radical centrism"* and the importance of picking up valuable aspects of different political environments (here, Dugin could serve as comparison). Ryan England has wittily spoken of "class realism," and stated that the Alt-Left champions rights, not feelings. Political correctness is described as a problem, and mass immigration as a weapon in a class war.

The appearance of the Alt-Left is a necessity given the Alt-Right's lack of interest in the issue of money-power. This is likely due to the fact that many of the Alt-Right are former neoreactionaries or libertarians, and that the Alt-Right was conceived in America. However, as Bay Area Guy reminds us, there are far bigger fish to fry than feminists and fat acceptance activists—or even Jews. Moreover, the Alt-Left phenomenon might help some Bernie Sanders supporters and others on the Left to embrace at least parts of the Alt-Right perspective. On the other hand the Alt-Left is suffering from the same maladies as the Left at large, such as spiritual emptiness. Their analysis is often quite one-dimensional.

Meme Magic and Private Language

If you control the memes of a society, you control that society.
— LAWRENCE MURRAY

A key success factor is the Alt-Right's use of memes: shareable pictures and text, referencing various aspects of politics and pop culture. Such memes are a defining characteristic of the late postmodern era in which pop culture has become constantly self-referential. On 4chan, memes have long been an everyday occurrence, and through a collective, organic process the swarm of users has created a multiplicity of new memes, while existing ones are constantly recreated. This process involves an element akin to the natural selection of genes; depending on their properties, some memes proliferate and become ubiquitous, while most quietly sink into oblivion. The apparent connection between this selection process and the collective unconscious is still uncharted territory, not least of all since it involves processes which are massively collective and largely anonymous.

The postmodern era is sometimes described as borderline illiterate; people lose their reading ability while sounds and pictures battle for their attention. Memes are an expression of this development, which in turn is at its core a step in the Great Worsening. At the same time this opens new possibilities to dodge the gatekeepers of the collective unconscious, bypass the official ideology and the taboos of the *ersatz*-religions. A picture of a band of orcs with a speech bubble containing the phrase *"where are the White women"* and the caption *"immigration is rape culture"* can be just as effective as a more elaborated text, which at any rate is almost exclusively read by those already in the loop. Here memes act as a tool for rapidly establishing novel associations. Many memes convey various aspects of the modern world and modern man. This entails tragic figures and situations, like the *"Forever Alone"* meme, the *"Foul Bachelor Frog,"* and the superficially expressionless, actually uncannily suggestive face of *Wojak*. In several characters the lack of self-respect and discipline is obvious, as is the type Evola spoke of as fickle, and void of a sovereign within. The banality of the modern world and its general degeneration are expressed incisively by the Foul Bachelor Frog: "Fell asleep in yesterday's clothes, woke up in today's clothes." Similarly the ever lonely Forever Alone character ex-presses the collapse of dating and the atomization following in its wake.

The meme lords of the Alt-Right have utilized several memes por-traying the modern world and poking fun at anything from political correctness to African-American culture. However, one soon detects a will to something else—a struggle for another, distinct anthropol-ogy. Man, though void of a sovereign within, consciously struggles by way of memes to regain control. During Trump's presidential campaign elaborate Trump memes were created, in which the can-didate appeared as a Roman emperor as well as the "God Emperor" from the science-fantasy board game *Warhammer 40K*. These memes joined a heroic, regal, and masculine aesthetic—something for which our time is unconsciously longing—with optimism and faith in the *"Trumpquake."* We have already dealt with the cuck meme earlier in this chapter. A *"normie"* or *"normfag"* is any outsider to the Alt-Right or Chan culture. Many within the Alt-Right also adopted the *Harambe* meme, in memory of the silverback gorilla which was shot dead when a black child fell down into the gorilla's pen. Initially mocking Afrocentrists who assert that all civilization originated in Africa, the *"We Wuz Kangz"* meme was created, and has later been used to mock, among others, Whites who believe everything of value in the world originated in Europe. *White genocide, woke,* and *"the current year"* are other often encountered memes. The latter is a scornful reference to liberals who unironically might use a phrase like "after all, this is 2017," as if it were an argument. The Memescape quickly shifts, meaning that by the time you read this new memes and mutations will surely already long have out-replicated the memes mentioned here.

Most memes are entertaining, not rarely using absurd and tongue-in-cheek undertones. Meanwhile, memes are as self-referential as other pop culture, and eagerly combine elements of African-American culture, historical National Socialism, Hollywood productions and Japanese anime. The Alt-Right, their tweeters and trolls in particular, are associated with the politically *incorrect.* This comprises everything that most bothers the politically *correct*; their sorest points, what they hold most sacred. This is often done ironically, in an attempt to *trigger* the politically correct. One idea within metapolitics is that this tactic is necessary to drain politically correct demons and accusations of their meaning. Every troll posting pictures of a Hitler-saluting Pokemon is not necessarily a Nazi—many times this is just irony. Add the generational aspect: those who take the trolls seriously simultaneously betray themselves as being what in 1968 would have been called *bourgeois* or a *square.* Today, it is more likely *normfag.* The irony can have several layers. Andrew Anglin of the *Daily Stormer* has spoken of "unironic Nazis disguised as ironic Nazis."

The Alt-Right also has a close relation to anime—Japanese animated cartoons. These are intently used in meme-making, for instance by letting female anime characters express various politically incorrect statements. There is a logic behind this. Western entertainment has gone through a radical degeneration and politicization, which more often than not makes it part of the problem. Japanese entertainment, anime included, has rarely gone through this process, and can with some exceptions be seen as sound and exciting. Unsurprisingly, Japanese cartoonists like Kentaro Miura and Makoto Yukimura with *Berserk* and *Vinland Saga* captured the essence of our Nordic archetypes and legends significantly better than current European cartoonists. The Japanese aesthetics also express striving toward self-discipline and beauty in ways rarely seen in Western pop culture. Lawrence Murray writes on the current state of "Anomie, Anime and the Alt-Right" in a worthwhile article with the same title first published on *The Right Stuff*. Murray notes, among many other things, how anime is still based on archetypes and characters struggling to reach some kind of goal, while much of the most popular Western entertainment productions seem to have strayed from this tried and true formula, replacing *the hero's journey* with *"the coastal progressive agenda."* The Alt-Right has nicknamed such politicized entertainment *poz*, after gay slang meaning "HIV positive."

From Pepe to Kek

> Essentially a meme functions like a rune.
>
> — HANNIBAL BATEMAN

Speaking of memes, the Alt-Right has come to be particularly closely associated with the frog known as *Pepe*. Pepe is originally a cartoon character that became appropriated by the meme culture and, accordingly, developed in multifarious directions. The Alt-Right created a host of derivative memes on the theme Pepe, Trump, and MAGA (*Make America Great Again*, Trump's campaign slogan). Pepe is an example of an *everyman* character, which can be placed in any situation or role one can think of. Given the anthropological crisis and the herd society, Pepe may represent any or all of us. Modern man adapts to the situations in which he finds himself, as malleable as a Homer Simpson or a Pepe.

Interestingly enough, a seemingly *not entirely* ironic cult emerged in which Pepe plays a central part. Highly improbable connections were found, linking Pepe to the ancient Egyptian deity Kek—commonly represented as a frog or a frog-headed man. Coincidentally, "KEK" had already to a significant degree replaced the expression "LOL" ("*Laughing Out Loud*") as a way to express laughter or amusement on the Internet, this without any conscious connection whatsoever to the ancient deity. Later it was discovered how an ancient Egyptian frog figurine bore a hieroglyphic inscription uncannily reminiscent of a desktop computer setup with a human figure seemingly using the computer to the left, and, to the right, a symbol in the shape of a double helix, not unlike a current representation of the DNA molecule. Improbable number combinations also appeared in connection with Pepe, Kek, and the Alt-Right. Kek is an ancient deity, and Pepe is his avatar.

The story is indeed intriguing, and reminiscent of Jung's canonical essay "Wotan" as well as Aleister Crowley's encounter with a mysterious entity in Egypt, an entity which was to dictate *The Book of the Law* to the Crowleys. "Wotan" and *The Book of the Law* both came into being toward the ends of their respective eras, at times when the coming collapse of the existing orders still loomed in the shadows. One might suspect that the collective and anonymous meme processes are connected with various archetypes within the collective unconscious, archetypes which by now are behind the Alt-Right. It has also been said that Kek communicates with his believers through improbabilities, a mode of communication resounding well with the notion of Kek being a deity of chaos. A chaos deity, but one known also as the *raiser up of the light*. Some voices within the Alt-Right have however called for caution regarding Kek, proposing that the process of collective, anonymous and often rage-fueled shitposting has actually tapped into a collective *Id,* and that what has been conjured is "an older god"—a deity more ancient than Kek whose long-term plans might not necessarily align with those of the Alt-Right. Aurini mentions in his Youtube video *"Pepe, Kek, and the Rise of an Elder God"* the chaos deity *Azathoth*, who will be familiar to Lovecraft readers.

Such an interpretation might be one-sided, and could miss the fact that the emotions behind Internet posting are not merely hatred but also hope and longing for justice and something better. Jung held that Wotan might initially seem primitive, but that in time further aspects would come into sight. Wotan is a god of war and death, but also a god of wisdom, intoxication and magic. One-sided or not, the perspective could however be of some use, seeing that if the appearance of the chaos deity Kek has a connection to the collective unconscious, the question is how one could go on to visualize those patently unsound undercurrents of the collective unconscious which are currently manifesting as ethnomasochism and self-loathing. Regarding these, words like *perverted* and *demonic* are doubtlessly warranted.

Self-improvement

> Cynicism, which regards hero worship as comical, is always shadowed by a sense of physical inferiority. It is a fact that contemptuous speech of heroes slips from the mouths of men who do not consider themselves physically fit to become heroes. Invariably, cynicism is related to feeble muscles or obesity, while the cult of the hero and a mighty nihilism are always related to a mighty body and well-tempered muscles.
>
> — YUKIO MISHIMA

One theme the Alt-Right has adopted from the manosphere is the interest in self-improvement. The personal *is* political. Many take an interest in anything from classical literature to how the individual is affected by porn consumption. Three core areas are identifiable—these overlap the three Indo-European societal functions, but the two systems are only partly analogous.

The first identifiable core area is the interest in Greco-Roman heritage, history at large, and just a general understanding of the workings of humans and their societies. Figures from the Alt-Right as well as from the manosphere regularly recommend "books for men." In an era which intently strives for a break with much of history and a disposal of our long memories, studying it is an act of defiance. While many of their opponents lack historical perspectives, proponents of the Alt-Right can often draw parallels between, for example, the Roman era and the current. There is not rarely a Christian element involved; more rarely a pagan. To follow the Alt-Right is an educational experience regardless of whether one's interest lies in history, psychology, economy or politics. This core area contributes to an ideal of masculinity which includes the personal cultivation of general knowledge as one of its integral parts.

The second area is the aspiration to physical self-improvement, primarily pursued by studying martial arts and lifting weights. The question *"Does he even lift?"* and numerous variations, has long been part of the realm of memes. To varying degrees, this area corresponds to the Indo-European warrior function. At the same time, it's a reminder of the connection between the personal and the political, which within the Alt-Right is explicit. A person who *does not even lift* is often viewed with suspicion. This is sometimes taken further, in lengthy forum threads concerning what profiles within the Alt-Right have "pedo faces," are overweight, or just seem gay. Fundamentally, however, the tendency toward self-improvement is sound and beneficial, contributing to a new generation of alpha males. Quite a few

Alt-Right profiles are body builders, such as Swedish Youtuber "The Golden One" (Marcus Follin) and the tweeting gym nudist Bronze Age Pervert. The Alt-Right embraces an aesthetic distinguished by ideals of strength and health, order and discipline. The hedonistic aspect of this aesthetic's concurrent mainstream stands in stark contrast to it; it is often somewhat ironically referred to as *"fashy,"* after historical Fascism. For instance, the hairstyle donned by Richard Spencer and many others—shortly cropped in the back and sides while longer and neatly combed on top—is recognized as a *fashy* hairstyle.

Thirdly, there is the area concerning the human ability called *game*—the art of attracting women. Some practitioners pursue increased game for purely hedonistic motives, but many also realize the fact that the man who fails to form a family is practically infertile, and as such he becomes the breaker of an unimaginably long chain of successful reproduction—the first loser in the succession of winners who were his forebears. Thus, Christians too find this area interesting when adapted to a Christian perspective. It is also noted that that which impresses women often also impresses other men: the ideal is to become an alpha male. Connected to this third area is also the interest in certain diets as well as in financial success.

In this regard, the Alt-Right overlaps with a number of lifestyle blogs which often share parts of its conception-of-the-world. For example, Vox Day collaborates with Mike Cernovich of *Danger & Play.* Cernovich writes about things like how to develop a beneficial mindset—called *Gorilla Mindset* or *MAGA Mindset*—and how to achieve an impressive physique. The starting point is the will to live a life one really wishes to live. The outlook of these lifestyle blogs is reminiscent of earlier attempts to break free from the mindless, vapid monotony of the modern world, but now more often within the framework of capitalism than in opposition to it. Many of these blogs focus on financial freedom; among others we find Victor Pride, who besides taunting political correctness also writes about physical exercise and business enterprise. Many also bring up downright geographical escape from the United States, the possibilities of living in the Philippines or other low-cost, non-feminist countries. One success factor of these blogs is that they offer readers practical advice that might improve their lives. Most people wish for free and healthy lives; few wish for lives of loneliness and despair. At the same time several genuine celebrities have emerged from and around the Alt-Right—celebrities whose fame is, remarkably, wholly independent of establishment media.

The Socio-Sexual Model

To women, sex is a confirmation of love. To men, love is a confirmation of sex.

— Chateau Heartiste

The Alt-Right is shaped by influences from the different spheres out of which it emerged, and benefits from practices learned from 4chan, as well as perspectives adopted from the neoreactionary movement and the manosphere. One recurring theme taken from the manosphere is a conception-of-the-world in which relations between the sexes play a central part. This worldview differs markedly from the egalitarian, and contains for instance a theory of socio-sexual hierarchy which permeates society. Each human individual possesses an *SMV*, a Sexual Market Value, and men and women assess SMV differently. For example, the looks of a woman are generally of greater importance to a man than the looks of a man are to a woman.

All men are not equally attractive; there exist a smaller number of *alpha males* compared to the greater number of *beta males*. Beside the alphas and betas there are also the *omegas*—a pitiful group which sometimes, as we have read, turn into wizards at thirty. The manosphere assesses that most women are *hypergamous*, meaning they constantly pursue relationships with males higher on the alpha-scale. This circumstance is handled by different societies in several distinct

ways. The historically European way of handling it was to instate monogamous marriage as the norm. This meant that beta males were able
to form families together with common women. Monogamy is seen as
a stabilizing factor, politically as well as economically. Unmarried beta
males roaming aimlessly without a family to support can be an explosive
force—as is evident in many societies in which polygyny is prevalent.
The incentive of such single men to invest time and other resources in
their civilization is largely diminished compared to that of family men.
However, the historical socio-sexual solution that expressed itself in
the norm of monogamy has collapsed in Europe, as well as in the West
at large, giving leeway to the female propensity to hypergamy. This collapse coincides with a ubiquitous feminism which confuses beta males
and women alike about the nature of relationships; it also coincides
with the emergence of so-called welfare states which are eager to take
on the responsibility—and thereby the power—of breadwinners. The
consequences have been described by author F. Roger Devlin as an
Africanization of mating patterns, marked by polygamous and volatile
relationships and a decline in investment in the resulting children.

Chateau Heartiste has used the socio-sexual model to explain the
phenomenon of so-called *white knights*: men who rush to the defense
of feminist women against perceived "sexists." Heartiste's assessment is
that white knights are often men who are unaware of their true sexual
motivations—and were they to become aware, the outcome of their
efforts would greatly disappoint them. The *cuck* phenomenon too can
be described in socio-sexual terms—it is not alpha males who become
cuckservatives. Also significant are the socio-sexual components of
ethnic relations. If White males are encouraged to feminize while
other males are not, this will have consequences—not least of all for
the aforementioned White males and their scant progeny.

In light of this, use of the socio-sexual model can indeed be deemed
fruitful. The model is also an expression of a clearly anti-egalitarian
conception-of-the-world, closely related to the theory of evolutionary

psychology proposed by blogger and author *Anonymous Conservative* (henceforth *AC*). The theory has gained some acclaim within the Alt-Right—one person who has expressed his appreciation for it is Matt Forney. The theory grows out of what biologists call *r/K selection theory*, which AC applies to the human species. Here, *r* (rate of reproduction of the organism) and *K* (carrying capacity of the habitat) are proposed classes of reproduction strategies, each strategy bringing its respective advantages and disadvantages in particular types of environments.

K-strategies benefit life in predictable but challenging environments and entail the rearing of comparably low numbers of offspring, allowing greater parental investment in each young. Monogamy is a common trait, as are complex social systems. Wolves and elephants are examples of species with a clear propensity for *K*-strategies; individuals of both species are selected for successful competition over meager resources.

Conversely, *r*-strategies are associated with environments in which resources are abundant but in which sudden events might at any time eradicate large swathes of a population. Under such conditions, rearing the largest possible number of offspring in the shortest period of time is often a necessity for survival, even though this strategy unavoidably comes at the cost of lower possible parental investment in each young. Adaptations facilitating successful competition are unlikely to be advantageous, seeing as how conditions are subject to sudden change, quickly rendering such adaptations obsolete. Common *r*-selected traits are promiscuous mating patterns and a disinclination to competition.

Applying the *r/K* selection theory to the human species, AC construes how *r* and *K* strategies correspond with the behavior and values of liberals and conservatives, respectively. Differing attitudes toward free markets, gun control, promiscuity, and much else are all thought to be explicable through the notion that liberals are dominantly *r*-selected while conservatives are dominantly *K*-selected. The apprehension that *r*-selected groups not rarely play *K*-selected groups off against one another is worth noting, which would explain the affinity among liberals for Islamists. The cycles of history, too, may be construed as a story of how cultures dominated by K-selected individuals, molded by hard times, create *good times*—times which allow for the proliferation of r-selected individuals within the culture. In turn, this proliferation of less monogamously inclined individuals predictably leads to a decline of family structures and, by further extension, society as a whole. Moreover, AC argues that r-selected people tend to betray their society to its enemies. The conflicts and calamities following such betrayal then come to constitute the next historical instance of *hard times*—times of the kind which recurringly mold cultures dominated by *K-selected* individuals. In this respect, the r/K selection theory as applied by AC to the human species is indeed reminiscent of Glubb's *life cycle of empires*, as well as Turchin's *secular cycles* and Volkmar Weiss' *population cycle*.

Adjacent to the socio-sexual model and theories of r/K-selection we encounter what may be called *Lombroso's revenge*. For decades, the field developed by physician Cesare Lombroso (1835–1909), *criminal anthropology*, with its concern over connections between certain physical characteristics and certain behaviors, was viewed as pure pseudoscience. In recent years, however, scientific evidence has actually begun to prove Lombroso right on some points. The evidence not only shows connections between appearance and criminality,[5] but also connections between appearance and pedophilia.[6] As expressed by *Chateau Heartiste*: "Physiognomy is real." Although the discovered correlations are in no way perfect, it is sometimes possible to discern who is intelligent and who is a pedophile. The findings are intriguing in and of themselves, but are also somewhat alarming as regards the connections between *science and politics*; sometimes, it seems, it is the

---

5   Valla, Ceci & Williams (2011). The Accuracy of Inferences About Criminality Based on Appearance. *Journal of Social, Evolutionary, and Cultural Psychology*.

6   Dyshniku, Murray, Fazio, et al. (2015). Minor Physical Anomalies as a Window into the Prenatal Origins of Pedophilia. *Archives of Sexual Behavior*.

outcome of a world war that consigns a field of study to the pillory of pseudoscience for the better part of a century.

The Generational Aspect

Generation Alt-Right is one with nothing to lose and everything to gain.
— HANNIBAL BATEMAN

To a high degree, the Alt-Right consists of younger males. Like the identitarian generation in Europe, they have experienced the consequences of political correctness, mass immigration, and the tenets of '68 in general. Their parents, on the other hand, have often experienced a better world than that of their children, and they still relate to this world. The parental generation assumes that this better world is the normal state of affairs, and that any deviation is temporary. For instance, they have a limited, and often positive, experience of multiculturalism. They may persuade themselves that they took part in shaping today's society, either through their participation in the events in and following 1968 or in the so called anti-fascism of the 1990s. To young men of European descent the situation is markedly different: they are almost invisible in current pop culture, and in the public discourse they are considered as either being humdrum or privileged "racists."

Several proponents of the Alt-Right have shone light on the generational aspect, not rarely with reference to the research conducted by Strauss and Howe on the matter. Vox Day has noted that the millennials are subject to the roughest economical conditions of any generation since the Great Depression of the 1930s. This may explain many of their evident troubles. Their less frequent sexual activity, for instance, could have something to do with fewer of them having been able to move out of their parents' homes. They drive less because they cannot afford the costs. They do not save money, as this does not seem meaningful, and so on. Hannibal Bateman expounds on the matter in his article "Generation Alt-Right," published on Radix. The members

of his generation were denied a past as well as a future, and many of
them grew tired of it. Some rediscovered socialism. These are often
so called Bernie Bros, who supported Bernie Sanders during the 2016
election. Others moved to the right. All had one thing in common:
they sought an answer to the question *"Who am I?"* seeing that such
answers were not offered freely by their society.

Here is to be found, in America as in Europe, an element of generational revolt. Matt Forney has spoken of the *gerontocracy*—how
the boomers of '68 co-opted and monopolized the whole of society.
He describes them as the most narcissistic and greedy generation in
American history. A similar generational divide partly exists *within*
the Alt-Right, in which an older generation of immigration critics do
not always appreciate the antics of a younger generation of trolls. This
is somewhat reminiscent of the relationship between older Leftists and
the rebels of '68; the latter used the catchphrase, "Don't trust anyone
over 30." The situation has not, however, become as hostile as it once
was in West Germany, where professor Adorno was confronted with
an *unpleasant* generation of students, putting it mildly, during what
were to become his last years. On August 6, 1969, in his 66th year,
Adorno suffered a heart attack which proved fatal.

William Strauss and Neil Howe through their studies on the significance of generations have reconnected with a fundamentally traditional subject. Most readers have, sometime or other, encountered
the theory of the three generations, according to which the first makes
a fortune, the second conserves it, and, finally, the third squanders it.
Glubb as well as Turchin make use of generations to make sense of
history. Strauss and Howe have expounded on their own theory in
works like *Generations* and *The Fourth Turning*. Their central concept
is, unsurprisingly, *generations*. A generation consists of people born
during a certain period of time—a period of about 20 years, during
which they experience the same deciding trends and events during
the same phase of their lives. It might be that they experienced a world

war or a depression during their childhood. Thus they develop similar ways of viewing the world, and share a sense of commonality. After their conception-of-the-world has formed, it only changes incrementally. Strauss and Howe have identified a recurring pattern in British and American history, in which four types of generations have succeeded each other in repeated order since the 1400s. The theorists have imaginatively named these four generational types *Prophets, Nomads, Heroes* and *Artists*.

Prophets grow up following a greater crisis. During their childhood they are indulged and receive much attention, and as young adults they tend to dream up their own crusades, demanding change of society and its norms. One such fanciful revolution was that of '68, and the generation behind it was, of course, the *Baby Boomers*. The ensuing generation, named *Nomads* by Strauss and Howe, conversely grow up *during* such a revolution—when parents have much time for their own, personal, interests but less for their children. Thus generations of Nomads witness the downsides of the revolution; their members are not indulged but rather neglected, and are later perceived as threats and trouble. Strauss and Howe first called it "Generation 13" to express the sense of a dangerous generation, but the term that stuck was *Generation X*. Generation X was the generation associated with gangsta rap, black metal, and skinheads. The previous Nomad generation was the one Gertrude Stein called *"the lost generation"*—the generation of Ernest Hemingway and countless others, famous and infamous alike. A generation of *Heroes* grow up while their society is crumbling, during eras of individualism and *laissez-faire*. These are the *Millennials* of today, also known as *Generation Y*. The *Artists* are born during a crisis. These are *Generation Z*, hammered out by the "War on Terror" and the recession of 2008.

It is notable that *Generation Z* (at times humurously referred to by some within the Alt-Right, with emblematic irreverence, as *Generation Zyklon*) already is one of the most conservative generations alive. As the values of a generation are shaped mainly by early experiences, they are also very resistant to reform. It is for instance a giant leap for a baby boomer to reassess the multicultural dream— to realize that *"we've been trying this for 50 years, and it still doesn't work!"* To Generation Z, on the other hand, what was revolutionary in '68 is now run-of-the-mill. It is what they have grown up with and often also grown tired of. They do not see drugs or *"the sexual revolution"* as emancipating, but tend to be more skeptical about drug use, transsexualism, et cetera. There are even indications that the younger they are, the more adverse American members of Generation Z are to immigration. Among those born in 2000–2003, 25% replied in a survey that immigration hurts America, compared to 20% of those born 1991–1996 (and 43% of those born before 1965). This is telling, not least because Generation Z in the United States is also the generation most marked by ethnic diversity; barely more than half of them are White, compared to 73% of boomers. Generation Z grew up during the recession, and their parents are often members of "Generation 13" who have imparted their skepticism toward boomer utopianism to their children. This entails that the generation is more conservative, financially as well as on matters like drugs, et cetera. In one survey, they were more supportive of Trump than of Clinton. They also tend to be independent, and many consider starting their own businesses. By and large they constitute a promising generation, carrying the potential to conduct the crucial normalization of society which their parents failed to achieve. Generation Z might very well, and fortuitously enough, be followed by *Generation Alpha.*

Strauss and Howe also elaborated a theory of the *Fourth Turning*— four recurring phases which in turn shape the respective generational types. These phases are identified as the *High,* the *Awakening,* the *Unraveling,* and the *Crisis.* Times following the end of a crisis are marked by optimism, strong institutions, and a spirit of high hopes for the future. Such times constitute instances of the *First Turning.* It was during such a period of *High* that the would-be rebels of '68 grew up. Their subsequent *Awakening* commenced in the 1960s, and by 1968 it had reached critical mass. This second turning was a rebellion against social norms that boomers, as they came of age, perceived as stuffy and old-fashioned, and against anything they saw as vapid or unauthentic. Rebellion, however, leads to a weakening of institutions and a diminished sense of belonging and society-wide affinity. Following this comes a period of individualism and societal fragmentation. The spread of neoliberalism and postmodernism entailed an almost literal *Unraveling* of the established order, as the fabric of thought as well as of custom—and even reality itself—all were to be intently and methodically deconstructed to show that even the most beautiful and elaborate fabric consists of silly, mundane fibers. This unraveling constituted much of the third turning, and by then many former *hippies* had already transformed into *yuppies*. What inevitably follows according to the theory is the fourth turning: the *Crisis*. This crisis is already underway, and it is up to an alliance of generations to manage the crisis so that a new *High* may ensue. Signs that such an alliance might be possible are not entirely absent, not least of all because significant portions of the boomers of '68 are finally beginning to realize what actual consequences their once youthful utopianism had when it was implemented.

Success Factors and Pitfalls

> Kick a dog enough and you end up with a bad-tempered dog. Acknowledging the fact doesn't mean you support kicking dogs—or bad-tempered dogs.
> — Nick Land on the Alt-Right as "an inevitable outcome of Cathedral overreach"

The Alt-Right has reached critical mass. Partly this is due to historical factors such as the generational aspect, the demographic shift, the

Internet, and an establishment which has run amok. Partly it is also
due to the use of tactics and strategies appropriate to these historical
factors. The Alt-Right has turned its back on *Cuckservatism*: toward
those who hate one's guts there exists no nuanced approach. Neither
can their self-description be taken seriously: they claim to be "anti-
racist" and to champion justice, but their actions reveal a deep-seated
hatred of Europe as well as of Europeans. Such conditions call for
more offensive tactics. The reaching of a critical mass means that a
market has opened up for options alternative to the dot-com giants.
These giants are often prone to hampering the Right, or even to
downright kicking it off their platforms. Facebook and Twitter have
both clearly demonstrated this tendency. Vox Day calls alternatives to
them *Alt-Tech,* with examples like the Twitter-contender *Gab* and the
crowdfunding site for journalism *WeSearchr.*

Another success factor has been the ability to raise a *big tent*,
with the Alt-Lite reaching normies while other corners of the tent
elaborate a more fundamental critique of current society. This division
of labor has made it possible for Spencer to play the role of eloquent
and wholesome spokesman, while on other fronts anonymous trolls
continue undermining political correctness by way of—in a double
sense—offensive memes. At the same time there are indications that,
since the Trump victory, the big tent rests on shaky ground. Sections of
the Alt-Lite rather see themselves being accepted more by Trump than
by the Alt-Right proper, while sections of the Alt-Right proper seek
more orthodoxy and purism, among other things regarding the choice
of allies. Both these trends jeopardize the Alt-Right's forcefulness: the
Alt-Lite risks being co-opted and hamstrung by the establishment,
while the Alt-Right risks being once and for all banished to the political ghetto.

Yet another success factor is the vitality and originality of the perspective of the Alt-Right. For decades society has been dominated by a
simplistic conception-of-the-world, not only far removed from reality

but in many respects also downright *boring*. A subdued demand for something new has been brewing, and the Alt-Right offers several new and exciting perspectives on anything from the political to the socio-sexual. Spencer has said that the Alt-Right is in many ways situated similarly to the New Left; it dedicates itself to mentioning the unmentionable and thinking the unthinkable. This is all reminiscent of Guillaume Faye's realization that "now, *we* own the monopoly on rebellious thought." And such thought is indeed in great demand, in particular when conveyed with wit and confidence.

The realization of the Alt-Right that *the personal is political* is also a success factor; he who has not already transformed himself can in no convincing way tell others how to transform society. Ideals like strength, virility, beauty, and *Courage to Be* set the Alt-Right apart from most established political environments, a condition which produces real people superior to most of what their opponents can deliver. In the long term, this particular tendency will likely prove to be of immense value. However, the personal might become *too* political, as when parts of the Alt-Right attack allies for being homosexual, or attacking prominent profiles within the movement for even *looking* gay. There is a constant risk of over-radicalization and hubris, in particular under the protection of anonymity. Whatever degree the Alt-Right is vulnerable to entryism, it is more "Cartman Nazis" than it is individual Jews that pose the threat. An indispensable and complex analysis risks being reduced to "the (((Jews)))" and thence, like so many others before it, losing all potential for real influence. Colin Liddell has commented that the Alt-Right needs not trigger anyone with Hitler memes—the opposition is so extreme that it is sufficient to focus on mature identitarianism and traditionalism, and to humanely and honestly shed light on issues regarding race and Jewish influence. The intended audience will absorb the message, while the opposition will be triggered regardless of how humanely and maturely the message is being expressed.

The Internet has been an important refuge, and has been crucial for the flourishing of the Alt-Right. But unless the Alt-Right steps out into the physical world, *meatspace*, it will meet the same fate as neoreaction. The Alt-Right is also vulnerable in the long term if left at the mercy of Facebook and Twitter, and if participants experience the constant threat of doxxing. Luckily there are signs that the movement is moving in the right direction in this regard, with increasing local initiatives such as conferences and the like.

The Alt-Right has occurred as a defensive reaction—and it is little surprise given the cornered position of the European and European-descended peoples. However, this entails a focus often turned toward negative things—threats and the enemy. Issues like ecology are conspicuously absent. One constant risk is that of purity-spiraling, a tendency which is observable in the internal criticism targeting proponents who co-operate with homosexuals and Jews. Were this criticism to become dominant, the Alt-Right would lose its relevance as well as its ability to extend its reach to wider coalitions. Today's leading proponents generally seem to realize this. The greater risk is how this might change with future rapid growth. In short, the danger is that when identitarianism is imported into America it transforms into something reminiscent of National Socialism—a blind alley, humanly as well as politically. A likely reason for this is that race is a more central category in the Anglosphere than in historical Europe. The National Socialism of the NSDAP was partly a German adaption to that Anglo-Saxon conception-of-the-world which Hitler and Günther both viewed with ambivalence. In a way, an Anglo-Saxon National Socialism would constitute a re-importation of ideas once exported to Germany. Nevertheless this circumstance does not make the ideas any better.

Regarding this matter, Bruce Charlton has directed a relevant warning to the Alt-Right. Charlton writes that the Alt-Right has to choose between either becoming *spiritual* or becoming what its enemies claim it already is. Charlton's impression is that large swathes of the movement are marked by materialism, anti-altruism, and reductionism. What normally motivates people is primarily an ideal, and secondarily fear and hatred. Unless the Alt-Right finds an ideal it will find itself dependent on fear and hatred as its unifiers. Such tendencies are already visible, but, as has been shown above, so also are forceful counter-tendencies. One could add that the Alt-Right is in need of a significant admixture of *Deep Right* in the sense of ecology, Tradition, or Spirituality as a safeguard against degeneration toward mere group-egoism and a lack of empathy that few historical men of the Right would have found appealing.

Early 2017 saw a notable event very relevant to this point, when the site AltRight.com was launched by Richard Spencer and William Regnery as well as a number of fellows linked to Arktos and/or Sweden, such as Tor Westman, Henrik Palmgren and Daniel Friberg. The articles published thus far have been promising, not least of all since the American Alt-Right as well as the European New Right and the Russian Right are all represented. For the Alt-Right to once and for all remedy its teething troubles it needs the perspectives of the New Right, but likewise the New Right needs the insights of the Alt-Right to gain political relevance. In any case, the Alt-Right has much to teach those aspiring to create a vigorous and cogent postmodern movement of resistance.

Chapter 13

The Immigrants in the New Europe

> It's very good that there are yellow French, black French, brown French
> ... but only as long as they are small minorities. Otherwise, France ceases
> to be France. After all, we are primarily a European people of the white
> race, with Greek and Latin culture, and Christian religion. Try mixing
> oil and vinegar. Shake the bottle. They will separate again.
>
> — DE GAULLE ON INTEGRATION

After decades of mass immigration we have a situation in Europe in which the ethnic and social components of the identity no longer overlap. For example, there are people who are part of Danish society, but not part of the Danish *ethnos*. There are also large groups that are neither members of Danish society nor the Danish *ethnos*, and who live in more or less hostile parallel societies to which the Danish *ethnos* pay monthly tributes in the form of welfare checks. This situation can be dealt with in different ways, both by the ethnic Danes and by the immigrants who are part of Danish society (and who after some generations will have merged into the Danish *ethnos*). Some of these make a career as politically correct pundits, always characterized by *ressentiment* against what they cannot become. Others identify themselves with the natives of Europe.

The latter usually have the advantage of getting away with saying things that the white Europeans are not allowed to say. You can find them in many countries (in Denmark we have Naser Khader as an example). They tend to become very popular, as they allow native immigration critics to signal that they are not racists, and as they can be considered confirmation of the dream of the possibility of integration: "If Naser Khader can do it, everyone can." This is admittedly wishful thinking, and the more Khaders there are, the more difficult its realization becomes. Individuals and entire minority groups are very different phenomena. But the tendency is of interest, even though it varies. For example, Xavier Naidoo is closer to "conspiracy theory" positions than to Camel Bechikh's Muslim patriotism.

Éric Zemmour — the Reactionary

I have understood that it is not my words that matter, but my thoughts. Not even my thoughts, but my underlying motives.

— ZEMMOUR, IDENTIFYING POLITICAL CORRECTNESS AS AN OUTLOOK

One of the most interesting representatives of this trend is Éric Zemmour. Zemmour belongs to a family of Berber Jews, originally from Algeria. Like many other Jewish families, Zemmour's followed along the French *pied-noirs* when they left a decolonized North Africa. Zemmour has made a career as a journalist and author, but he has gradually become increasingly controversial. Zemmour's contacts with French justice also show how intolerant it has become; he has been convicted several times for rather harmless statements of opinion.

Zemmour described how France was feminized and castrated in the essay "Le Premier Sexe," a reference to *The Second Sex* of Simone de Beauvoir. He has since then focused much on the Great Replacement and Islamization, as well as the ideologies behind them. Zemmour has had a lot of sharp things to say about the Left and anti-racism. Anti-racism appears to him as the Leftist strategy to conceal that it has embraced neoliberalism and made peace with capitalism, which is an insight worthy of being taken to heart. Zemmour writes:

> Anti-racism was the smoke screen that concealed the socialists' submission under the liberal forces. Anti-racists share a common ground with international finance: the abolition of borders. Along with all kinds of progressives, they destroyed the last obstacles to market power: families, nations, states. The former served the interests of the latter, the useful idiots of capitalism that they are.

The "Left" facilitates the reduction of man into an atomized consumer. Zemmour has also identified the metapolitical methods of the politically correct in the *"three Ds."* In French there are *Dérision, Déconstruction*, and *Destruction*—deride, deconstruct, and destroy. This too is a useful insight, whether you want to defend yourself against this method or even apply parts of it.

Zemmour describes himself as an anti-liberal also in terms of the economy—a reactionary close to Gaullism and Bonapartism, who is able also to find value in some of Marxism's analyses. Twenty years of privatization and liberalism have weakened France. A national order has been abandoned and disassembled, both socially, politically and culturally. For Zemmour, the Left is dead, because it abandoned the workers and the nation. Neither the elite nor the people can fight anymore, and many have adopted the English language. Over all, language plays a role in Zemmour's analysis; he notes, among other things, that the choice of first name plays a role in determining identity. If you choose to name your children with Arabic or English names, this is a symbolic distance from everything French. Such a distance has been encouraged for decades, and Zemmour believes that the result will be the division along ethnic lines. He writes:

> ... the celebration of multiculturalism, the constant criticism of France, the degradation of the school and the French language, the weakening of patriotism—all this has made people go back to their roots, to religion and to local communities. Because we wanted to destroy the

nation we will get the tribes. And the tribes will wage war. All tribes, not just the Jewish and the Arabic ones.

He believes that this could lead to civil war, and has said that he has received information from a reliable source that the French military has been in contact with his Israeli colleagues to prepare for this ("Operation Ronce"). At the same time, he reminds us that this demographic replacement is a symptom, and that we are well advised to identify the underlying disease. Zemmour has cited the Senegalese poet and politician Senghor's words, *"in order to be colonized, one must first have been colonizable."* What and who made France into a colonizable country? Among other things, Zemmour brings up Christopher Lasch's theory of the "revolt of the elites" against the people to explain this.

Zemmour not only looks at Islamism, but also at the established French Judaism. He believes that the recurring reminders of historical tragedies had the effect of creating a contest in victimhood, with Dieudonné as the clearest example. All in all, he is a fascinating figure who constantly challenges the politically correct rules of allowable opinion, whether regarding the existence of races or the fact that "humanitarian interventions" are usually rhetoric concealing neocolonialism. Zemmour's books have gained significant popularity and have succeeded in spreading a reactionary and Gaullistic perspective to wider circles. Zemmour is a reactionary, and a well-read one; only a handful attain his level in this respect. It usually takes a few generations before you get enough training to become a Zemmour.

Akif Pirinçci — the Libertarian

Integration is a word invented by the green Left. There is only assimilation; a state or a community can not work if everyone does their own thing. It is not enough only to speak German—something the history of

the multiethnic states shows. A society or state can only work through
assimilation, but assimilation is voluntary.

— Pirinçci

Closer to a classic liberal position we find the Turkish-German author
Akif Pirinçci. Pirinçci has lived in Germany since he was a small child;
his parents taught him to be grateful for the opportunity they received.
He also has children with a German woman. Pirinçci has been successful in his new homeland, through his popular books about Francis, the
cat detective. Germany's most expensive animated film, made in 1993,
was based on the first book, *Felidae*. It is an interesting film, with many
interesting themes, such as animal cruelty, cults, and the relationship
between abuse and revenge. It is not suitable for children, however.

Since early 2010, Pirinçci has been involved in the German social
debate. He has contributed to, among other things, the Conservative
Junge Freiheit and Classical Liberal *eigentümlich frei*, he has also written for the blog *Achse des Guten*. In Germany there is a significant
overlap between classical liberalism and more national conservative
new Right.

Pirinçci's main thesis is that Germany has gone mad and is dominated by politically correct enclaves, which use ugly methods to silence
critics and control the debate. This is also the title of his first, more
political book, *Germany Gone Mad: The Crazy Cult around Women,
Homosexuals, and Immigrants*, from 2014. The writing is fierce and
exhorting, describing and responding to the ideas of the official ideology. Pirinçci is both entertaining and disrespectful, a true iconoclast.
What the politically correct sees as holy, he deems to be stupidities, and
he is open with it too. He writes about what great "progress" it is that
gay policemen can now be open with their sexuality. In the past, many
policemen did not speak openly about their position: *"Noooo, is it true?
That's terrible! So when I'm illegally parked somewhere, I'll get a note saying 'It's illegal to stop here—also I'm a hard homo.' It will put everything
in another light, like, in a metaphysical way, you know."* Pirinçci is often

an effective, albeit somewhat vulgar, satirist. This applies not least to his feigned and exaggerated compassion with the different "questions" of the PC-"Left": "But noooooo! Is it *really* true? How *terrible!*"

Pirinçci leans heavily towards classical liberalism, not least of all by focusing on the *high-tax-state*. Someone has to pay for the replacement of the native stock with people from the global south, and these unimaginable costs will turn Germany into a slave state. Pirinçci's analysis of the German high-tax-state is, again, marked by classical liberalism: he notes that it is only roughly one in eight Germans that provides for the rest (unemployed, state employees, children, et cetera). This also means that many Germans see themselves as a "middle class" without actually being so. The fake middle class, which to a large degree is supported by tax-redistribution, tends to push away the real middle class from, among other things, the finer residential areas; it is the tax funds of the latter that are used to indoctrinate the former through state television, provide for a mediocre "intelligentia," and turn their own children against them. Here we recognize Moldbug's distinction between Vaisyas and Brahmins.

But it's to the actual middle class that Pirinçci turns. His analysis is based on the notion that "*fear is a choice.*" The German citizen is afraid. Afraid of being called a Nazi, afraid of being beaten, afraid of a visit from the tax department, afraid of criticism from the EU. But, in reality, it is he or she that has the power, both domestically and in the EU. Pirinçci therefore advises the middle class to take collective action, in the form of a tax boycott. A lone tax dodger is put in jail, but what does the state do when there are hundreds of thousands? Without the high-tax-state, Pirinçci believes that many of the other problems would solve themselves. Demand for ideology-producing "gender mainstreaming," and the like, is likely to be limited in a free market. Likewise, the number of divorces would decrease when such a phenomenon is linked to real economic consequences. Many of the immigrants who do not share Pirinçci's feelings for Germany, or his financial success, would return home if the state handouts were canceled. Et cetera. Here we recognize the reasoning from Hoppe and Rothbard, and the question *"How do we strangle the beast?"* Pirinçi's analysis is also shared by the philosopher Sloterdijk, who talked about how Germany goes from being a tax state to a debt state.

In 2016, Pirinçi released the book *Umvolkung*, entitled "How the Germans calmly and quietly get replaced." *Umvolkung* is a term from the Third Reich, when whole populations were moved around as chess pieces across the map. "Reich-Germans," "Slavs," "Jews" and others. By means of the same concept, Pirinçi identifies how the same attitude permeates our time, when large groups of predominantly Arab men are moved into historic Germany. He has previously been interested in the demographic aspect, and talked about "bio-Germans" to describe the native stock. Already in *Germany Gone Mad*, he theorized about the dysgenic consequences of Islam, describing the immigrant murder of native youth from an evolutionary perspective. It is about struggle for territory, and in a normal situation this would lead to a reaction from the exposed group, and an ensuing balance. But in Germany, the hegemony of political correctness prevents the emergence of such resistance and balance. Which thus requires human lives.

Pirinçi has in recent years been subjected to a *de facto* attempt at professional blacklisting, in which major bookshop chains have stopped selling his books, even his fictional books about cat detectives. But he has found new channels to reach the public, including lectures.

Bassam Tibi — the Patrician

> Calling someone racist is a very effective weapon in Germany. Islamists know this.
>
> — Bassam Tibi

Zemmour and Pirinçi are men of the Right, though Zemmour has more in common with the genuine tradition of the Right than the more libertarian-leaning Pirinçci. But even people with a Leftist background have responded to the massive population replacement. Among these we find Bassam Tibi. Tibi came to Germany in 1962, and belongs to a Sunni patrimonial lineage from Syria. He has compared his lineage to the Hanseatic Buddenbrooks family (in Thomas Mann's novel). In Germany, Tibi became part of the Left; he is a political scientist and has known several of the heavy Leftist figures such as Adorno, Horkheimer, and Bloch.

Tibi is a Muslim, and has previously talked about the need to reform Islam, as well as the need for a German *Leitkultur* to enable integration. At the same time, he has criticized the European tradition of racism, and the difficulty of truly becoming a part of Germany. But the massive migration of recent years has brought things to a head even for Tibi. In an interview with Welt, Tibi told him that he had talked to thousands of Syrians in the last year. Many were antisemites, not a single one a physician or engineer. Tibi talked about the parallel societies, about how maybe 5 or 10% of Muslims in Germany live as he does, as Europeans. The rest do not.

Tibi was critical of Angela Merkel's unilateral decision to open the borders. He said that *"with this decision, Germany changes. It is already seen in Göttingen: the city was formerly a student city, 20% foreigners, an idyllic city. Today it looks like a refugee camp, where Afghan or Eritrean gangs roam the streets, and one witnesses it with fear. The community of Göttingen is destroyed ... Over time, these groups have become gangs ... Göttingen has in just a year become a city filled with crime. And for that we have Frau Merkel to thank."*

Tibi believes that the reformed Islam he had previously hoped for, a Euro-Islam, is today no longer a possibility. The Muslim leaders with whom Merkel and others demonstrate side by side have never been interested in Euro-Islam. And with the massive influx of men from cultures in which violence against women is woven into the conception of inter-group conflicts, it becomes even more impossible. These men thought that in Germany, both a luxury car and a "nice blonde woman" were waiting for them, and their disappointment is directed towards the women of German men. *"Patriarchally minded men from misogynic cultures can never be integrated,"* states Tibi.

Tibi's perspective is interesting, and reminds us that the ethnic issue is not a Right-Left question. He reconnects to his former teacher Horkheimer, who called Europe *"an island of freedom in an ocean of dictatorships."* This freedom is threatened by what Tibi calls a demographic avalanche. He also addresses issues such as the change of cityscape, the groups of wandering young men, the aspect Giddens calls "ethnic poverty," the parallel communities. For many years, Tibi has turned against both Islamism, traditional Islam, and European racism and advocated for a synthesis of Islam and European values. Today, inverse racism seems to have led to a demographic situation that makes such a synthesis obviously impossible.

Like Zemmour, Tibi is a single voice. He takes part in the struggle of ideas, and lends certain ideas respectability as a recognized scientist, but he is also a one-man army. At the same time, these men are part of the establishment, which gives them added weight.

Égalité et Réconciliation

> It was clear from the Maastricht Treaty that the enemy is global financial capitalism, for which Europe is a Trojan horse. It was also clear that the majority of the French understood this. It was clear to me that the only politician who can fight this system is a nationalist, independent of the world of finance, institutionalized politics, and the media ... Jean-Marie Le Pen.
>
> — Alain Soral

Outside the establishment, there are Alain Soral and Dieudonné M'bala M'bala. In this context, they may be particularly interesting because there is also an institution around them in the form of *Égalité et Réconciliation.*

Alain Soral has made films and written books. He was originally a Marxist, and later influenced by communist theoretician Michel Clouscard. Clouscard's theory was that the movement of 1968 wasn't really a socialist movement, but was rather a part of the development of a *capitalisme de la séduction* and a *libéralism libertaire*—a "seductive capitalism" with a superstructure of "permissive liberalism." Clouscard captured these concepts of capitalism's change, which coincides with public morality. From a Victorian morality to a "liberty," in which new markets and goods are created in line with the "un-victorianization" of society's morality. New attitudes exemplify this change, such as that toward sexual minorities, drugs, and eating without working, as well as toward the earlier morality characterized by self-control, moderation, and independence. This older morality formed exemplary entrepreneurs and workers, but not exemplary consumers. This, of course, means that such matters as the "sexual revolution," 1968, and the new tolerance for LGBT-groups end up partially in a different light. Rather than merely being an expression of freedom and tolerance, they also appear to be intimately linked to the changed interests of capitalism. At the same time, Clouscard noted that despite this permissive ideology, for many this was still about purchasing power; for many, it meant that *"all is permissible but nothing is possible,"* even though the rebels had taken up the slogan of *"it's forbidden to forbid."*

Soral interpreted and further developed Clouscard, whose theory resembles both Zemmour's and Houellebecq's insights. It has proven to be a fruitful model, which explains, *inter alia*, how "freedom" meant that the market's logic would invade new social spheres such as family and society. The author Michel Houellebecq has described this with words pointing to the manosphere:

> In our society ... sex undoubtedly represents a second differentiation system, completely independent of money, and it acts as an equally ruthless differentiation system. Just like unchallenged liberalism, sexual

liberalism can, and for similar reasons, lead to total impoverishment. Some make love every day, others five, six times in their lives, or never. Some make love with lots of women, others with none. That is what is called "the law of the market." In an economic system where redundancies are prohibited, virtually everyone can find their place. In a sexual system where infidelity is prohibited, virtually everyone can find a companion.

The form of Communism that the younger Soral supported was at the same time patriotic. But it was disassembled, at a time when according to Soral the need for anti-liberalism was greater than ever. Soral describes how the French Right and the French Left converged to become virtually identical, embracing what he calls a dominant ideology. This ideology is based on economic liberalization through the EU. It also builds on the unconditional belief in open borders, reduced national sovereignty, and the imperative to multi-culturalism. In order to conceal that the established parties agree on a dominant ideology, the alleged conflict between "Right" and "Left" serves an ideological function. Those who are not *"liberal, globalists, human rights fundamentalists, pro-American, and pro-Zionist"* are excluded from establishment and television.

Clouscard, too, inverted the old Marxist attitude towards the state. Previously, according to him, the state had been the tool that a class could use to repress another; with globalization the state could instead become a tool to counter globalism. This meant that Soral could imagine a nationalist Marxism. He approached Front National and was a member of the party's Central Committee for a while. But he eventually left Front National as he did not share their view of Islam as a threat. His belief was that the specter of ethnic conflict between ethnic French and Muslims would be something that the global empire could manipulate and exploit to hurt France in the same way that ethno-religious conflicts had previously been used to break up Yugoslavia. His ideal is Michel Aoun and Hassan Nasrallah, the Christian and

Shiite Lebanese leader who worked together instead of perpetuating a civil war. Soral is a pronounced anti-imperialist, and has written a book about the modern empire.

Soral describes himself as right-wing and left-wing at the same time. His values belong to the Right; values such as patriotism, honor, and virtue. Economically, he is to the Left, and on the side of the workers against the capital. "*Gauche du travail, droite des valeurs*,"[7] as expressed in French. He believes that many French Muslims, in practice, have the same conception-of-the-world as French Catholics, and that their interests are overlapping. On the other hand, he draws a clear boundary around what he calls "Islamo-scum": Americanized and/or fundamentalist, and anti-French Muslims. Soral views the Shiite axis, with Iran, Syria and Hezbollah, as a valuable opposition to the American Empire. He believes that this empire often exploits ethnic and religious divisions, and that it may use the conflict between native and Muslim French against France. He is critical of what he calls *communitarianism*, that is the creation of organized "states inside of the state," such as Muslim special interests, or Jewish, gay, native, feminist ones, et cetera. One concern here is that anti-communitarianism is so closely linked to anti-Zionism, which is easily perceived as threatening by those who simultaneously are patriots and Jews (for example, you may wonder why Kontre Kulture sells Drumont's *La France juive*).

Soral has said that Front National can engage in party politics, leaving the metapolitics and the avant-garde to Égalité et Réconciliation. Consequently, the group has gathered a number of system critics. There are the above-mentioned Shiite circles, the artist Zeon, Pierre Jovanovic, and the Afro-French ethno-differentialist Kemi Seba. There are also the survivalists Piero San Giorgio and Gabriele Adinolfi. E&R is open to patriotic Muslims, and Soral has estimated that they represent maybe a third of the group's members.

---

7   French: "Left in labor, Right in values." —Ed.

Dieudonné

> The French Revolution is my tradition. It is a French attitude that you
> need a revolution. I'm deeply French.
>
> — DIEUDONNÉ

Dieudonné M'bala M'bala was for a long time one of France's most popular comedians. Since he began to touch politically incorrect themes in his sketches, he has been excluded from the public space, but has become instead a very popular underground comedian. Dieudonné began his political path as an anti-racist, but gradually came to reassess Front National and the nation state which the party defends. Today he concentrates mainly on reacting against communitarianism—the political organizing of special interests such as feminists, Zionists, anti-racists, and LGBTX-movements—and demanding special benefits, both real and symbolic (including statutory protection against criticism). Dieudonné sets the French Republican tradition against this; this has brought him accusations of anti-semitism. He is an entertaining comedian; unfortunately only a few of his performances are translated into English.

As the political establishment has lost more and more of its legitimacy, Dieudonné and Soral have gained in popularity, in the suburbs as well as among young people, and also in the French military and police. Dieudonné's characteristic gesture, la quenelle, has become cool, and even the military takes selfies when performing it in different places. The establishment has attempted to describe it as a reverse Hitler salute, but this has only made them look ridiculous.

Overall, E&R is an interesting phenomenon in today's Europe. Similar attempts have been made in other countries, where the Old Left has allied with Muslims. George Galloway and the Respect Party give an example, with old socialists and Muslims united in a party. Even the Swedish Green Party is an example; but here shortcomings in strategy come to the fore. The Islamists who became members of the Green

Party seem to have been entryists rather than being honestly interested in a Swedish green party. Such an alliance between native Progressive and Immigrant Muslims is not sustainable over time, not least of all for demographic reasons and because of entryism. However, this risk is less for E&R, as there are few gains associated with infiltrating an environment so demonized in the eyes of the establishment.

Soral is also an example of how an Old Left can move towards a New Right; Dieudonné is an example of how an anti-racist can reevaluate the importance of the sovereign nation state. Similar trends are to be found in several other European countries. More interesting than Galloway is the German Jürgen Elsässer, who once stood near the so-called "*Antideutsche*." He has, however, turned against this anti-racism related movement over the years, and today has adopted a view of society's fundamental conflict that resembles Soral's. In 2009 he founded "*Volksinitiative gegen das Finanzkapital*," welcoming both the Right and Muslims. Like Soral and Dieudonné, he sees the nation state as an important weapon to defend the people against global financial capitalism; and, like these, he has moved away from the toxic frame of political correctness, whose main function, anyway, is just to criticize everyone on the basis of political labels and/or religion.

Chapter 14

Dugin and the Fourth Political Theory

If you are pro global liberal hegemony you are the enemy.

— Dugin

Most of the movements we have studied so far are lacking what Machiavelli described as "weapons and money." Because of that they differ from Russian philosopher Alexander Dugin and the groups surrounding him. Dugin is a geopolitician, a professor in sociology, and he is politically active. He is sometimes described as Putin's adviser, which, however, seems to be an overstatement. Nonetheless, he has connections in the Russian power apparatus, and contacts in several other countries. He has built a network of ideas, institutions, and people around the basis of a deeply anti-liberal project. To understand the success behind his project we must consider the situation in Russia after the fall of the Soviet Union.

The Post-Soviet Background

...defense of the national interests of Russia is today organically merging with the struggle for socialism and Soviet types of democracy.

— Communist Party of the Russian Federation

The fall of the Soviet Union was for many Russians catastrophic. The economy deteriorated rapidly and at the same the time Russia's control of its destiny seemed threatened. Oligarchs controlled most of the economy and life expectancy was decreasing. The situation was politically acute, and for a while Russia even seemed to be crumbling.

In terms of conception-of-the-world, the Soviet Union had a different situation in comparison to Western Europe and the United States. The crisis was political and economic, and unlike in the West, post-Marxism had never taken hold. For example, the Soviet anthropologists did not embrace the fundamentally misleading theories regarding the human races and physical anthropology of Franz Boas. Human rights ideologies or queer theory had not gained credibility either. It is interesting that even before the fall of the Soviet Union, some circles in the Red Empire had started replacing Marxism with other ideas. When the communist parties in Western Europe started being influenced by American cultural Marxism, the Soviet Union was already developing in another direction. In the 1960s new ruralists had carried out a veritable conservative revolution that, among other things, completely dissociated from Western liberalism and instead acknowledged a new orthodox and ecological conception-of-the-world. This tendency is not unique—consider for example the ultra-nationalistic Juche ideology in North Korea and Romanian National Communism—but it had a geopolitical importance in the Soviet Union that was unmatched elsewhere.

When the Russian conception-of-the-world was crumbling, the Communist Party updated their program, moving toward a more national communistic view, combining patriotism and socialism. The party now states that different people will fulfill socialism on the basis of their historical continuity (a position which is compatible with both Spengler and the older Marx). To start from Lenin's theory on imperialism easily leads one to a positive view of national liberation movements. The geopolitical analysis of the communist party also gives Russia and the new Soviet Union an important global position as opponents to imperialism. During the fall of the Soviet Union, communists and radical nationalists were often on the same side; this was called the "brown-red alliance." Many nationalists are still socially aware and many communists are still nationalists. The consensus in Russia—what Gramsci called "the common sense"—is completely different from that of the West. In Russia, the consensus is a combination of cultural conservatism and social economy, whereas in the West it's the opposite—neoliberalism combined with political correctness.

Dugin

> The type of person I have in mind has nothing to do with the world of the bourgeoisie.
>
> — Julius Evola

During the 1980s a young Dugin was involved with the dissident movement; he was an anti-communist interested in Nietzsche, Evola, the Conservative Revolutionaries, and the New Right. Early on, Dugin had an interest in geopolitics, and because of this his thoughts on Communism changed upon the dissolution of the Soviet Union. The Soviet Union had been a land-based power, whereas the United States was an ocean-based power with values accompanying its status as such. Dugin reevaluated the historical role of the Soviet Union and the role that Marxism had played. He was now also interested in the so-called eurasianists with Savitskij and Troubetskoj, who held similar views on the Soviet Union.

In the early 1990s Dugin was one of the founders of the National Bolshevik Party, an attempt to combine ideas from the radical Left and the radical Right, which has similarities with the National Bolsheviks in Germany and the radical Germans surrounding Ernst Niekisch during the early 20th century. In 1998 Dugin left the National Bolsheviks and got closer to the corridors of power by becoming an adviser to the Duma. After Putin came into power, Dugin supported him with advice and recommendations. Dugin has consequently urged Putin to develop a full fledged conception-of-the-world and to push further in conflicts, both inside and outside of Russia.

Today Dugin is the leader of the International Eurasian Movement as well as the Center for Conservative Studies. He is an academic and the author of the geopolitical handbook *Foundations of Geopolitics*. On a metapolitical level Dugin is very active, making contacts both in Russia and internationally, including with Persian academics, Russian-Israeli Zionists, the North American New Right, and parts of the Greek left-wing party Syriza. Dugin co-wrote the new program for the Communist Party of the Russian Federations, he invited both Thiriart and de Benoist to Moscow. His geopolitical handbook is used by the Russian military.

Being a Russian-Orthodox Old Believer, Dugin also expresses admiration for Shia Islam and Iran. In Dugin's circles there are leaders of the Russian Muslims, Kalmykian Buddhists, as well as Jews and Catholics. Lately it seems that Dugin has approached the religious conception-of-the-world, for better or worse. Among other things his eschatological view has grown strong and his views on postmodernism as Satanism could prevent him from reaching readers from the Left. During the Ukrainian conflict Dugin was repeatedly brought to the media's attention. He was falsely described as Putin's close adviser and was put on sanction lists for supporting the separatists in Donbass. The sentimental Glenn Beck, among others, explained that Dugin was a really awful person. All things considered, Dugin is a very productive and educated man, and he is well worth a closer look.

The Fourth Political Theory

A conservative is a committed carrier of his national culture and tries to live according to its norms.

— DUGIN

Alongside of his work on geopolitics, Dugin is best known as the founder of the *Fourth Political Theory*. He claims that throughout modernity we have witnessed three political theories: liberalism, socialism, and Fascism. Since all three are inadequate, Dugin thought a new synthesis was needed. This view is not new. Even Marx could be thought of as a founder of a Fourth Political Theory, with elements from the conservatism of Hegel, the liberalism of Ricardo, and French socialism. Niekisch combined nationalism and Bolshevism. Rothbard sought allies in both the New Left as well as amongst the populists. Adinolfi and others developed a Third Position. The Hegelian and the National Marxist Reinhold Oberlercher has with his program tried to implement both the liberal, conservative, and socialist revolutions of the people. The position of de Benoist could also be called a Fourth Position, if we include non-conformists and personalists such as Mounier in the first political theory in a broader sense, socialists such as Proudhon and Sorel in the second, and the Conservative Revolutionaries in the third. Therefore, Dugin's approach is included in a longer tradition of synthesis, but is interesting in its own right.

When analyzing the pros and cons of the first three political theories Dugin finds that liberalism is built upon a false premise, on the individual. Liberalism has today exhausted its potential and is proceeding into postmodernism right before our eyes; at the same time it is spreading all over the world, erasing all unique and ancient cultures. Dugin considers postmodernism to be demonical. Ecological and cultural diversity is extinguished by a confirmative liberalism which, at the same time, is reducing man to a contemptible being. Instead of the individualities of early liberalism and modernity, we are today facing shattered sub- and trans-individual phenomena, constantly controlled by consumer society and various collective emotions. Postmodern man has lost meaning to life, as well as identity and a sense of higher values. This is a logical consequence of liberalism. Dugin can be read in combination with Domenico Losurdo's analysis of liberalism. Losurdo has undermined parts of the official mythology, showing that the American Revolution worsened the situation for large parts of the population, and that liberalism coexisted with slavery for a long time.

Losurdo's view is that liberalism historically has led to increased freedom for some but heavily reduced freedom for others. This concerns not only American slaves but also the poor Englishmen who lost both their freedom and their lives. Today there exist similar groups who do not benefit from freedom in a liberal sense.

The second political theory, socialism, was for a long time an opponent to liberalism, but one that did not enjoy final success. According to Dugin, the central concept of socialism is the social class. He empathizes with its positive aspects such as Soviet Communism and its anti-bourgeoisie and "spartan" elements. This is valuable reading for every socialist and could contribute to a necessary reinterpretation of what the real conflict during the Cold War was about. Was it really the classless society, or was it an alternative civilizational model, a new Sparta? This question would lie in the subconscious for many socialists and anti-imperialists, which would explain the confusion after the fall of the Soviet Union. Dugin's critique of the second theory is that it tried to create social justice without God. Soviet Communism was also missing a purposeful geopolitical theory and strategy, as well as an understanding of the ethnic question. Marxist Communism was never able to consciously understand why it was so successful in various agrarian communities. Dugin makes the argument that Communism in these countries took advantage of various ethnic and religious myths, for instance Russian-Orthodox and Jewish Messianism, but that the communists rarely understood this. Some socialists have approached Dugin's project, the most interesting being the Italian Costanzo Preve, a communist who focuses on what he described as a paradigm shift in the later Marx. While the middle-aged Marx saw the social class as the actor, the later Marx was influenced by studies of Russia and various "primitive peoples" to also see *society* as a possible actor. The consequence of such a shift in paradigm is of importance, as Lasch and Piccone implied. Preve called himself a communitarian and a communist, and was interested in the connection between socialism and geopolitics.

The third political theory was historical Fascism, which for a short period threatened the liberal order and was quenched through massive violence. The central concepts are race and the state. Here, Dugin finds positive aspects similar to the second theory. His main critique is its chauvinistic racism, which led to inhumanities and crucial mistakes. In Russia such racism would bring about a shattered empire, and the subjugation of its former parts to America. At the same time Dugin is not an anti-racist; he has written many positive words on some of the predecessors of the third political theory and has no problem cooperating with North American White Nationalists. Several of Dugin's influences come from the third theory, from Carl Schmitt and Heidegger to Wirth and the Ahnenerbe.

At the same time he analyzes how all these theories were modern even though both of the challengers were so to a lesser degree. He also describes why they failed to defeat liberalism; today he sees them as spent. Nowadays there are smaller groups that imitate either Lenin or Hitler, but larger movements will probably never arise. Dugin, however, noted that there is much value in the margins of those two ideologies; however, their valuable aspects must be liberated from the dead wholes. In many ways, it is a creative de- and reconstruction that Dugin is suggesting. Dugin notes that in the margin of these theories were thinkers that could still be of value when creating a fourth challenger, for instance Herman Wirth and the National Bolsheviks. One could also suggest the German father of cooperation Schulze-Delitzsch as a valuable thinker from the first theory, Proudhon, from the second (if anarchism actually fits in the category "second political theory") and Hans F. K. Günther from the third. As can be seen, the approach is fruitful and offers quite a few rewarding thought experiments. Dugin can, among other things, demonstrate how these modern theories had parts in common. For example how the racism of National Socialism had obvious parallels in liberal ideology, in its contempt of the poor, the ugly, and "developing countries." He also shows how our established conservatives of today are to be considered as liberals.

Dugin's project becomes yet more interesting when starting from Günther's thoughts on the impossibility of undoing or overcoming a historical era without simultaneously fulfilling it. This is extremely clear in relation to the two newer political theories. Dugin's thoughts on multipolarity and the right of civilizations to choose their own economic models takes the best from the historical Left's anti-imperialism and anti-capitalism, but also further develops them by removing their worst aspects. In the same way, focus on *ethnos*, civilizations, and geopolitics, but this time without chauvinistic racism and antisemitism, could be the fulfillment of the best historical Fascisms. From a similar perspective, Dugin's own version of 4PT also seems problematic, since his relationship with the first political theory is very critical. Dugin's anti-liberalism is so far reaching that it becomes alien for the northern and Western European ideals of freedom. Those constructing a 4PT for their own country should reconnect also to the liberal tradition, for example de Jouvenel or Rothbard. Freedom is a central Indo-European value, older than both urbanization and thalassocracies. In a Fourth Political Theory conservative freedoms must be included, such as freedom of speech, et cetera—not least of all because they are threatened in many "liberal" societies.

When contemplating Dugin's 4PT one should consider his anthropology as being at the core of it. According to Dugin, a human life is dignified under certain circumstances, but the modern world reduces it to something else. This is, from my point of view, the core of Dugin's conception-of-the-world and the motor of his tireless activism. Being a human is to be included in something bigger, some human kinship with a connection to the Sacred. Dugin's anthropology is versatile: being a person means being connected to politics, spirituality, and to social matters. However, with modern society comes the "post-society" in which the individual is shattered and destroyed. For Dugin this is a nightmare, something diabolical. Postmodernism is Satanism, with a will to do nothing, in which all differences must be dissolved and reconstructed, even though it is these differences and nuances that makes us human. The experience of the fall of the Soviet Union has led Dugin to regard the opponent as very powerful; it has after all defeated two political theories (and changed the first one beyond recognition). Therefore there is a natural need for allies. A benevolent interpretation of the 4PT is that Dugin is looking for friends rather than enemies. He is attempting to form a broad alliance including everyone, from old Marxists like Costanzo Preve to German identitarians—an alliance in which both Jews and Muslims have a position.

Dugin's willingness to create a synthesis comes through in his views on Julius Evola. He describes Evola as an impressive character, a traditionalist telling us to revolt against the modern world, against liberalism, materialism, and egalitarianism. At the same time Dugin thinks that the Left—a Left that is against the bourgeoisie, liberalism and capitalism—should also read Evola. According to Dugin, Evola's support for the conservatives and the capitalists rather than the proletarians and socialists is built on a misunderstanding. Evola confuses classes and castes, and fails to understand that workers are really people from the peasant caste being driven from their homes. Therefore workers cannot be identified with the fourth caste, those Evola saw as Shudras. The modern world is the bourgeoisie. Dugin reminds one of the Indian-influenced economist Ravi Batra, who states that the plutocratic concentration of riches, and the lawlessness associated with it, drives proletarianized warriors and priests to lead the masses in revolt, starting a new era of war. Batra thinks that not only proletarianized farmers exist, but warriors and priests as well. Dugin's new interpretation of Evola is in dispute however, as Brazilian philosopher Olavo de Carvalho instead identifies the capitalists with Kshatriyas and sees the intelligentsia and the bureaucrats as the threat.

It is interesting that Dugin does not consider conservatism as a political theory of its own. This is especially interesting, since he often describes himself as a conservative. One can argue that the Fourth Political Theory is conservatism combined with features from all three theories. Its central category is Heidegger's *Dasein*, instead of abstractions: it concerns our real identities; Dugin starts from *ethnos* and from religious tradition. One possible concern here is that *Dasein* is too difficult a concept to communicate, as compared with, for example, class. Dugin speaks of a conservative revolution, of the need for a new ideology and a new elite. As conservatives he includes parts of the Russian Left. What separates Dugin from many Western European conservatives is that he imagines that conservatives have a historical mission, that their project has a direction. It is not only about always just being ten steps behind the radical Western left-liberalism.

Dugin's relationship to nationalism and the nation state is an ambivalent one. He welcomes all allies against globalism, but basically his idea is the old European imperium. Such empires unify coordination of military defenses and foreign affairs with significant autonomy for the parts, which, according to Dugin, are often ethnic. This is Dugin's solution to the question of how to unify a continental perspective, which is necessary to meet the sea-based power, with respect for peculiar natures and *ethnos*, which is in many ways the reason for disagreement with the sea-based power to begin with. This is how he describes the difference between autonomy and sovereignty. For the lesser people in Russia he imagines autonomy as the ideal, through which they themselves are responsible for economy and education; full sovereignty is not an issue, since they are too small to be really independent in practice. This concerns not least the military. Here he partly reminds us of Thiriart's distinction between empire and dominion, as well as of the ideas of federations within the anarchist tradition. Dugin has a complex relationship to the question of *ethos*; he is an ethno-pluralist but not necessarily an ethno-nationalist.

At the same time, Dugin emphasize that the Fourth Political Theory will manifest differently in different countries, since cultures and their histories differ. A Swedish 4PT would probably find inspiration in both the Young Right as well as in C. J. L. Almqvist's classic *Den svenska fattigdomen* (On Swedish Poverty). The latter could favorably be compared to Dugin's ideas of a "poor north" and the true Nordic. A Swedish 4PT would also have interest in Strindberg and a deconstruction of the social-democratic experience which would identify both positive and negative aspects of the same. The rich tradition of poetry in Sweden would also be necessarily included, in which Ekelund, Ekelöf, and Hermelin would appear as valuable civilizational critics. Likely it would also reconnect to Swedish Gothicism and dive deeply into both the Swedish Lutheranism as well as the pagan heritage.

Dugin and Putin

> We can see that many Euro-Atlantic states have chosen a path by which they deny—or even fight—against their own roots, including their Christian roots that are the foundation of Western civilization … and these countries try to push this model on other countries, globally. I am deeply concerned that this will lead directly to the degradation and primitivization of culture, which would deepen the demographic and moral crisis in the West.
>
> — PUTIN

The relationship that Dugin has to Putin is interesting for several reasons. He supports the president but also critiques aspects of his politics. In *Putin vs Putin*, Dugin not only describes Putin's historical role, but also how he again and again fails to fulfill it. Dugin describes the situation preceding Putin's leadership as catastrophic—a one-sided capitulation without historic precedent. For a time the existence of the Russian Federation was at stake, and Atlanticists were infiltrating the government. Neoliberal economists enforced a "shock therapy," which was catastrophic for the Russians, and the constituent republics seemed to be breaking off from the federation. This came to a head in the Chechen Republic. The situation was marked by a corrupt elite loyal to the United States. It was often anti-Russian in its attitude, and much of its time was spent in looting and silently watching as the country was shattered and weakened. In short, it was constituted by what in late Marxist theory are called *compradors*, but within a very short time frame. The situation was so obviously pathological that it was only a matter of time before the masses would react. It was then that some authorities gathered to find a new model that could maintain the legitimacy of the system without compromising the people. The model of choice was "patriotism + liberalism." A new leader would emerge, who would continue the economical politics that was turning Russia into a colony, but now with a patriotic image. That leader was Putin.

Putin, however, turned out to be more independent than expected. His patriotism and realism meant that he could successfully defend the interests of Russia against the oligarchs, against certain governors with separatist ambitions, against anti-Russian media, against Chechen agitators, and against the United States. Soon Dugin came to regard him as a good leader for Russia, and Dugin has now supported him for many years. There have not been any alternatives, and as a person Putin is quite superior as compared to Obama or Merkel. Putin's historical role is to defend Russia. Putin has some features that makes him particularly fit to fulfill this role. He is a Christian conservative, has a past in the secret service, and is a realist when it comes to international relationships. During his years as a leader, Putin has spoken straightforwardly about everything from NATO's destructive politics and its attempt to create a unipolar world, to what the current policies in the West are leading to in the form of demographic and moral crisis.

However, Dugin thinks that Putin lacks an intentional geopolitical principle. Putin handles practical politics, like the increasing integration with neighboring countries and the outmaneuvering of the oligarchs that for a while took over both natural resources and policy-making. A well formulated vision is missing, a clear geopolitical heritage. Because of that, Dugin is uncertain of the future of Russia. Among other things, his uncertainty includes Putin's relatively liberal economic policy and his careful position with regard to Ukraine. This is what Dugin means with *Putin vs Putin*—the historical role of Putin vs Putin the real person and his politics. Dugin wants Putin to develop a genuine conception-of-the-world, which is necessary if a Russian path is ever going to be actualized. That would also mean that Putin could more easily leave a legacy to his successor.

Novorossiya

> The republics of Donetsk, Luhansk, and Kharkiv will be holy places for the Russian cultures, the Russian spirit and the Russian renaissance identity.
>
> — Dugin

Dugin received an explosive geopolitical punch with the events after Maidan in Ukraine 2014, when the president was removed from office and the leadership of the coup moved closer to NATO and the EU, and began to question the rights of the Russian-speaking citizens. The following events, during which parts of Donbass broke loose from Ukraine and a civil war started, were a real baptism of fire for the Fourth Political Theory and its supporters. Their role has been compared with that of Spain in 1936-1939. Dugin was wholeheartedly on the side of the separatist republicans, and warned of the existence of fifth and sixth columns in Russia. The fifth column is the relatively small group of liberals called "the Englishman within" and the sixth column is more dangerous, lying as it does within the corridors of power.

Volunteers with different ideologies from many countries have fought for the independence of the republic of Donbass. Using Dugin's terminology, this has implicated both the second and third political theories, including everything from National Socialists to communists, orthodox Christians and pagans. This confirms in many ways his theory of a Fourth Political Theory and new lines of conflict. It is worth mentioning that this also includes the opposing side, which comprises everything from Ukrainian nationalists and National Socialists that had traveled there for that occasion, to Crimean Tatar Muslims, Jihadi that had gone there in support, Zionist oligarchs and Atlanticist liberals—although the latter group is rarely seen on the battlefield anymore.

Even on the Internet one has been able to follow the emergence of a sphere in which the support for the new Russian republics goes beyond historical categories such as "Left" and "Right." It is here that we can find for instance The Saker, a former military specialist describing himself as an orthodox "monarchist of the people" in the tradition of Dostoyevsky. The Saker is involved in both Ukraine and Syria, driven by a resistance to a monumentally trite and dangerous establishment. What makes him represent a new historical reality—what de Benoist would call transversal—is that he is cited by people from the Left and the Right. Parts of the Old Right and the Old Left sympathize with the new Russian separatists, as well as parts of the New Right and the New Left.

Geopolitics and Eurasia

The Russians were separated from the West religiously through Byzantium, and geopolitically thanks to the Mongols and Turks.

— TRUBETSKOY

Dugin is an eminent geopolitician. His geopolitics often cross over to metaphysical geography, but at the same time he is both knowledgeable and realistic in his analyses. His geopolitical handbook contains the best presentation of the history of geopolitical theory I have read, in which all the more established names such as Rudolf Kjellén, Alfred Mahan, Huntington, and Fukuyama are described in detail. Dugin also discuss important geopoliticians that have been European patriots, from Lohausen and Parvulesco to the Gaullist geopolitics and the New Right. Dugin compares geopolitics and Marxism, claiming that both disclose aspects of reality beyond the rhetorical: behind the speeches on "rogue states" and "human rights" there are often real interests at play.

The core of Dugin's geopolitics is the distinction between tellurocracy and thalassocracy, between land-based and sea-based powers. This has a long history; it goes back to the wars between Sparta and Athens, Rome and Carthage. Those powers develop different types of civilizations and values, and the conservative Dugin wholeheartedly sides with the land-based powers. Tellurocracy, "the eternal Rome," is imprinted with conservatism, holism, idealism, heroism, collectivism (for example *ethnos* instead if individuals), and values such as faith, honor, and loyalty. Dugin also refers to it as military-authoritarian, and describes it as an ideaocracy. Regardless of whether it's Soviet Communism or the German Reich, the continental power is driven by an idea. Thalassocracy is instead driven by individualism, change, and the value of merchants. The sea-based powers also tend to become oligarchies, controlled by financial powers, regardless of whether we are looking at Carthage or the United States. Dugin describes Thalassocracy as "democratic." This implies that one, as a conservative, should be aware of the connection between ideology and geopolitics; the struggle between hedonism and heroism also has a geopolitical aspect.

Dugin believes that our time-period is being shaped by the Thalassocracies' attempt to dominate the world. Against this attempt stands Russia (when he wrote the handbook he was rather skeptical about China as an ally, but that was some decades ago). The Russian Federation is central in many geopolitical theories, since the so-called Heartland is located there. From the Heartland the entirety of Eurasia can be reached and empires can be built; because of this, American foreign policy has for a long time tried to stop the growth of a Eurasian power. In Halford Mackinder's words:

> Those who control Eastern Europe control the Heartland; those who control the Heartland control the world islands, and those who control the world islands control the world.

A central part of this theory concerns the so-called Rimlands, the Eurasian coasts. Spykman stated that "he who controls the Rimlands controls Eurasia." Hence the attempts to contain the Soviet Union, and the attempts on the part of the Soviet Union to reach warm water ports. With Russia as a starting point Dugin strives for the growth of a bloc of resistance, *inter alia* around the shoulder Moscow-Tehran-Yerevan.

Starting with Savitsky's geopolitics, Dugin postulates that the mistake of the Third Reich was putting blood at the center and underestimating the importance of soil. This occurred because the circle around Haushofer did not receive attention. Savitsky spoke of topogenesis, of the importance of geography for the creation of order. Dugin cites Thiriart:

> It is necessary to create a synthesis of non-Marxist Communism with non-racist National Socialism.

Dugin's geopolitics partly starts with geography, partly with religions and partly with *ethnos*. This reminds one of Lohausen's way of "thinking in people" and "thinking in continents." For instance, he mentions in the analysis of Ukraine that there is a geopolitical danger in Crimea's belonging to Ukraine, but also in the potential friction between the different ethnic and religious loyalties in the country (from Crimean Tatars to Russians). The conclusion is that Ukraine, geopolitically, lacks a *raison dêtre*, but also that a union between Russia and Ukraine is problematic. Better then to reconstruct the region. Regarding the

Baltic Region, Dugin uses Kjellén as a starting point and considers the region as being tied to Germany. The goal here is, instead, a Baltic Sea area consisting of Finland, Sweden, Estonia, Denmark, Norway, Karelia, and Germany, around a recreated Prussia. This could even mean that Russia would give up parts of Kaliningrad. However, he views Poland and Lithuania as belonging to another cultural and historical setting. Settings, religions, and ethnos are the recurring concepts in Dugin´s geopolitical analysis, together with civilizations. The economical aspect plays a relatively small part, which is logical in an expression of the perspective of the land-based powers.

It is interesting that Dugin's geopolitics often has metaphysical aspects, as in *The Mysteries of Eurasia*. He mentions Hyperborea, the mystical north, and its characteristics (light, purity, and unity). He also brings up its connection to a certain Nordic type of person, described as a *Sonnenmensch*. Here Dugin comes close to both Ariosophists and Nordicists in their description of the Nordic person. However, unlike them he states that this originally was a race, but it is more like a human type today. He also brings up the traditional view of America as "the greenland," "the land of the dead," "the false Atlantis," and notes the dismal significance of its discovery through Columbus. The distinction between sea and land plays a central role with Dugin, and he also speaks of such things as different types of civilizations connected to the forest and the steppe. Dugin mentions how the "rich North" stands against the "poor South," but talks also about the possibility of a "poor North." He is then referring to an ascetic North, struggling against the values of money in favor of timeless values. It is often an intriguing read, even though it is permeated by a far-driven dualism.

Dugin continues further to develop the theories of the so-called Eurasianists, who were often Russian intellectuals in exile. They thought of civilizations as unique units. From this followed their turning against the liberal claim of universality. Liberalism had been created in a specific civilization and was not necessarily applicable in Russia. Several Eurasianists predicted that Russian civilization would outlive the Soviet experiment and that Russia would return to monarchy and faith, among other things through an inner change of Bolshevism to a temporary "Left-Eurasianism." One interesting predecessor of Eurasianism was Piotr Savitsky. He thought that the West was affected by a dangerous delusion: while other civilizations strove to subordinate the economy to other values, economy, in the form of a "militant economism," had run amok in the West. Both liberalism and Marxism were expressions of this, both being examples of one-dimensional economism. The economic growth that followed came at a high cost in terms of spiritual and human values. Savitsky viewed Russia as the heir, not only to the other Rome—Byzantium—but also to Genghis Khan. Geopolitically this meant that Russia had acquired the same territory as the Mongols once had. Trubetskoy is similar to Savitsky; he emphasizes that a system seeking social justice without God is not sustainable. He thought that Russia was a civilization of its own, and saw the West as a threat towards the rest of the world, and at the same time he described orthodox Russia as an ideaocracy. Dugin noticed that the secularized Christianity of the West was the source of liberalism and that the secularized Christianity of the East was the source of Communism. He does not consider this a coincidence.

Dugin describes the globalist project as a threat against all unique cultures of the world and all civilizations, and states that a regional phenomenon, liberalism, is spreading throughout the world. He considers neo-Eurasianism as an opposition against this process, a way of defending the diversity of "nations, cultures, religions, languages, values and philosophical systems." Globalization entails a unipolar and Atlanticist process. In contrast to this Dugin wants a pluriverse, a multipolar world. Eventually he imagines a few geopolitical zones— Schmittian *Grossraums*, with North- and South-America as one, and Europe together with Africa and the Middle-East as the second. It is interesting that after the victory of Trump he has changed his view on the United States; he now speaks of the "swamp"—an expression he has borrowed from the new president. The swamp was earlier localized in the United States, but is now deterritorialized. Dugin defines the swamp as liberalism, postmodern culture, and the transnational capital, while Trump seems to refer to the corrupt elites as the swamp. The definitions are at least partly overlapping. Dugin's distinction between land- and sea-based powers reminds us also of the crack within the United States, between a relatively land-based middle America and the more liberal coasts. It concerns both different social models and different views of the world, which is worth considering when we come in the next chapter to make the acquaintance of Sam Francis.

Ethno-sociology

> Ethno-sociology is not only the sociology of ethnic groups. It is something completely different—it is a special method for the study of human societies as the development of their original and basic ethnic structure.
>
> — DUGIN

One useful and exciting initiative from Dugin is what he refers to as ethno-sociology. He has developed a sociology and anthropology starting from important thinkers like Bachofen, Tönnies, Geertz, Dumézil, and Gumilev. Dugin describes *ethnos* as the first step in the history of a society, but also as the foundation in every society, including complex societies that are no longer formally built upon ethnic groups, but which instead describe themselves as nations or communities. Dugin defines ethnos as a group of people who think they have a shared heritage—something which they could have to varying degrees. They have shared traditions; Dugin describes the holy as the essence of *ethnos*. In the pure *ethnos* there is no individual; *ethnos* is unity.

History reveals that the pure ethnic society is disappearing, although the ethnic remains and affects its development, even when it is not visible. The first step is the rise of a people. Like Gumplowicz and

Gobineau, Dugin views the people as the result of a struggle between two distinct *ethnos*. One *ethnos* conquers another and the state emerges. The process continues, however, with the nation and society, and after that civil society, global society, and then the post-society. At this point we find ourselves in a context that is post-human, post-identitarian, and post-individual. Without Dugin's ethno-sociological perspective it can be difficult to understand his views on *Dasein*, on imperium and autonomy, and his belief that postmodernism is satanic. *Dasein* and *ethnos*, are intertwined; the autonomy for small *ethnos* also becomes logical given the results of ethno-sociology. In a good society *ethnos* does not act blindly, but consciously. Dugin's views on postmodernism as satanical are also logical, given its connection to the post-human.

Many of the thinkers mentioned by Dugin are highly interesting, not least Lev Gumilev, who was the son of the poets Nikolay Gumilev and Anna Akhmatova. His father was executed by the Bolsheviks when Lev was nine years old, and his mother was subject to long-lasting persecutions that also affected the boy. He grew up in the gulag archipelago but would later make an academic career as a historian, geographer, and ethnologist. Gumilev took an interest in the people of the steppe, and studied, among others the Khazars. He also studied ethno-genesis—the birth and development of ethnic groups—especially in connection to their geographical environment and the biosphere. This association is of interest and can be linked to thoughts on bio-regionalism and ethno-development. An ethnic group is therefore a part of its natural environment and can coexist with it. When newcomers arrive there is often a change in this environment, since they are lacking the relationship that the original inhabitants have. This provides an additional ecologically based argument *against* large-scale immigration, and *for* the real autonomy of ethnic groups and local communities. Ethnic groups have, according to Gumilev, their own development. Many of the ethnic groups that today seem primitive and stable, are in the final phase, the phase of relics, which in theory could last forever. So the question Gumilev asks himself is when the African Khoisan people had their acmatic phase.

Gumilev describes how ethnic groups historically have created communities that, when living among each other, thought of each other as closely related. The Greek city-states fought limited civil wars, reserving full-scale wars mainly for the "barbarians." After the victory against the Persians, the Greeks who had fought side by side with the Persians were executed, while the Persian soldiers were spared, the first being traitors and the latter strangers. During Medieval times the Catholic people of Europe were so close that they could fight side-by-side in the Crusades, while the surrounding world called them "Franks." Even during periods of political fragmentation, the Muslim world enjoyed a similar kinship. Similar traits have been found amongst the steppe people and in the orthodox sphere around the Byzantines. Gumilev calls these groups of *ethnos*, *super-ethnos*—a concept that bears a strong resemblance to Peter Turchin's meta-ethnic groups.

The concept of *super-ethnos* is both interesting and relevant. We saw how a European *super-ethnos* was shaped during the 1930s, when so-called nationalists wanted to avoid a war between brothers, and when they could fight together against Eastern Bolshevism. This *super-ethnos* had historical preconditions for also including the Slavic peoples, possibly also parts of the Middle East and North Africa. Today we see something similar: both the European Union and the collaboration between nationalistic parties of the European descendant's world are built upon the European peoples forming a *super-ethnos*. Gumilev also describes how ethnic groups sometimes can create sub-ethnic elements, which have the ability to undertake specific tasks. In Europe this has mainly concerned the aristocracy; in the Ottoman world it is tempting to include the Janissaries as a sub-ethnic group. Gumilev includes the Cossacks, Pomors, and Siberians as Russian sub-ethnic groups. These groups had their own traits, but were still a part of the Russian *ethnos*.

One can also see that Gumilev does not mean to say that the appearance of a *super-ethnos* demands that the different ethnic groups be intertwined. He differs for example from Francis Parker Yockey, who claimed that a European Empire presupposes the formation of a European nation and a European race. Gumilev proceeds from other *super-ethnos*, in which the subsumed ethnic groups, even though high in solidarity, consisted of separate groups. This also has relevance for the Eurasian project, which is based on historically close relationships between the Russian *ethnos* and the steppe peoples. Dugin seems to think that Russia, with its imperial tradition, has the prerequisites to form an alliance and a *super-ethnos* that can stand against the American empire and global capitalism.

The X-factor that Gumilev wants to identify in the births and lives of the ethnic groups he studies, he finds in what calls *passionarity*: an individual who puts his self-preservation on the back shelf, and who is capable of fighting and dying for something greater than himself has passionarity or drive. This "something greater" can be both power and honor, and for this reason Gumilev includes Napoleon, Sulla, and Alexander the Great in this type of men. It can also be religion, which similarly drove Jan Hus and Jean d'Arc. Gumilev cannot fully explain why larger groups with higher drive show up at certain points in history rather than at others, but he notes that in order for them to succeed with their project they must be surrounded by others with at least almost as high a drive. The Vikings are a good example of this, also the men and women surrounding Muhammad and Jean d'Arc. The curse of Hannibal was that his men did not have enough drive, regardless of his own courage and capacity.

This driving force can also affect larger groups, through what Gumilev calls induced drive. This is a form of imitation, and its effect vanishes when the source is removed. This drive is also a source for the emergence of new kinships that eventually transform into ethnic groups. At the same time, as a trait it is always vulnerable. People with high drive expose themselves to such great risks that they tend to become extinct, and therefore periods of high drive are followed by calmer periods. Gumilev notes that the Icelandic descendants of the Vikings were later unable to defend themselves, neither against Algerian nor Danish pirates.

What can keep the driving force in an ethnic group high is if its carriers produce many children before heading out to war and dying. Gumilev states that in Medieval Europe, this often took the shape of bastards, illegitimate sons of the aristocrats, who not rarely led their own units. Over time the degree of drive decreases and the *ethnos* moves towards the relics phase. Gumilev sorts people into three groups: those with high drive, those with low but stable drive ("individuals with harmony"), and those with "sub-drive," the latter being strictly inferior. Gumilev gives the proletarians of late Rome as an example, who were always demanding bread and circus, and refused to acknowledge the situation of Rome or to defend their homeland. Gumilev notes that neither he himself nor anyone else has mourned over the fact that Gaiseric slaughtered these elements.

Gumilev also studies the different types of ethnic relationships. Generally he does not consider marriage across ethnic lines as something positive; rather it tends to precipitate negative and dissolute tendencies. When two or more ethnic groups coexist, this tends to cause conflict, what Gumilev calls *xenia*. One example of *xenia* is the coexistence of Walloons and Flemings, both of which belong to the European *super-ethnos,* but which still have a strained relationship. When two *super-ethnos* collide the situation is even more problematic. Then one *super-ethnos* usually abolishes the other. One can bear this in mind when considering the European immigration policies that, for instance, have led to millions of members of the Muslim *super-ethnos* residing in the heart of Europe. Regardless of one's opinion about this, the conflicts that have arisen are completely predictable.

An exceptional case of coexistence of different *super-ethnos* is the creation of what Gumilev refers to as a *chimera*, which means that a group from one *super-ethnos* conquers a group from another *super-ethnos*. Gumilev thinks that chimeras are deeply negative. He cites the Christian Germans power over Baltic heathens as an example, as well as early Bulgaria. Other examples are slave communities, and in the present time mass immigration is the cause of the rise of new chimeras.

Dugin's ethno-sociological perspective has enabled cooperation with many of the population groups of the old Soviet Union. To no one's surprise, there is a division of the Eurasian movement in, for instance, Tatarstan. Chechen godfather and nationalist Noukhaev also approached Dugin's Eurasianism toward the end of his life. This without abandoning his loyalty towards his people and his faith, and without ceasing to see himself as a barbarian superior to the decadent West.

The Saker has emphasized that Russia is a civilization rather than a nation, and that Eurasia can be compared to an ocean. An ocean of steppes with islands of cities. The ethnic groups form different islands, but have no absolute borders. The Saker's view is akin to Dugin's remark that "nation as a concept is capitalist and Western." Dugin will not abandon what transcends the nation, *ethnos*, nor the civilization that can unite them. At the same time he turns against the theory of the struggle of the civilizations. He states that they are united by a common enemy in the form of liberalism and degeneration.

What Can We Learn from Dugin?

It can be difficult for an American or Western European to directly imitate Dugin's recipe for success, since it is built upon special historical circumstances. To some extent Richard Spencer and the Alternative Right are trying to keep the same relationship to Trump that Dugin has to Putin (Weev speaks of an "Evolan criticism," inspired by how Evola in his time criticized Mussolini from the Right). It is not an impossibility, even though the situation in the disintegrated Soviet Union was different from that of the United States of today. Russian and Anglo-Saxon conceptions-of-the-world also differ on many points.

What we can take out of Dugin's thought is the Fourth Political Theory as a concept. There are elements in older ideologies that can be useful today, but one does not have to buy the entire package. One can create one's own synthesis. Today's growing populism is in a way a synthetic type of populism, with elements from nationalism, socialism and liberalism. Even Trump has a flexible relationship to the already established opinions in American politics. This also means that we do not need to be restricted to the older lines of conflict and alliances. Dugin seeks friends to a greater extent than enemies, and has gathered Christian, Muslims, and Jews around his project. In a similar way it would be possible for the American Right to separate parts of the Democrat alliance, for example Afro-Americans or Asian-Americans, and instead get them on their side. Then the creation of an American imperium can begin, with autonomy for the different American people. In Europe the situation is different; there it is less about the historical European peoples and more about newcomers. However, Dugin's thoughts of a *super-ethnos* can be of value here as well.

Dugin is also an exemplary metapolitician. He has tied both quality people and a number of valuable institutions to his project. This ranges from media to think tanks and educational alternatives, which could perpetuate the anti-liberal consensus. His ideas constitute a whole and an alternative to liberalism. Connecting to this is, to borrow an expression from Thiriart, a "Piedmont of our time," independent Russia. The relationship to Russia is both good and bad. On one hand Russia is a threatened and resourceful challenger to the globalists, on the other hand it can be difficult to know where Russian imperialism ends and 4PT begins.

One of Dugin's factors for success is that he obviously has fun while writing, which also makes it fun to read him. When he mixes Ariosophical thoughts about Hyperborea and the North with national communistic and anti-imperial thoughts, Dugin is genuinely rewarding. His clear anthropological ideals are also appealing; his geopolitical reasoning is especially relevant for those wanting to understand and influence our time.

Dugin answers challenges from both Maurras and Castoriadis. He is a theist Christian and gives religion a central place in his conception-of-the-world. His focus on imperium, *ethnos* and autonomy is also an innovative respond to Castoriadis. Dugin is however not without some flaws. He does not write much about ecology or economy, and can sometimes have an overly dualistic tendency. The North European ideal of freedom is not as important for Dugin. Robert Steuckers has described a partially alternative Eurasianism that proceeds from the theory that the Indo-Europeans were the first to control the Eurasian steppes. When the Cossacks arrived that was in a sense a *reconquista*. Such Eurasianism is more Indo-European and freedom-oriented. In conclusion, Dugin is very much a rewarding acquaintance, especially when considering the appeal of adjusting his thoughts to one's own reality and one's own part of the world with seriousness.

Chapter 15

Trump

I don't have time for political correctness.

— Donald Trump

The American presidential election of 2016 was characterized by deep polarization. To both sides, it was *real* in a way that no other election had been in recent years. It was expected to be a watershed moment in American electoral history and many White Americans in particular saw it as the last chance to take their country back. This feeling had, ironically, been reinforced by liberals and the politically correct who gloatingly and repeatedly reminded this group that they were soon to become a minority in the United States.

Victory and the presidency went to Donald Trump, celebrity and billionaire. During the campaign he broke the conventions of how a presidential candidate was supposed to express opinions, which traditionally required a candidate to employ political correctness as both rulebook and discourse. Among other things, he noted that *"when Mexico sends its people they're not sending their best,"* he called Hillary Clinton a corrupt liar, and he promised to "drain the swamp" (the swamp here being the corrupt establishment). This riled up many journalists, Brahmins, and members of the New Class, but also made him beloved to many parts of the American people. They had long since tired of political correctness, and Trump became a representative of the people, in spite of his fortune. Similarly, he is a leading figure for a kind of populism, both in the American tradition and globally, which is gaining ground. But who is this Trump, and how would we view him through a historical lens?

Trump's Background

> Without passion, you don't have energy; without energy, you have noth-
> ing. Nothing great in the world has been accomplished without passion!
> — DONALD TRUMP

Donald Trump, born in 1946 of both German and Scottish ancestry,
comes from a wealthy family. His father was a real estate businessman. Donald was lively and tough as a child, and would attend the
New York Military Academy. He has appointed many generals to
high positions in his administration, saying that he appreciates the
military way of thinking. After attending the Academy he studied
economics at the University of Pennsylvania, before taking over the
family business in 1971. In Moldbugian terms, Trump has features of
both *Vaisya, Brahmin,* and *Optimate.* His German roots are especially
interesting if we consider HBD-theory: if White America consists of
different "nations," the German-American nation has been politically
marginalized since the Second World War. During this time, Trump
has spent his adult life in Jewish and Yankee circles. In many ways
there is a certain Janus quality to the man, with each foot in a different
environment.

Trump has been involved in many real estate deals, including the
construction of Trump Tower. He has also done business pertaining
to sports and beauty pageants. His participation in wrestling shows
and the TV-show *The Apprentice,* as well as his books on how to get
rich, have made him famous to many Americans. On a number of oc-
casions he has shown interest in starting a political career, either as a
Republican or as part of the Reform Party.

Trump is a Protestant. In one interview he called the denomination
"a wonderful religion." He has Jewish grandchildren and a daughter
who has converted to Judaism, which he has described as something
positive. Trump is not a traditionalist, but there are some interesting
aspects to him. In *How to get Rich* he brings up his relationship to Carl

Jung, whom he warmly recommends, and notes that psychology is useful when trying to understand one's environment. Jung is useful for achieving personal growth. Trump also mentions the Jungian concept of the *persona*, the "mask" with which we face the world, and the risk that we *become* our persona. He quotes Jung:

> Your vision will become clear only when you look into your heart. Whoever looks outside, dreams. Who looks inside awakens.

The connections between Trump and the fairly Anglo-Saxon tradition of positive thinking are also of interest. He heartily recommends Norman Vincent Peale, a proponent of a particular combination of psychology and Christianity. James O'Meara of Counter-Currents has written a series of articles linking Peale to Neville Goddard, a more metaphysical author. Among other things, Goddard related "The Law," a technique for creating your own reality through visualization of a desired condition. He interpreted the Bible esoterically, referenced Blake, and emphasized the connection between God and fantasy—the human capacity to imagine different things. Like the founders of Theosophy and modern day Nation of Islam, Goddard is supposed to have come into contact with the timeless Tradition through mystical teachers. In Goddard's case, it was an Ethiopian Jew named Abdullah who taught him Hebrew, Kabbalah, and how to interpret the Bible esoterically. The link between Abdullah and Trump is rather indirect, but it serves as an interesting little piece in the history of ideas and forms part of the background of today's positive thinking. It is clear that Trump assumes that life can to a large extent be influenced by the attitude and energy one faces it with.

Trump as a person has been described in many different ways. He can often seem like a pompous boor, an impertinent narcissist who speaks before he thinks. The co-author of *Art of the Deal* would eventually come to compare their joint venture to putting lipstick on a pig. This isn't the whole truth, however. Trump himself has mentioned how much it meant to him when an expert said of his buildings that they show he has an eye for beauty. In *How to get Rich* Trump relates how our society contains too many distractions and too much noise, and states that we have trouble handling silence. As a result, he tries to set aside three hours a day for uninterrupted contemplation and spends much time reading. He underscores the importance of positive thinking—of what he, like CasaPound, calls *altitude*. There is a link here to Nietzsche's warning against *ressentiment*, and Trump believes it is important to let go of negativity as swiftly as possible. He compares negativity with both bacteria and fear, but he has also brought up the importance of sometimes being able to avenge injustices, as well as his unwillingness to shake hands with people.

To a European, Trump may seem strange. He is open about his success. In both speeches and books he adapts his language so that it is intelligible to a ten-year-old, even though he is well-read and possesses a higher education, which suggests that he has made a deliberate attempt to reach the entire population rather than just parts of it. The Trumpian self-image is quite alien to us Europeans, but is less remarkable in America. The man himself speaks of it with a certain dispassion and claims that if you are to succeed you can't be too humble. When he describes his employees, however, he reveals a certain humility. Here he seems more like a general than just an employer, which may prove an interesting characteristic when he moves from being a businessman to being a president. Considering his interest in Jung and his habit of speaking of himself in third person, it may in any case be hard to determine where Trump the *persona* ends and Trump the person begins.

The Background to Trump

> To those on the Left that pushed identity politics too far: Live by the
> Sword, Die by the Sword.
>
> — STEVE HSU

Trump is often described, pejoratively, as a populist. This may seem strange since populism and democracy should be synonymous and most of those who mock populism see themselves as democrats. Those who call him a populist often neglect to mention the reasons that a populist could attain the presidency in this day, since that would suggest the failures of the politicians with whom the accusers identify, and indeed the failure of the entire liberal order.

The support for Trump is very much a reaction to both failure and betrayal. This is partly related to the social elite having interests that diverge from those of the people. Among other things, the elites want to replace the people with cheaper labor—which is obviously not in the best interest of the people. However, this phenomenon can also be explained by the interplay between meta- and sociopolitics, and what Faye has called a blocked society. The elite adopts a certain world view, not just to keep the people in check, but also to maintain unity within the elite itself. This can lead to the elite losing its capacity to think clearly—it finds itself lacking both the terminology and the ability to understand when the prevailing policies will lead to disaster. The problem is further aggravated when the leadership style is collectivist and pursues conformity.

In the United States, the main issue is demographic displacement. In 1980, half of all White Americans lived in a county in which nine out of ten were White. Today, it is only a quarter. The speed of change has been made clear to many, who are also given reminders by a gloating liberal Left. From a historical and sociological perspective, it would be more remarkable were people *not* to notice that they were undergoing such a displacement, than for them to do so.

At the same time, the establishment has evolved into what Trump calls a swamp. Their interests are not those of the people and they are more loyal to each other, whether the part of the establishment in question is Goldman Sachs, the military-industrial complex, the two major parties, or the press. In practice, it has long been impossible for the people to solve this problem by voting, but this fact still acts as a fertile breeding ground for both populism and general antipathy against politicians. In parallel with this, the emergence of the Internet and alternative media has made a third power possible. This became apparent during the election campaign, when Wikileaks revealed a number of disconcerting facts about the Clinton camp and their ties to the media. The media was now partially outplayed as creators of *common sense*.

The problems that have made Trump's election victory possible do not pertain uniquely to the United States. They have, to varying degrees, stricken every country inhabited by people of European ancestry; they are connected to the liberal order. As a result there are similar forms of populism in most of these countries, even though one can distinguish between an older and a younger tradition in Europe. The older is represented by NPD in Germany, BNP in Great Britain, and Golden Dawn in Greece. It is typically characterized by a more ethnic definition of the nation and skepticism toward both Atlanticism and liberalism, and commonly toward Israel, as well. The younger tradition is represented by, among others, UKIP in Great Britain, and AfD in Germany. It is generally more liberal in its conception-of-the-world and has a more open definition of the nation. In Duginian terms, the older tradition is often an expression of the third political theory while the younger is a critique of aspects of current policy from the perspective of the first political theory. This means that as long as the liberal order works, if barely, parties like AfD will be more respectable and gain more voters than NPD, but when the crisis becomes obvious the situation might be the reverse. In this context, Trump should be considered much closer to UKIP than to the BNP, even though he personally is different from the leaders of most European parties.

Trump as a Modern Day Napoleon?

Drain the swamp.

— Donald Trump

In *Great Again* Donald Trump describes the United States as a land with large problems. Its infrastructure brings the Third World to mind, unemployment is widespread, and neither enemies nor allies respect the country any more. He holds the establishment, politicians, and the media in particular responsible. Against this state of affairs he pits the middle class and the country's workers, whom he promises to help.

It is interesting to compare Trump with Dugin's thoughts on a Fourth Political Theory. There are, to some extent, links between his politics and a 4PT with clearly American features. Such a thing has considerably stronger liberal features than its Russian counterpart. Trump is primarily a liberal, especially in matters pertaining to economics and historical liberties, such as the right to bear arms and the freedom of speech. Trump's economic policy is also liberal at its heart—he has strong faith in the power of competition. He is critical of the worsening conditions of the school system, with teachers suffering reduced authority, and education becoming politicized. He is also critical of powerful teachers' unions, however, and supports the right to pick one's school. Trump also supports a simplification of the tax system, which would make it easier to understand and reduce the tax burden of the poor while at the same time creating economic growth. Trump's plan for creating jobs through extensive investments in infrastructure and the military is also fundamentally compatible with liberalism. The focus on poorly functioning infrastructure is reminiscent of older liberals like List and Naumann. In many ways, Trump's is an older version of liberalism than today's postmodern liberal establishment, in every sense, from nation to gun laws.

Trump's liberalism is not unconditional, however. He has been accused of being a protectionist, and has criticized the free movement of both people and capital. He looks upon the export of jobs from the United States with disapproval, and he has been outspoken on the vulnerable situation of American labor. What we see here is a vaguely socialist streak in Trump, since he prioritizes the social over the economic in this case. Trump connects with antiwar activists both on the Old Right and the New Left. The Trump that wrote *Great Again* does not seem ill-disposed toward a war with Iran, though, and he describes that country's nuclear program as a deadly threat to Israel. Trump also finds the market lacking when it comes to the sick, and he believes that the poor, too, must have access to health care. He has, for many years, also been an activist for the country's veterans.

Trump also connects with the third political theory, though not much. He is an opponent of abortion, he is a nationalist, and he speaks positively about God and the military, but not much else. Many *idées fixes* of the second and third political theory are conspicuously absent with Trump. He is an American exceptionalist, though, and often returns to the point that America is both a "very special place" and the "best country in the world." A close relationship to Israel also seems to be of central importance to Trump.

All things considered, "Trumpism" is more liberal than the second or third political theory. The first political theory, liberalism, has historically been compatible both with nationalism, with a Christianity which does not intrude in the political sphere, with certain interventions in the market, and with protectionism. It has, in the form of political correctness, mutated into a version which pits itself against both Christianity and protectionism, and in light of this Trump represents a return to an older liberalism.

Geopolitically it is still unclear whether Trump is an isolationist or if he is going to employ an aggressive foreign policy against countries like China and Iran. *Great Again* suggests that he both wants the United States to possess such a military superiority that everybody respects the country, and that he does not want to make commitments to allies who don't want to share in the costs. Trump seems to represent a hegemonic repositioning, wherein the hegemon of the global system would adopt policies characterized more by self-interest. This is more than a bit related to the fact that the United States can no longer afford to shoulder the responsibilities of being a hegemon, a phenomenon which has historically led to world war and a new hegemon assuming the mantle.

If the Russian 4PT is imperial and uses autonomous ethnic groups as a starting point, the Trumpian counterpart is more liberal. His concern for both White and Black Americans seems genuine, as when in Detroit he expressed his view that the African American church had for centuries been the conscience of the nation. In contrast to Dugin, Trump speaks of "communities" instead of *ethnos*. In common with Dugin, Trump in any case prefers to seek friends rather than enemies, and it's not impossible that he will one day succeed in breaking up the Democrats' ethnic alliance/historical bloc. Whether it is Asians, Hispanics, or African-Americans who go over to the Republicans remains to be seen. As far as Blacks are concerned, there is one potential group who could leave the democratic camp: the so called *hoteps*. A *hotep* is typically a Black man who turns away from both victim mentality, Black Lives Matter, as well as feminism, and instead focuses on self-improvement and genuine Black Power, including economic independence. It was originally intended as a pejorative, but the hoteps have made it their own. Many hoteps supported Trump during the election in order to annoy Black liberals, among other reasons. There are actually good reasons for Blacks to support Trump's immigration policy, since they are subject to brutal ethnic cleansing by Hispanic gangs in many cities. For example, the mythical Compton is no longer a Black area. On Twitter there is occasional contact between hoteps and the Alt-Right.

Trump's break with historical American conservatism is also implied in the phenomenon *LGBT for Trump*. As early as 2011 he spoke in front of the Conservative Political Action Committee after being invited by an organization for gay conservatives and their friends. In short, Trump does not focus on people's private lives, but on questions of *realpolitik* like trade and migration. That Milo Yiannopoulos has stepped forward as a Trump supporter should not be cause for surprise. On the whole, we can see that in our time parts of the LGBT-collective are adopting conservative and nationalist opinions. Internally, this is seen as a great problem. In queer theory circles there is talk of everything from "homonationalism" to "pink-washing," but the existence of conservative gays follows logically from the fact that human sexuality is only a limited part of who we are.

Trump won about 25% of the Jewish vote, and has taken Israel's side against Iran. This could be an expression of something Guillaume Faye considers in *The New Jewish Question*: many Jews today have common interests with Whites in matters like law and order, and immigration. America's Jews are in many cases well on their way to making the same journey that Italians and Irishmen once made, and being absorbed into the White collective. The exception seems to be the deeply religious Orthodox Jews, but Trump gained more votes among them than among other denominations—in particular among New York's Orthodox and Russian Jews. These have been compared with the White voters of the Rust Belt. Here we also find a difference between American and European Jewry: the British Jews who voted for Brexit made up a far larger part of their group than American Jews who voted for Trump.

As far as the Chinese voters are concerned, Trump was popular among those born in China. Many of them felt that the American Left had gone off the rails in matters like sexual standards and morality, while there is also a conflict between Blacks and Chinese in many parts of the United States. The Chinese are seen as easy pickings by Black criminals, and there is also an aspect of ethnic *ressentiment*. This has become obvious during riots, during which Asian business owners have been attacked. At the same time, many Asians privately look on Blacks with contempt, among others, since they don't live up to the Asian standards of discipline and drive. John Derbyshire wrote some years ago about a possible "Arctic alliance" between North Asians and Europeans, and it is possible that an eventual Trumpian historical bloc may show aspects of such a thing.

The core of Trump's historical bloc is however the White voters. It is also their interests he represents. He received more than 50% of the White votes, and as far as the White voters without higher education are concerned his lead was impressive. In this way there was a class aspect to the election. Despite the fact that the Democrats are seen as a left-wing party in Europe, things are not so simple in the United States. Interestingly, Trump also won among White women voters, which could be the beginning of a larger change in which European women turn away from political correctness and mass immigration.

It is an interesting question as to whether Trump is an expression of the historical phase which Spengler called Caesarism, or if he is rather a part of the political category Marx described as Bonapartism. Most things indicate that the Trump phenomenon is probably a type of Bonapartism, at least for now. That is, assuming the members of the Swamp don't force him to cross the Rubicon, something he suggested he was ready to do during the election campaign should victory have been stolen from him through electoral fraud. His tendency to nominate generals is also of interest here, and suggests that he realizes the gravity of the situation.

Spengler's description of Caesarism is relevant here. It arises in an era when money has seized power over society, through democracy. Long has the global city and the economy dominated politics, but finally it becomes apparent that Man's political side is stronger. *"The sword is victorious over money, the master-will subdues again the plunderer-will,"* wrote Spengler. Spengler called the dominance of money capitalism, and he called *"the will to call into life a mighty politico-economic order that transcends all class interests"* socialism. If Trump really had been a Caesar, as many of his more fanciful and creative supporters have suggested by likening him to a God-Emperor, he would according to Spengler's terminology also have been a socialist for the new millennium. Spengler's succinct and dramatic portrayal of the struggle between money and the sword, between finance and blood, reminds us, though, that Trump is not a Caesar. Today money has a considerable power over our societies and the world, but Trump's challenge is not of such an existential nature that a compromise would be impossible. For now. However, his closer ties to the military rather than the deep state, in the form of the CIA or oligarchs like Soros, suggest that the day when money and sword will clash in America draws closer.

Trump and Sam Francis

Trump has been described as a part of a larger populist wave exemplified by things like Brexit and various anti-immigration parties in Europe. He is also a good example of the strategy Sam Francis once developed for the Republicans. Francis believed that the Republicans ought to abandon their almost religious belief in "the market" as well their courtship with Christian fundamentalists (the former is an example of their loyalty to money-power; the latter is what Viereck described as the original sin of the Right—accommodations to the hysterical Left). Instead, they were to focus on *realpolitik* which improves the lot of the middle sections of society, or *Middle America*. Both Trump and Francis can be considered proponents of the American brand of populism.

The American type of populism has deep roots, but it is also a motley tradition. Parts of the New Left found a more realistic way forward through a more postmodern populism, among them Lasch and Piccone. However, populism has also been connected with everything from segregationism, to states' rights, and the like. It can be both right-wing and left-wing, often both. There is an American political tradition which is reminiscent of Marxism but puts the middle class, often explicitly the White middle class, front and center in political change. It quite simply replaces the Marxian proletariat as a revolutionary subject. Lawrence Dennis wrote about this matter as early as the 1930s with regard to the relevant movements in Europe, and declared that bankers should restrain themselves in their treatment of the middle class:

> Little do they realize that the discomfiture of the middle classes can turn into a Roman holiday at which the big bankers will be supplying and not enjoying the fun. The big business leaders and bankers never would be missed, while the middle classes cannot be liquidated.

Dennis pre-dated Francis, but they have a lot in common. Francis was recognized as a talented writer, and was for a time adviser to Pat Buchanan. Francis was racially conscious and wrote about the importance both of pivoting towards Middle America and encouraging an ethnic consciousness among the Whites of the country. Given that the tradition Francis was part of, through James Burnham, has an origin in Marxist class analysis, there is nothing wrong with describing it as right-wing Marxism—with Marx read from the Right. This is applicable to such a degree that Paul Gottfried can quote Francis' evaluation of a certain Marxist *"closer to the Right than anyone in the Heritage Foundation."* To the extent that Francis was a right-wing Marxist, his ideas still lacked the utopian component of the original Marxism. Burnham and Francis were also more influenced by Vilfredo Pareto and Mosca, and their studies of elites and power. Francis' whole work was a fruitful synthesis of Marx, Spengler, Gramsci, and Pareto. It should come as no surprise that his masterpiece *Leviathan* is described as the *Das Kapital* of the Alt-Right in a review on Social Matter. It has the potential of becoming just that. Among other things it explains both the Alt-Right and the Trump phenomenon.

Francis wrote a number of articles on topical political subjects of his day, wherein he, among other things, coined the term anarchotyranny and brought up the violence against Whites in American prisons. Furthermore, he left behind a long analysis, which was posthumously published in 2016 as *Leviathan and Its Enemies*. It is a very useful analysis of our present. Without using the term, Francis makes use of the Marxist view of means of production replacing each other. What Marx described as capitalist Francis calls *bourgeois*, and the preceding state he calls *prescriptive* rather than feudal or traditional. In contrast to Marx, though, Francis maintains that the bourgeois society was not replaced by the socialist, and later classless, society, but rather that something completely different took place. The bourgeois society was not large scale in the same sense as ours; capitalists had a physical relationship to their property and a personal relationship to their employees far more often than today. The society of the masses and its grand scales did not just entail a quantitative change, however, but a qualitative one as well.

Big business is no longer run by its owners, who by the way can be so many that they lack both the ability and the will to run an increasingly complex business. Instead it is run by a professional class that Francis described as *managerial*. They are highly educated and have their own interests and values. This is not just happening in big businesses. The government, too, has seen its maintenance taken over by similar groups, as have the large organizations. Francis frequently grounds his thoughts on the three spheres of politics, culture, and economy when he deals with aspects of power. Politics, culture, and economy are all taken over by managers, a collective Francis calls the *New Class*. As opposed to those conservatives who want big business but don't want the state, Francis emphasizes that their common interests include the New Class in the economic sphere and that the line between New Class in the state and in big business has become blurred. Like Marx, Francis views the means of production as singular entities, and the one we are living under is not the one that existed in the 19th century. The means of production which we inhabit is the managerial, the technocratic. The New Class has carried out a veritable revolution against the ruling class which preceded it, the bourgeois. This partly explains their anti-bourgeois world view—they had to portray their rivals as being worse than them. Francis also notes that the technocratic revolution has been expressed differently in different countries. Soviet Communism and National Socialism were also technocratic revolutions, but the means used were considerably more brutal. Francis speaks here of hard technocracy rather than our soft version. Anyhow, this brings to mind the fundamentally totalitarian tendency of the system.

Francis describes the world view of the technocrats as being, among other things, *managerial humanism*. It is cosmopolitan and hedonistic. It is also characterized both by the idea that everything can be continually improved through administrative reforms, and the notion that Man is highly malleable by his environment. The New Class always has an interest in invading new social and cultural spheres, by finding problems that their members can solve through administration and therapy. Such problems can be anything from child care to racism. Francis even suggests that the New Class is *accelerationist*, that in contrast to historical elites it has an interest in society constantly changing. Their agenda is also globalist, their technocratic structures constantly open to including new countries. A new result of this accelerationism is that society becomes fragmented and damaged, the natural communities lose their autonomy. Family, the local community, the group—these are all invaded by the New Class and forced to see their functions transferred to the state, the big business, or the mass-organization. According to Francis, the New Class will annihilate society in the long run. The immigration project of our day seems to be the logical and ultimate challenge for it.

Initially the remnants of the bourgeoisie fought against the New Class, but gradually large parts defected to the New Class in ways similar to how parts of the nobility once became capitalists. Francis instead identifies a new challenger in what he calls the post-bourgeois proletariat and Middle American radicals. The post-bourgeois proletariat is different from the Marxist proletariat in that the former is part of the new mass-society. The members of this new proletariat will often times work with large businesses or the government and are frequently dependent on government programs and subsidies. That said, with Toynbee's definition of the term they are a proletariat because they don't share the world view of the New Class. In this way, they are strangers in their own society, but they are many. Neither are they necessarily proletarians in the economic sense: many of them belong to the middle class.

It is mainly from the post-bourgeois proletariat that the Middle American radicals are recruited. Here Francis brings up a study by Donald I. Warren. These radicals are often North European or Italian, in many cases men, and have rarely graduated from college. They are pitted against both the elite and the underclasses, and maintain that between these there is a collaboration directed against their own group of honest, regular people. These radicals don't have any real issue with the existence of mass-organizations, and they rarely turn against the nucleus of the welfare state. On the other hand, they do have a problem both with the elites that manage the mass-organizations and with the values of those elites. Based on a study from 1990, Francis identifies this group as a latent presence in both parties. They have historically voted for George Wallace, Ronald Reagan, Pat Buchanan, and Donald Trump, among others. If the world view of the New Class is hedonistic and cosmopolitan, the post-bourgeois radicals are instead marked by asceticism and solidarism. For them, identities are important, as are family and nation, and increasingly also race. Francis notes that the New Class almost forces the post-bourgeois proletariat to become class- and self-aware, as the former poses a social and existential threat to the latter by opening the borders.

According to Francis, the New Class has considerable weaknesses in comparison to historical elites. One part of the equation is the accelerationist component, which provokes resistance and damages the society that they rule. Another piece of the puzzle is the fact that the New Class rules by way of manipulation. If elites are described by Pareto as foxes or lions the New Class is made up of foxes, because they use manipulation to solve problems. Sometimes they can ally with groups of lions to defeat other groups of lions. This means that the New Class has a hard time handling the problems it creates when they need to be solved with violence or force. A modern example is the inability to handle Jihadism in Europe. What's more, the New Class often views Jihadists as a group of lions useful against the lions of post-bourgeois proletariat. Francis also maintains that a substantial economic crisis might be something the New Class would be unable to handle. After that, the post-bourgeois proletariat and their radicals could take over—radicals that are, *nota bene*, to the Right on many cultural issues, but on the Left in many matters of economics, just as Soral suggests with his *Gauche du travail, droite des valeurs.* It is a matter of radicals who are lions as against the foxes of the New Class.

Francis helps explain the new populism: it is, to a high degree, a phenomenon of the post-bourgeois proletariat. The New Class has pressed these segments of the population too hard, both in real terms and in symbolic terms; now comes the reaction. Furthermore, this reminds us of Moldbug's Brahmins and Vaisyas, and Francis, too, describes the alliance between Brahmins and Dalits. But it also reminds us of the myths of our ancestors; there Loki is the manipulator *par excellence*—after a time of cooperation with the gods he instead aligns himself with their enemies. He then collaborates with, among others, Angrboda—the giantess who breeds trolls in the Járnviðr (Iron-wood). The alliance between the manipulator and the daemonic feminine can also describe our time, like an explosion of the open violence that has been lurking in the background. Against this stands Thor, friend of the stable middle layers and a classic lion, as does Odin, king of the gods and in many ways a fox. Odin reminds us of the importance of being *both* lion and fox, especially as regards the Middle American radicals and their chances at success. Such a combination, with a dash of inspiration from our ancestral myths, could perhaps be described as a *wolf*.

It is worth noting that Trump's populism, as opposed to the Middle American radicals, does not show much interest in the *Lumpenproletariat*. Both Moldbug and Francis maintained that the alliance between the technocrats/Brahmins and the underclass/Dalits was of vital importance; Trump instead focuses on those who hold power. This could be positive since he, as a result, seems like a populist who "punches up" rather than down. Meanwhile, it is worth wondering if creating a split in the New Class might be possible, since there is an obvious conflict between ethnic and class interests among many of its members today. The existence of such subversive elements in the ruling class could play a valuable historical role. Moldbug's project was in many ways an attempt at dividing the Brahmin caste.

Trump and Metapolitics

The biggest demographic group opposing Trump—including the ones on the street—are young people. Objectively speaking, young people are the dumbest people within every demographic group. I was dumber

when I was younger. So were you ... People my age, we have seen one
fake media scare after another.

— SCOTT ADAMS

Trump is also interesting as a metapolitician. His metapolitics are
adapted to the United States, but he can be a rewarding object of study
for others as well. His metapolitics have been described as characterized by *winning*, by success. Evola wrote in his day of the metaphysics
of victory. Trump is a degenerate form of this, yet he is still a form of
it. Victory has a pivotal role to play among Indo-Europeans, even if it
has suffered the same assault as *thumos* during the liberal half-century.
Trump heralds the return of success, summarized in the phrase *Make
America Great Again*. His followers seem to have longed for a genuine
leader and as a result they have tied him to traditionally royal symbols.
He has been been associated with lions, described as a "golden don,"
and the Alt-Right calls him God-Emperor. There are elements of both
irony and naïve projection here, but also a regal symbolism and a
strong degree of influence from the collective unconscious.

Trump has been described both as an alpha male and a "shitlord."
Others, too, have adopted his uncompromising image and propensity for boasting at his own success. This tendency is a double-edged
sword—in many ways it expresses the African-Americanization of the
United States. This behavior isn't particularly Nordic, to loop back to
Günther. But in an era distinguished by men, especially White men,
being expected to apologize for their existence and to go to the back of
the line, both truly and symbolically, the return of the shitlord is not
purely negative. Hopefully it's just a phase, though. The combination of
shitlords and capitalism or shitlords and foreign policy might become
an unpleasant experience for everyone involved.

According to Aristotle, dialectics and rhetoric are separate phenomena. Arguments capable of convincing an honest person won't
necessarily convince a crowd. Especially not if those arguments are
mediated by hostile journalists with their own agenda. Trump's victory

may be described as an effective use of rhetoric and the consequence of an ability to manipulate the media. Scott Adams is famous for creating the comic strip *Dilbert*, but he is also interested in hypnosis and persuasion. He was one of the few who could credibly explain and predict the Trump phenomenon. His analysis of Trump is predicated on Trump being what Adams calls a Master Persuader. Given this, Adams views it as natural that Trump sometimes strays from the truth. People aren't particularly rational and facts will oftentimes play a negligible role. (It might be added that Trump wasn't alone in his flexible relationship to the truth.) What is most important are those impressions that are created or become entrenched. Adams brings to mind Gustave Le Bon's old analyses of the psychology of the masses. Among other things Adams notes that Trump should not pick anyone with a mustache or greater charisma than himself to be among his closest men. Those who haven't studied the art of persuasion might therefore see Trump as a dangerous and irrational maniac without any grasp of the facts. Adams maintains that the opposite is the case: Trump is rational, and what worked best during the election campaign is not something he will pursue as president. Adams also gives examples of how Trump used the media. He had a limited budget and a hostile journalist caste to deal with, and still he managed to make them report both on his campaign and on the topics he wanted to impress on the public. One example is the issue of non-citizens voting for Clinton. Trump didn't have any real idea of how many these might have been, but he made the media talk about it until it became a recognized fact that many non-citizens voted for Clinton.

Adams has also described how Trump has made use of the method *pace and lead*, which entails Trump at first speaking and acting like the group he wants to impact. For example, he expresses himself categorically on Muslims and comes across as authoritative among people who are skeptical towards Islam. That's just the first step, pace. After that he *leads* the people whose trust he has won. Albeit not necessarily to the extremes he has suggested. For example, Adams maintains that Trump most probably takes climate change seriously, in spite of his statements to the contrary. This implies a problem with democracy: voters aren't rational and honesty rarely works. But it also says something about the secret behind Trump's success. He himself has described his method as *truthful hyperbole.*

With a hostile journalist caste against him it was also natural for Trump to align himself with alternative media in the form of Breitbart. Breitbart has been described as part of the Alt-Right, but that is only true in a very generous definition of the term. It is, however, a part of alternative media, with a critical attitude toward the establishment. Today, such initiatives have reached a critical mass, and like Breitbart they can help a populist politician reach success. Here Trump probably helps us understand why the Sweden-Democrats are stuck in a rut: their attitude towards the Breitbarts of Sweden, such as Fria Tider, is condescending, and nothing like an invitation to cooperate. Conscious synergies rarely emerge. The Sweden-Democrats' relationship to the establishment is instead characterized by an attitude that would make the Alt-Right call them cucks. Through cooperation with Breitbart, Trump came into contact with Stephen Bannon, one of Breitbart's more interesting figures. When Trump appointed Bannon as his chief of staff it was a positive move. Among other things, Bannon has a positive attitude to many European nationalist parties. Contact with Marion Maréchal-Le Pen also seems to have been Bannon's idea. It was supposedly Bannon who wrote Trump's populist inauguration speech.

Trump also handled hostile media by holding rallies during which he could meet voters directly, instead of depending on journalists to transmit his message. These rallies were a successful measure and saw high attendance numbers. Some people have formed a group called Bikers for Trump, which quickly gained thousands of members and promised to protect him when so-called Leftists threatened to attack his inauguration ceremony. True to his usual habit, Trump has not disavowed them.

Success and Risk Factors

> The worst thing you can possibly do in a deal is seem desperate to make it. That makes the other guy smell blood, and then you're dead.
>
> — DONALD TRUMP

At the core of Trump's successes lies *thumos*. He is an alpha male who doesn't apologize when he is confronted with accusations from globalists and the New Class. This means that he could manipulate them effectively during the election campaign and say things that would provoke them. His remarks would be reported with much ado, while many voters never found them particularly offensive. This was a balancing act, but one Trump handled well. What he said might have seemed shocking at first glance— "He says Mexicans are rapists!"—but upon closer inspection would be regarded as his stating the obvious ("OK, some Mexicans *are* rapists"). The preconditions for Trump's success were the legitimacy crisis, political corruption, and demographic replacement—things which Habermas, Michels, and Spengler have described. There was a large portion of voters who did not feel represented by the elites, and which had previously voted for various Republican or Democratic candidates for lack of better alternatives. This group gave Trump a voice, but that wouldn't have been possible without his *thumos*, charisma, and rebelliousness.

At the same time, the Trumpian strategy can be difficult for others to imitate. Based on Glubb's historical timetable, Trump belong in two eras—here, too, he has a Janus quality. He is a celebrity, something which is almost a prerequisite for a political career like his in our era of decadence, but he is also a business leader, a magnate who brings to mind the era of commerce. To some degree he's a historical atavism. To someone without money or fame Trump's strategy can be difficult to reproduce. It would have to be adapted to that person's own situation (one should, of course, always follow the neoreactionary motto—*"Become worthy"*—and accumulate various resources in the process). Trump's victory also improves conditions for others to follow his example.

The Achilles' heel of Bonapartism is the inability to leave behind an enduring heritage, with regard to both ideas, people, and institutions. This has been obvious when it comes to malcontent parties like (in Sweden) New Democracy and the Sweden-Democrats, which rarely act metapolitically. When it comes to Trump, the risk is not as great, since he has a background as a creator of enduring things and seems predisposed to leaving behind a dynasty. His relationship to Breitbart also suggests an understanding of the importance of having his own media, his own institutions. In the long run, Trump will have to break the hold which the Cathedral or the swamp has taken on the Americans' world view. Helpful advice is available from Hoppe and Putin. The former, in *What Must Be Done*, has brought up the need to cut off funding to a hostile academia; the latter has, through his treatment of the powerful oligarchs, shown how Soros & co should be dealt with if they do not willingly relinquish the political sphere to the democratically elected.

At the same time, Trump's politics have a number of worrying elements. He has used threatening rhetoric against Iran and expressed positive views on certain kinds of torture. He hardly seems to be a friend of the environment. On the other hand, the things Adams says about Trump's rhetoric make it hard to determine what he honestly means and what is *pacing and leading*. Trump has also assumed the presidency in a deeply divided country. His victory was met with protests and demonstrations in parts of the country and the CIA's allegations that Russia helped him win the election suggest that he does not have the support of the American deep state (consisting of the CIA, NSA, and others). What's more, he has several especially resourceful

American oligarchs against him, including George Soros. In a way, Trump's situation is reminiscent of that of the early Putin, but without his enemy initially feeling safe. Soros and other globalists have been involved in numerous "color revolutions" in other countries, from Ukraine to Georgia. There is talk that the same method could now be used in America, a so-called purple revolution. This means that Trump's nominations of liberals and globalists don't necessarily say a lot about what policies he intends to employ. Initially he is probably interested in dividing the Soros camp. We will gradually be able to decide who President Trump really is. In other words, there are, going forward, good reasons to employ Dugin's model from *Putin vs Putin* to interpret the Trump phenomenon. It will then be a matter of *Trump vs Trump*, the role Trump has according to Spengler and Francis versus the policies that Trump as a person will deliver. His early presidency suggests, therefore, that he intends to deliver the policies his voters have demanded, both in the form of a wall against Mexico and withdrawals from free trade agreements.

We'll also gradually get to know if the scenario in America is going to be *Fenrist* or *Odinist*, if you'll recall chapters 1 and 11. Political violence can be viewed as a wolf, and like Fenrir it can be unleashed. There are signs of this all over the Western world, with increasing polarization and hatred against White men, a hatred which is gradually bringing its mirror image to life. When Soros, the CIA, Black Lives Matter, and others show that they don't accept the elected ruler it will mean a step toward a Fenrist development, wherein American society could explode. But this violence can also be subordinated to the legitimate leader, like Odin's wolves, Gere and Freke, or the wolf warriors among our ancestors. These are still potentially dangerous, always with one leg in the daemonic sphere, but they also serve an important function. Trump's contacts with the American military suggest that this is the scenario he's pursuing, wherein the legitimate power has the monopoly on violence and only has to use it in exceptional cases. That is the Odinist scenario. As the liberal order starts working ever more poorly, the issue of the monopoly on violence will increasingly take center stage, and we can well imagine scenarios with military coups even in Europe and the United States. That's nothing to fantasize about or regard with wishful thinking, but one should be aware of it and to some extent plan for it. Especially if one has the personality type our Indian cousins would have called *kshatriya*.

Chapter 16

The 21st Century Begins

Nothing is lost until all is lost.

— Curzio Malaparte

Our review of the liberal order and its challengers is approaching its end. Hopefully, these various challengers have inspired, both when it comes to their solutions to different problems, and the methods and strategies they have developed. In this way, this book can serve as a toolbox, from which each can retrieve whatever suits his own situation and character. For example, I myself stand closer to the de Benoist and CasaPound in the view of economy, but if the more liberal reader was able to discover and explore Club d'Horloge, de Jouvenel, or Moldbug further, this is also positive.

The various groups we have encountered remind us of several things. Not least of all they remind us of the importance of a historical perspective. What historical epoch do we find ourselves in today? This means that the strategies that might have worked for the Left during the 1960s do not necessarily work right out of the box today. The 60s had strong features of what Glubb calls the era of intellect: intellectuals influenced society and enjoyed respect. We, however, live in the era of decadence, which means that we, for good and bad, can make use of memes, for instance, referring to pop-culture. At the same time, the transformation when moving from one era to another is not absolute; the importance of intellectual work remains. Not least when we target people with, to quote Greg Johnson, *"an IQ over 120."* If we fail to understand our time, we cannot develop properly functioning strategies. Glubb's perspective also reminds us that the era of decadence is the embryo of the warrior (or pioneer) era. We notice this in such diverse environments as the CasaPound and the Alt-Right, as well as the increasing polarization, and Fenrir's increased presence, in our societies.

But the historical time-perspective must also be combined with Hoppe's thoughts about time preference. One problem mentioned earlier was that system critics were often excessively pessimistic and defeatist: *"Everything is lost, everyone else is stupid, hope they go under,"* was not an unusual attitude. For the moment, we will leave aside the possibility that this "everyone else is stupid" might be related to one's own inability to communicate one's message. Hopefully, the previous chapters have contributed to kindling a sense of optimism; as Maurras expressed it: *"Despair in politics is the absolute stupidity."* And today there are many reasons for optimism. The establishment currently finds itself thrown into a legitimacy crisis that has just begun. At the same time, in several countries there are more or less well developed and complete alternatives, which can take over after current establishments fail. We begin to see the outlines of what Steuckers called "new teams." Trump's victory, Brexit, and the success of national conservatives, especially in Eastern Europe, point to this. The big risk today is not optimism; optimism is a healthy attribute. Instead, the risk is high time preference—wanting everything *now*—and an inability to realize that we still have a long and hard fight ahead of us. The establishments have had decades after decades to indoctrinate our compatriots, and they still have almost unbelievable resources at hand. The risk that parts of the establishment neutralize the popular dissatisfaction by incorporating parts of an establishment-critical rhetoric are significant. High time preferences are often linked to an inability to correctly understand the Trump-phenomenon, and not seldom to a certain kind of hubris: one thinks something like, *"Trump won the election by saying whatever comes into his mind, so I'll do that too: the Jews are lying about the Holocaust!"* to take an exaggerated example. One fails to recognize here, first of all, that one is not a famous billionaire, and second, that Trump was very aware of what he did say and what he didn't. Hubris leads to poor metapolitics and the inability to make a correct assessment regarding what shape the "common sense" of the people is currently in.

Identifying the historical situation within which we act is only the first step. The next step would be to ask the eternal question, *"Who am I?"*, perhaps inspired by Richard Spencer's effective call to *become who we are*. One can proceed further with the help of psychological personality theories, like the schematic development of Jung's *Psychological Types,* the *Myers-Briggs Test.* One can assume Pareto's distinction, asking if one is a fox or a lion—both groups have their strong and weak sides. One can also assume Dumézil's description of our ancestors' conception-of-the-world: to which of the three functions do I belong? Am I a thinker (or a mystic even)? Am I a warrior? Am I an entrepreneur or a member of the honorable people—the middle layers? Am I a bard? An academic? Am I even, when I see myself in the mirror, a *pariah?* The answers to these questions are crucial for how to best benefit others. It is crucial to create synergies between these types of people, rather than conflicts. They are all needed, each and every one, in a successful movement. Historically there has been the tendency for these groups to misunderstand one another; intellectuals might look down on street activists or vice versa. My impression, however, is that these tendencies have become weaker as the seriousness of the situation has become overbearing; but one should be aware of the value of a smooth division of labor and mutual respect. If you are not a warrior, thinker, leader, bard, or any of these things, you should at least consider the possibility of being a patron; as Machiavelli reminds us, we need both weapons *and money* to build our own institutions and broad cadres of personnel to challenge liberalism in time.

The question of who we are also reminds us that the personal is the political in more than one sense. Most of us have grown up in an estranged consumer society, and to some extent we have to answer "yes" to the question of whether we are what would once have been called *pariahs* (or degenerates). To this we can react in two ways: we can become offended and claim that such conceptions and such a perspective are "Fascism"; the politically correct "Left" has reacted in this precise way for decades, and we know what it has done to them. But one can also make an active choice to get better, work with one's degenerate sides and *"become worthy."* Here too, Dumézil has much value to offer: our goal is a complete and versatile person who can function at a decent level in several contexts. But Günther too is a valuable acquaintance, one who reminds us of our ancestors' human ideal. This has been called *megalopsychos, stormenska* (literally great, or superior, man) and *humanitas*, and is characterized by such qualities as balance, faithfulness, courage, and greatness. The latter is not the least significant; there are limits to how a great man behaves also against his opponents. Linked to this is what you can call Don Colacho's dilemma. Colacho—really Nicolás Gómez Dávila—was a Colombian reactionary and an author of vigorous aphorisms. These are very rewarding, but at the same time he puts the reactionary reader into a dilemma. The modern world is the world of the masses, an epoch in such decline that *"adult public political discussion cannot be found in any country."* This also means that *"not all defeated men are decent, but all decent men are defeated."* Modern politics is about adapting to the masses, lowering oneself to their level, and promising free stuff in the form of other people's property. This is a genuine dilemma. The "Left" has rarely reflected on the relationship between means and ends, and was able to combine an utopian goal with complete nihilism regarding the means—with predictable results. A real Right is not as fortunate. To some extent, however, Colacho opens the possibility of a closer relationship between populists and reactionaries, when he notes that the people are dangerous when they are enthusiastic, but less so when they are afraid. Today's populism is very much about fear of the globalists' unstinting radicalism and its consequences, so reactionaries and populists have many common interests. This also follows from Francis and his description of Middle American radicalism as solidaric and ascetic.

The consumer society appears to many of the groups we have come to know as an enemy. Castoriadis did not describe our society as a consumer society, or as a society of the spectacle, but as a *society of oblivion*. We fill our time with amusements and distractions in order to avoid confronting reality, especially our own mortality. But the one who looks back on his life and finds that *"10 years I spent on Facebook and 10 years with HBO"* will probably not feel that this time was well spent. Reconquering one's time should therefore be a key goal; the personal is very political in terms of the consumer society and the attitude it fosters—an attitude that is simultaneously lax, unjustifiably optimistic, and infantile. Lasch spoke of narcissism, the Alt-Right of *poz*, Jung of primitivism, Evola of inversion of traditional values, Günther of *Artfremd*, and Adorno of the culture-industry as mass production—all this and more is shaping the attitudes of people today. But the consumer community can also be recreated in our own environments, in the form of the almost pornographic sessions of hate and despair that are the result of daily reminders of things such as rape and politically correct insanity. When you notice that you do not feel well because you have been exposed to this, and if you already have left political correctness behind, then it is high time to instead invest your time on self-improvement.

Castoriadis' dilemma (the alienation of people and state) is answered in various ways by the groups we have encountered. Generally, Soral, Trump, and Dugin have some different views on what their "we" are and how the relationships between different "we" should be organized. Metapolitically, it is important that this does not lead to conflicts, so that a historical bloc of groups with partially different goals can be maintained during the *Ragnarök* of the liberal order. This also means that the clash of civilizations should be avoided. Whether one is closest to Soral or Faye on the issue of *remigration*, it is important. Residence permits have been handed out in the last few years so generously and easily that in practice they have lost their meaning. It should be possible to recall them as easily, and this for a number of reasons will be strictly necessary for some of the countries we have become acquainted with.

The different answers to Castoriadis' dilemma also remind us of the existence of different national characters. There is an Anglo-Saxon attitude to the dilemma, which also characterizes the Alt-Right. But there is also a Russian, a German, and so on. This is not the only area in which national characters are important. For example, CasaPound's poetic and heroic appearance may be hard to copy in Sweden; the same applies to aspects of the Alt-Right and of the Fourth Political Theory. In short, the reader must reflect on his own nation and how it functions, and adapt strategies and metapolitics accordingly. This applies in particular to the Swedish reader, because in Sweden there is a historical tendency to uncritically imitate phenomena from abroad.

The groups with which we have acquainted ourselves also remind us of the importance of metapolitics, of creating and maintaining alliances, disseminating our concepts, analyzing and making an accurate assessment of the common sense of the people, and targeting the weak spots in the opponent. Here, our own ideas, institutions, and personnel are required; if one of these pillars is neglected, we are left to rely on those of our opponents, and we will over time be co-opted, or else we will degenerate into a ghetto-like existence. Gramsci and the New Right are indispensable teachers in this aspect, but they should be combined with Sorel's thoughts on the myth, with Le Bon's mass psychology, with Sloterdijk and Foucault's theories of the politics of language and discourses, and Francis', Dugin's, and Moldbug's thoughts about the relationship between groups and ideas. It is worth mentioning that we take a great risk if we focus entirely on politics and ignore metapolitics and culture. Tolkien and Lewis remind us of the meaning of our own culture based in our own myths—something we have seen only a few examples of so far. This also separates our situation from past renaissances, such as that of the Gothicists. In order to make a definite and lasting mark, we need music, fiction, poetry, and art that convey our myths and ideals. To the extent that these things already are *there* in popular culture, whether it is Batman, *300*, anime, Taylor Swift, or *Fight Club*, at any rate, both CasaPound and the meme creators of the Alt-Right have been good at finding them. But we also need something new, something that is our own.

Günther reminds us that we cannot overcome something without fulfilling it. In short, we should be aware of the historical and psychological function that liberalism fills, in order to replace it with something better. For example, in ethnomasochism we can identify a perverted quest for justice and anti-imperialism, which we can replace with an ethnopluralism that also takes our own interests seriously. To put forward pure self-interest as an alternative is, given our national characters, among other things, not sustainable in the long term. Günther's insight naturally leads to something like Dugin's Fourth Political Theory, which is not surprising as the old *völkisch* thinker, even back then, was positive about the cooperation between socialists and conservatives against liberalism. To use de Benoist's terms, we can be *transversal*, using the best from different environments in terms of analyses, tactics, and allies. As a common thread through all these chapters, we can trace the theme which might be called *1968 vs 1968*. The order that we have studied was founded around 1945 with liberal precursors, but underwent a transfiguration as a result of 1968. The 1968 generation has since been part of it as both yuppies and as older government officials and administrators of power. We can turn against them, even without concerning ourselves with the shortcomings that existed in 1945. But more promising is the attempt to understand what went wrong, because the result we have today is not what *they* wanted as young radicals. Something was wrong in their understanding of reality, but they also failed to take the link between what Marx called the social being and consciousness seriously. As rulers and a New Class, this was a crucial mistake. The time after 1968 can in any case be seen as this generation's revolt against, and compromise with, the system, and its catastrophic consequences.

Maurras' dilemma has also followed us through these chapters. The more philosophical paganism of the New Right is, in my eyes, perhaps the weakest point in its otherwise convincing ideological structure; but at the same time this means that everyone is free to combine the anti-liberal conception-of-the-world and metapolitics of the New Right with a religious tradition of his own choice. Here Jung, Klages, and Evola all have a lot of value to contribute. Related to this is the need for a Deep Right. We must reconnect to our hidden sources, both in terms of our long memories, our myths and the authentic Right. Economy and immigration can sometimes be of urgent importance, but we must not neglect the deeper aspects. We must devote ourselves to both defense and to reconstruction.

We need both "full spectrum dominance" and synergies; we need to control not only the street, but the Internet, the parliaments as well as the academy. This assumes the ability to divide labor. Synergies apply both within and between countries. In France, the New Right and the identitarians can be considered a good example of this; in the United States Trump and Breitbart. Success for one party in a synergistic relationship will mean success also for the others—and this is a good circle. Synergy between countries is partly due to the fact that the people of Europe are brother nations, and partly because they can have friends among other peoples. But such synergies are nothing that comes naturally; there are strong psychological and political trends that counteract them, including what Freud called the narcissism of small differences. For those who do not think metapolitically, nobody is as hateful as the one who *almost* thinks as we do ourselves.

Höfler, Donovan and others also remind us of the need for the *Männerbund*, as well as the fact that such can assume a number of forms. Blüher focused on the psychological aspect of loyalty between men, while for Höfler this was about a cultic community of warriors. Currently, Blüher's alliances can be easier to build than Höfler's, but this does not mean that for some it is not worth trying. However, the properly functioning *Männerbund*, as Schurtz reminded, always fills a concrete function, otherwise it is just a form of LARPing. On the other hand, the *Männerbund* may assume any of a whole range of functions; one obvious form, connected with *kshatriyas*, are the local vigilante-groups. A less obvious but also important form are associations of academics, writers, and the like, including our Swedish Gothicists and the circles around Lovecraft and Howard, on the one hand, and the Inklings around Tolkien and Lewis on the other. The *Männerbund* also remind us that almost all of those we have named in this book have been men. This is partly natural, given that we are speaking of a reaction to a feminist society, and that women rarely engage in system-critical politics. But there are also several interesting women in the milieus we have studied, such as Ann Coulter, Farida Belghoul, Emily Youcis, and Ann Sterzinger.

In the midst of all this, glaring at us, stands the fact that our society has lost *thumos*, because, according to Francis, it is ruled by manipulative foxes. There has come a long-awaited yearning for the return of *thumotic* people and collectives, and this partly explains the successes of CasaPound, the Alt-Right, and Trump. There is much that suggests our society will soon witness the return of the alpha males in public. Optimism and an affirmative outlook will then be valuable; and this is also healthier than communities that are built around fear and hatred. The 21st century may become a *thumotic* century—the person who feels the urge can translate this into action both in politics and culture. The 21st century might also be the century of personalities, following a liberal order characterized by a hydra of half-measures. That there will be an era belonging to the lions rather than the foxes seems more than likely. And this to such an extent that we should keep in mind that the good ruler, according to Machiavelli, needs both the fox's and the lion's characteristics.

Today we have good opportunities for victory. Nothing is guaranteed, but the combination of Spengler, Strauss-Howe, and Sam Francis reminds us that the post-bourgeois proletariat and the conservative Generation Z have a good chance to take over Faustian civilization, and to create a system based on ascetic, heroic, and solidaric values. The alternative is slavery and, in the end, complete annihilation—something Spengler touched on:

> "Lever doodt als Slav"—rather dead than a slave—is an old Frisian peasant proverb. The opposite has been the choice of every aged civilization, and every such civilization has had to realize how expensive that choice has been.

At the same time, we should not underestimate the importance of myth and magic, of the intervention of the gods in various forms. We have taken up both Kek and Wotan, as well as the effects of memes and Venner's conscious martyrdom. In conclusion, we are reminded of what made it possible for Surtr to destroy the world during *Ragnarök*: namely that Freyr had lost his sword. Freyr is a fascinating god, linked to royalty, fertility, and virility. Symbolically, one can interpret the loss of his sword in several ways. *Thumos* and the Deep Right are then the aspects needed for Freyr to keep immanent perdition at bay for yet some time. Our high culture can then turn the page, end the liberal chapter, and begin the next section of its history. The outlines of the forthcoming order have been suggested in several chapters; now it is up to us to realize them.

Index

OTHER BOOKS PUBLISHED BY ARKTOS

OTHER BOOKS PUBLISHED BY ARKTOS

LUDWIG KLAGES — *The Biocentric Worldview*

Cosmogonic Reflections

PIERRE KREBS — *Fighting for the Essence*

STEPHEN PAX LEONARD — *Travels in Cultural Nihilism*

PENTTI LINKOLA — *Can Life Prevail?*

H. P. LOVECRAFT — *The Conservative*

CHARLES MAURRAS — *The Future of the Intelligentsia
& For a French Awakening*

MICHAEL O'MEARA — *Guillaume Faye and the
Battle of Europe*

New Culture, New Right

BRIAN ANSE PATRICK — *The NRA and the Media*

Rise of the Anti-Media

*The Ten Commandments
of Propaganda*

Zombology

TITO PERDUE — *The Bent Pyramid*

Morning Crafts

Philip

William's House (vol. 1–4)

RAIDO — *A Handbook of Traditional Living*

STEVEN J. ROSEN — *The Agni and the Ecstasy*

The Jedi in the Lotus

RICHARD RUDGLEY — *Barbarians*

Essential Substances

Wildest Dreams

ERNST VON SALOMON — *It Cannot Be Stormed*

The Outlaws

SRI SRI RAVI SHANKAR — *Celebrating Silence*

Made in the USA
Columbia, SC
28 November 2024

47335547R00205